Shadows and Whispers:
Legendary Beasts, Creatures and Deities Across the World

A Fearsome Critters and Mythological Beasts Compendium

JG Baigent

Repartee Books, Independent

"The world is full of magic things, patiently waiting for our senses to grow sharper."— W.B. Yeats

Shadows and Whispers: Legendary Beasts, Creatures and Deities Across the World
Copyright © 2024 by JG Baigent. All Rights Reserved.

Contents

Introducing the Shadows   1
A Compendium of the Worlds Mythical Creatures

Part I. Shadows of North America

1. El Cucuy – The Boogeyman of the Spanish-Speaking World   7
   Spain, Portugal, and South America
2. The Basket Woman   13
   NorthWest Coast Native American Folklore
3. Adlet – The Dog-Men of Inuit Folklore   20
   Inuit Folklore
4. Skin-Walker – The Witch of Transformation   28
   Navajo Folklore
5. Squawkowtemus – The Swamp Siren   35
   Abenaki Folklore

Part II. Shadows of South East Asia

6. The Aswang   47
   Philippines Folklore
7. Rangda – The Balinese Demon Queen of the Leyaks   54
   Balinese Folklore
8. BatiBat – The Obese Hag Demon.   61
   Philippine Folklore
9. The Malay Penanggalan   68
   Malay Folklore
10. Hipag, the Vengeful Spirit   74
    Filipino Mythology

Part III. Shadows of South America

11. The Kayeri, Humanoid Plant Cryptid — 81
    Cryptid of Colombia and Venezuela
12. The Monster of Lake Tota – "Diablo Ballena" — 87
    Colombian Cryptid
13. The Capelobo Cryptid — 92
    Brazilian Folklore
14. The Cu Bird – The Tale of Vanity and the Lost Voice — 98
    Mexican Mythology
15. Guide to South American Shadows — 104
    South American Mythology

Part IV. Shadows of Oceania

16. The Bunyip - A Devouring Water Spirit — 115
    Australian Aboriginal Folklore
17. Taniwha, Creatures of Deep Rivers, Caves and Oceans — 121
    Māori Mythology
18. Ponaturi, Hostile, Goblin-like Creatures — 125
    Māori Mythology
19. Rainbow Serpent of the Dreamtime — 130
    Australian Aboriginal Mythology
20. Abere, the Fearsome Demoness — 135
    Melanesian Mythology

Part V. Shadows Of European Folklore

21. Androktasiai (Greek Mythology) — 145
    Greek Mythology
22. Erinyes, Embodiment of Vengeance — 149
    Greek Mythology
23. The Demogorgon — 153
    European Folklore

24. The Changeling 158
European Mythology

25. The Goblin, Grotesque Humanoid 163
European Folklore

26. Rawhead and Bloody Bones 169
European Folklore

27. The White Lady 174
European Folklore

28. The Wild Hunt 192
European Folklore

Part VI. Shadows of East Asia

29. Hanako-san: The Spirit of the School Lavatories 199
Japanese Urban Legend

30. Baku: The Dream-Eating Beast 204
Japanese Folklore

31. Nue: The Chimera of Nightmares 211
Japanese Mythology

32. Lake Tianchi Monster: The Mysterious Creature of Heaven Lake 217
Chinese Cryptid

33. Guide to Chinese Beasts: Legendary Creatures of Mythology 222
Chinese Mythology

34. Bạch Xà (White Snake) 255
Vietnamese Mythology

35. Gumiho, the Nine Tailed Fox 260
Korean Mythology

Part VII. Shadows of South Asia

36. Bangladeshi Ghosts: The Spirits that Haunt the Land 267
Bangladeshi Phantoms

37. Vetala: The Reanimated Spirits of the Dead 274
Hindu Mythology

38. Barmanou: The Wild Man of the Chitral and Karakoram — 281
Pakistani Folklore

39. Devil Bird (Ulama): Sri Lanka's Screaming Omen — 287
Sri Lankan Folklore

40. Asuras and Devas: A Cosmic Battle — 294
Hindu and Buddhist Mythology

41. Rakshasa, Naga and Matsya — 300
South Asian mythology

42. Vishnu, Shiva, and Maya — 307
South Asian Mythology

Part VIII. Shadows of Africa

43. Dingonek, East African Cryptid — 317
East African Cryptid

44. Tibicena, North African Demon — 323
North African Cryptid

45. Sasabonsam, Vampire of the Akan — 330
West African folklore

46. Obia, The Witches Creature — 335
West African folklore

47. Nyami Nyami – The Zambezi River God — 341
Southern African Mythology

Epilogue — 347
Shadows and Whispers

Shadows of Glossary — 348
Shadows and Whispers

Introducing the Shadows

A Compendium of the Worlds Mythical Creatures

From the ancient myths of distant lands to the whispered tales passed down through generations, mythical creatures have fascinated and terrified humanity for centuries. They are the monsters that lurk in the dark, the legends that spark our imagination, and the figures that embody our deepest fears. Some of these creatures are familiar, their names uttered with a mix of dread and awe—while others are more obscure, known only to those who dare to listen to the whispers of the forgotten past.

In this book, we delve into the captivating world of *mythical creatures* from *cultures around the globe*. Each creature is a living testament to the rich tapestry of human imagination, offering a glimpse into the unique fears, hopes, and values of the societies that birthed them. But this is not merely a collection of stories—this is a journey into the heart of darkness, a walk along the edge of the unknown.

Within these pages, you will encounter creatures that have haunted minds for centuries, lurking just beyond the edge of the known world. Some are *fearsome beasts*, others are *sly tricksters*, and some are *tragic figures* caught between the realms of life and death. From the shadowy rooftops of Spain to the mist-filled forests of Eastern Europe, each tale will transport you to a world where myth meets reality, where the boundary between the living and the supernatural is blurred.

But beware—these creatures are not confined to the pages of a book. They are the product of ancient beliefs, passed down through generations. And in some cases, it may be said that their legends never truly die. They wait, as creatures of myth often do, lurking in the corners of our world, ready to return at any time.

Are you ready to face the monsters that roam our nightmares? Turn the page, and let the journey begin...

PART I
SHADOWS OF NORTH AMERICA

The Creatures of Indigenous North American Folklore

In this first section we turn our attention to the vast landscapes of North America, we enter a world steeped in ancient myths and legends passed down through generations. From the dense forests of the north to the windswept plains and shadowed swamps, the creatures that roam these lands are as varied and powerful as the cultures that birthed them. In **the stories of Indigenous peoples**, creatures are not simply monsters or specters—they embody lessons, fears, and the natural balance of the world.

In this chapter, we meet some of the most chilling and captivating beings to emerge from the folklore of North America: **Squawkowtemus**, the eerie swamp spirit whose cries lure the unwary to their doom; the **Skin-walkers**, witches of Navajo legend who can transform into animals, blurring the lines between human and beast; the **Adlet**, the hybrid offspring of a woman and a dog, whose tragic origins shape the destinies of both human and canine worlds; the **Basket Woman**, a monstrous hag who captures disobedient children, carrying them away in her enormous basket to an untimely end; and **El Cucuy**, the Boogeyman of Spanish-speaking folklore, whose shadowy figure strikes terror into the hearts of children from Mexico to the southwestern United States.

Shadows of North America | 3

These creatures are not mere figments of imagination—they are deeply woven into the fabric of the cultures they inhabit, each with its own unique connection to the land and the people. They serve as warnings, guardians of societal norms, and reflections of the fears that shape human existence. As we journey through their stories, we will uncover the dark truths behind these legends, exploring the complex interplay of life, death, and the supernatural forces that govern both the natural world and the spiritual realm.

Step into the shadows, listen to the whispers in the wind, and prepare to encounter creatures that have roamed these lands for centuries. Welcome to a world where myth and reality collide, and where every shadow holds a story waiting to be told.

I.

El Cucuy – The Boogeyman of the Spanish-Speaking World

Spain, Portugal, and South America

El Cucuy – The Boogeyman

The legend of **El Cucuy**, known across Spain, Portugal, and much of South America, is an ancient and terrifying tale told to children to ensure they behave. The creature's name is derived from the Spanish word "cabeza," meaning "head," a reference to its shadowy, headless appearance. As an embodiment of fear, **El Cucuy is the archetypal Boogeyman**—a figure used to instill fear in children who misbehave or wander off at night.

First Sightings: While the origins of El Cucuy are difficult to pinpoint, it is believed that the creature has been part of the folklore in Spain and Portugal for centuries. The earliest known mentions of El Cucuy date back to the 16th century when Spanish and Portuguese colonizers spread the myth to their colonies in Latin America. In some cultures, El Cucuy is thought to have been an ancient spirit of vengeance, now twisted into the modern form of a nightmarish predator.

> **Habitat and Behavior:** El Cucuy is said to dwell in the shadows, lurking on rooftops, in dark alleys, or even inside closets, waiting for its next victim. It is particularly associated with nightfall, when children are alone and unaware of the dangers lurking just beyond their sight. Its movements are stealthy, a blur of shadow and silent whispers. The creature's eyes, glowing in the dark, can be the only visible sign of its presence before it strikes.

El Cucuy is often described as a thin, almost skeletal figure with large, hollow eyes. Some claim it has no visible head, ithers talk of a skull sitting on its neck, and glowing eyes that gives it an eerie, unsettling appearance. Some stories claim that it devours children whole, while others say it kidnaps them to keep as its own. In some regions, parents tell their children that El Cucuy will not only eat them but also carry their souls away if they misbehave.

Physical Description:

- **Appearance:** Shadowy figure with a large, gaping neck where its head should be, or skeletal face with glowing eyes.
- **Size:** Varies, but often depicted as large and looming, capable of moving swiftly and silently.
- **Abilities:** El Cucuy is said to have the ability to blend into shadows, making it nearly impossible to spot until it's too late. Its movements are fast and often accompanied by a chilling, ghostly laugh.
- **Tactics:** It hunts children who wander too far from safety or stay out too late. It uses the element of surprise to strike quickly, often swooping from rooftops or emerging from dark spaces.

> **Mythical Significance:** El Cucuy plays a role in reinforcing cultural values such as obedience and caution. Its legend is not merely a tale of terror but a means of ensuring that children stay close to home and heed the advice of their elders.

"The Whispering Roof"

The moon hung heavy over the small village nestled in the mountains of southern Spain, casting long shadows across the cobblestone streets. The air was thick with the scent of pine trees and damp earth, and all was still—too still. The town had long since fallen into slumber, save for one restless child.

Luna couldn't sleep. She tossed and turned beneath her blanket, her thoughts consumed by the stories her abuela had whispered to her when she was younger. Stories about El Cucuy—the shadowy creature that haunted the night, watching from rooftops, waiting for the slightest misstep. She'd heard it all before, but tonight, the air felt different, heavier. The whispers of the wind seemed to carry more weight, the shadows stretching unnaturally long.

Suddenly, a soft sound broke the silence—a scraping noise from above her window. Luna froze, her heart racing. She had heard it before, but this time it was closer. The roof... the sound was coming from the roof.

Trembling, she sat up in her bed, staring at the darkened window. The room was shrouded in deep shadows, and the only light came from the sliver of moonlight peeking through the curtains. She knew what the stories said. El Cucuy hunted the disobedient. El Cucuy preyed on those who dared to venture into the night.

Her mind raced. She had stayed up too late again, ignoring the curfew her parents had set. She was restless, wanting to explore the world outside her small room. Now, it seemed, her actions had caught the attention of something far more sinister than her abuela's warnings.

The scraping sound grew louder. Luna could hear a faint whispering now, like a voice calling her name from the darkness above. She pressed her ear against the wall, trying to make sense of it. The voice was low, guttural, like the wind through a hollow tree. "Luna… Luna…" it beckoned.

Without thinking, Luna leaped out of bed and rushed to the window, flinging open the shutters. The night air hit her face, cold and biting. She scanned the rooftops but saw nothing. Nothing but the flickering shadows of the trees and the faint glow of the moon.

But then, just as she was about to close the window, she saw it—a figure, barely a silhouette against the dark sky, moving swiftly across the rooftops. It was hunched, its long limbs stretching unnaturally as it glided from one rooftop to the next. Luna's breath caught in her throat as she realized what it was. El Cucuy.

The figure moved closer, and Luna felt her body freeze in place, unable to look away. She heard the voice again, louder this time, coming from right beneath her window. "Come out, little one," it crooned, its voice like a whisper of death. "I won't hurt you... yet."

Her heart pounded in her chest as she backed away from the window. She wanted to scream, to run, but her legs wouldn't move. El Cucuy was coming for her. She could feel it in her bones.

Luna stumbled backward, her foot catching on the edge of her bed. She fell, crashing to the floor, her heart racing faster than ever. The whispering grew louder, more insistent. "Luna... Luna... I am always here... waiting..."

Suddenly, the door to her room burst open, and her father appeared in the doorway, his face pale with worry. "Luna! What's wrong?"

Luna's voice was barely a whisper. "It's... it's El Cucuy... he's outside my window..."

Her father rushed to her side, his face filled with both concern and confusion. "It's just a story, hija. There's nothing out there. You've had a nightmare, that is all."

But Luna knew what she saw. The scraping on the roof had not been the wind, nor a bird. It had been El Cucuy, coming closer, drawn by her disobedience. He was still out there, watching, waiting. She could feel it—his cold presence pressing against the walls of her house, the night growing darker by the second.

Her father tried to comfort her, but Luna could only stare at the window, knowing the truth. El Cucuy was real, and it had not forgotten her.

From that night forward, Luna never dared stray far from her home after dusk. And as the years went by, she would tell the younger children in the village the story of that night. She would warn them of the shadowy figure who stalked the rooftops, his whispers drifting on the wind, reminding them always to be good... or else.

And sometimes, just when the moon is rising high in the sky, she would hear that scraping sound again, too faint for anyone else to hear—but loud enough to remind her that El Cucuy was never truly gone.

2.

The Basket Woman

NorthWest Coast Native American Folklore

In Native American folklore, the tale of Asin, often referred to as the "Basket Woman," has been passed down through generations as both a terrifying warning and a lesson in obedience. Asin is an ogre-like creature that roams the forests, seeking out disobedient children who have strayed too far from the safety of their communities. She is depicted as a massive, frightening figure with a large basket strapped to her back, which she uses to carry her captives away to her lair where she devours them.

Asin – The Basket Woman of Native American Folklore

The legend of Asin isn't just about fear; it carries deep cultural lessons. She represents the consequences of misbehavior, especially wandering alone in the wilderness or ignoring the guidance of elders. Her stories warn children of the dangers lurking outside their safe spaces and reinforce the importance of staying close to home and respecting social norms.

First Sightings: The origins of the Basket Woman can be traced back to various Native American tribes, including the Kwakiutl, Tlingit, Heiltsuk, Salish. Asin's presence in these cultures reflects a shared belief in using supernatural figures to reinforce societal norms. Although details vary across tribes, the core elements of the legend remain consistent—the monster's appearance, her basket, and the fate that awaits those she captures.

Habitat and Behavior:

Asin is said to live deep within the forests, away from human settlements, where she can silently track her prey. With her enormous basket strapped to her back, she sneaks through the trees, waiting for children to wander too far from the safety of the village. Her behavior is often described as sneaky and stealthy, using her large, silent feet to avoid detection.

Once she spots a disobedient child, she will pounce, scooping them up and tossing them into her basket. The child's cries for help are ignored as she retreats to her lair, where she plans to feast on the frightened, captured child.

Physical Description:

- **Appearance:** A massive, ogre-like creature with rough, weathered skin, wild hair, and enormous hands. Her most distinguishing feature is the large basket strapped to her back, big enough to hold several children.
- **Size:** Tall and imposing, towering over most humans, with a hunched, lumbering gait.
- **Abilities:** Asin is fast and deceptively quiet, using her stealth to approach children unnoticed. While she is strong enough to carry multiple children in her basket, she is not known for being particularly intelligent.
- **Weaknesses:** Many stories emphasize Asin's dim-witted nature, allowing children to outsmart her. In some versions, the children can escape by tricking her into looking away or using the basket against her.

Mythical Significance:

The legend of Asin serves as both a cautionary tale and a tool for teaching children about the importance of obedience and respect for boundaries. Asin's captures aren't just physical—they represent the consequences of straying too far from the safety and protection of the community. She acts as a supernatural enforcer of societal norms, ensuring that the young stay within the limits established by their culture.

However, Asin also reflects a more nuanced part of human nature—her vulnerability to cleverness and cunning, showing that even the most terrifying figures can be outwitted. These stories empower children with the idea that they can challenge or escape the monsters of their world, using their wit and resourcefulness.

"The Basket Woman's Catch"

The sun had dipped behind the mountains, casting the forest in a dusky twilight. A soft breeze whispered through the leaves, carrying the scent of pine and earth. It was the kind of evening that always made Kaiah feel uneasy—too quiet, too still. Her grandmother had always warned her to stay close to the camp after dark, to never wander alone into the woods. But tonight, Kaiah felt restless, as if something was calling her to the edge of the trees.

"You should stay inside, Kaiah" her grandmother had said earlier. "Asin is always watching. She never misses a chance to catch a lost child."

Kaiah had laughed it off, thinking it was just another of her grandmother's tales to keep her from running wild. "But I'm not lost," she had replied. "And I don't believe in monsters."

Her grandmother's eyes had narrowed, a deep, knowing look in them. "Then perhaps you should."

Now, standing just beyond the last row of camp shelters, Kaiah felt a strange tug of unease. The trees before her loomed tall and dark, and in their shadows, she thought she saw movement. She shrugged it off—just the wind, she told herself. But the air was thick now, heavy with a warning she couldn't quite place.

Without another thought, she stepped forward into the woods, feeling the ground beneath her feet shift from soft earth to the crunch of dead leaves. She had always wanted to explore deeper into the forest, to see the mysterious places her grandmother had spoken of in whispers, but she had never dared venture this far before.

As the shadows grew longer, Kaiah's curiosity bloomed. She found herself walking further and further, the village firelight fading behind her until only the sound of her breathing and the distant rustling of the trees filled the air. But then, she heard something else—a soft scraping noise, like something heavy dragging against the forest floor.

Kaiah stopped dead in her tracks, her heart suddenly pounding in her chest. She turned, but saw nothing. The woods were silent again, save for the occasional snap of a twig beneath her feet. She took a shaky breath, trying to calm herself, but the scraping continued, getting louder with each passing moment.

And then she saw her.

A towering figure stepped out from behind a tree, its eyes glowing faintly in the dim light. It was a woman—no, not a woman, something else. Her skin was rough and mottled, her hair wild and unkempt. But it was the large, weathered basket on her back that caught Kaiah's eye, its edges frayed, and the scent of old leather filling the air.

Kaiah's blood ran cold.

It was Asin—the Basket Woman.

The creature's massive hands reached for Kaiah, its mouth gaping open as it let out a low growl. "You've strayed too far," Asin's voice rumbled, sending a chill down Kaiah's spine. "Now, you belong to me."

Kaiah's heart raced, but in that moment, the lessons her grandmother had taught her came rushing back. Stay calm. Think. Don't panic.

As Asin bent down to scoop her up, Kaiah spotted a large rock lying just a few feet away. In one swift movement, she grabbed it and hurled it in the opposite direction. Asin's head whipped around, distracted by the sound of the rock clattering against the trees. Kaiah didn't hesitate. She bolted.

Her feet pounded against the earth as she sprinted through the forest, her breath coming in sharp gasps. She could hear Asin's heavy footsteps behind her, the scrape of the basket dragging across the ground. But Kaiah didn't dare look back. She kept running, weaving through the trees, pushing herself harder with every step.

In the distance, she saw the faint glow of her Grandmother's home fire. With a burst of energy, Kaiah rushed toward them, her lungs burning, her legs aching. She could hear Asin growing closer, but just as the shadow of the monster loomed behind her, Kaiah broke through the treeline and into the safety of the village.

She didn't stop until she reached her grandmother's door, slamming it shut behind her. As she leaned against the wooden frame, panting and shaking, her grandmother stood in the doorway, her face grim but relieved.

"I told you, Kaiah," she said softly, her voice carrying the weight of generations of wisdom. "The forest holds many dangers. And Asin is always watching, waiting for those who wander too far."

Kaiah swallowed hard, her heart still racing. She knew now that the stories were true. Asin was real—and she had almost become her next victim.

From that night on, Kaiah never wandered into the woods again, and she never doubted her grandmother's warnings. The forest was a place of mystery and danger, and Asin was always waiting in the shadows.

But sometimes, just sometimes, Kaiah could hear the soft scraping of a basket in the distance, and she would remember.

3.

Adlet – The Dog-Men of Inuit Folklore

Inuit Folklore

The Adlet, creatures born from a union between a human woman and a dog, occupies a unique place in Inuit mythology. Their origins are tied to a story of betrayal, survival, and revenge that spans generations. Known for their dog-like lower bodies and human upper halves, the Adlet are often depicted as both strange and terrifying, walking the thin line between human and animal. Their tale serves as a reminder of the harshness of nature, the complexities of family loyalty, and the consequences of defying societal expectations.

The Dog-Men

The story, primarily referred to as *The Girl and the Dogs* on the west coast of Greenland, tells of a woman named Niviarsiang, or *Uinigumissuitung* ("she who wouldn't take a husband"), who rejects all suitors and ultimately marries a dog, Ijirqang. From this union, ten children are born—five with the bodies of dogs and five with the hybrid form of the Adlet. This legendary tale explores the deep consequences of this unnatural union and sets the stage for the creation of an entire people.

First Sightings:

The story of the Adlet is widespread across the Greenland coast, with different versions of the tale told by various Inuit and Greenlandic communities. While the details of the Adlet's appearance and behaviors may vary, the core themes of family conflict, revenge, and the transformation of humans and animals remain central to their mythos. These creatures are often cited as the mythic ancestors of Scandinavian peoples, drawing a fascinating connection between the Inuit, the mysterious dog-like beings, and the wider world beyond the seas.

Habitat and Behavior:

The Adlet, like their parents, are creatures of duality. Their dog-like lower halves make them incredibly fast and agile, suited for the harsh northern environment, while their human upper halves endow them with intelligence and the ability to speak and interact with human societies. Despite their remarkable physical abilities, the Adlet are often portrayed as dangerous and aggressive, particularly when driven by the desire for revenge.

The Adlet's behavior mirrors the harshness of their origin. Born of a human woman and a dog, they carry both human and animalistic traits, making them unpredictable and often violent when angered. Their story is one of survival in a world where betrayal can lead to the creation of a new and formidable lineage.

Physical Description:

- **Appearance:** The Adlet have the body of a dog from the waist down, with powerful hind legs and a muscular, agile build. Their upper halves are humanoid, with faces and torsos resembling humans, though often marked by the canine characteristics of their father, such as sharp eyes, pointed ears, and a rough texture to their skin.
- **Size:** Adlet vary in size depending on their gender and age, but they are generally as tall as an average human, with their lower halves giving them a distinctive, quadrupedal stance when moving quickly.
- **Abilities:** Adlet are known for their speed and stamina, inherited from their dog ancestors. Their human upper halves allow them to wield tools and engage with the world around them in more complex ways than their purely canine counterparts. However, their mixed nature often leads to a struggle between their human intelligence and their primal, animal instincts.
- **Weaknesses:** The Adlet's mixed heritage can sometimes be a disadvantage, particularly when it comes to their sense of identity. They are often seen as monsters, both feared and reviled by humans, and their reputation for violence makes them isolated from both human and

animal worlds.

Mythical Significance:

The legend of the Adlet holds profound cultural significance, symbolizing the consequences of betrayal and the complex relationships between humans and nature. Niviarsiang's rejection of human suitors, her marriage to a dog, and the resulting birth of the Adlet challenge the boundaries of social norms and expectations in Inuit society. At its heart, the tale underscores the power of revenge and the unexpected transformation of one's actions into a new lineage.

The Adlet's story also reflects themes of survival and adaptability. Despite their violent origins, the Adlet are not entirely evil; they are creatures forged from the harshness of the world around them, and their very existence highlights the struggle for survival in a land that demands strength, resourcefulness, and resilience.

> The legend's resolution, in which the Adlet's fate is tied to the creation of Scandinavian ancestors, offers a connection between distant peoples and their shared mythological history. This connection to human migration and transformation reflects the deep sense of interconnectedness that is common in many indigenous traditions, where human and animal realms overlap and influence one another.

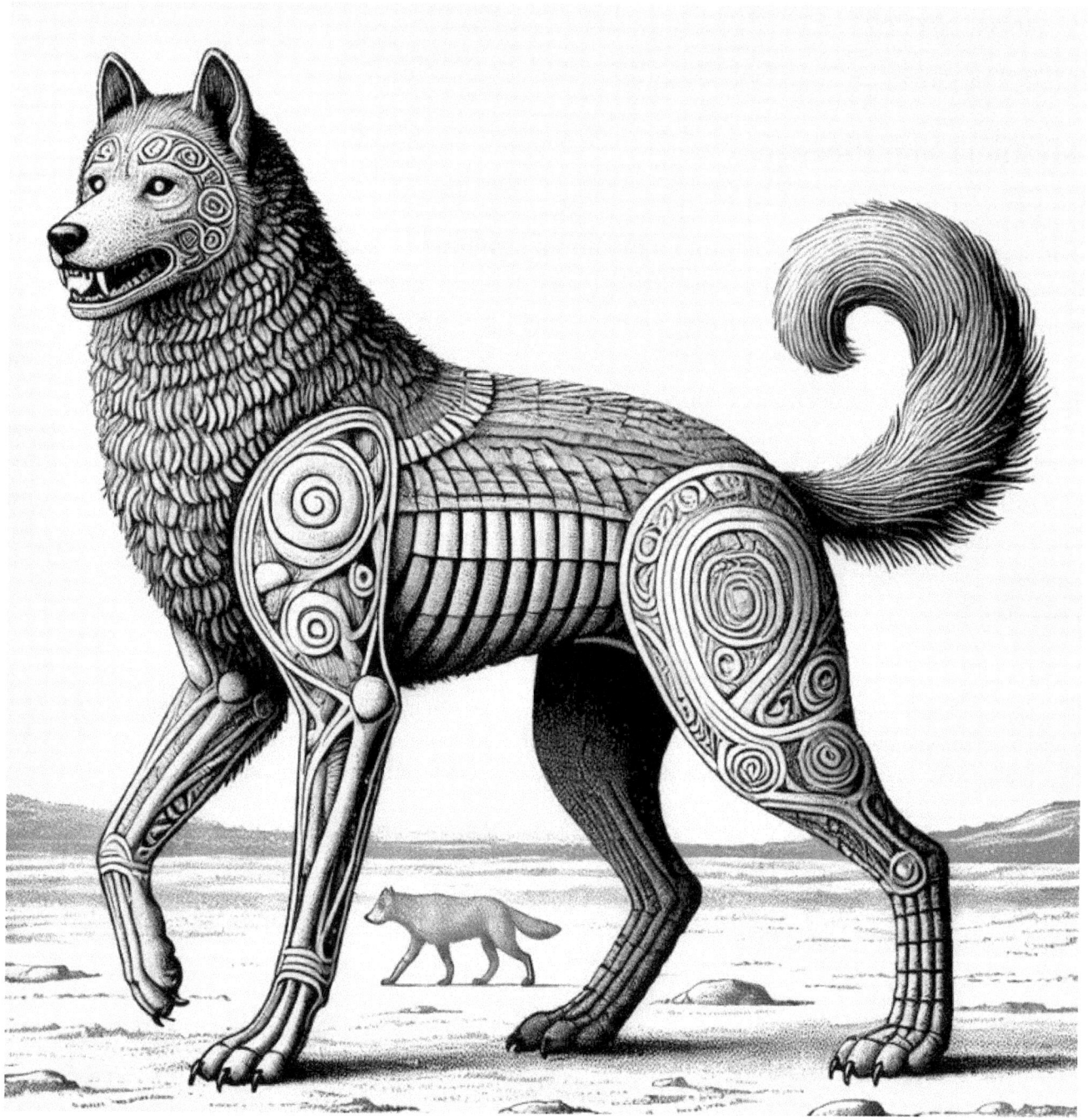

Ijirqang, Father of The Adlet Dog Men

"The Curse of the Adlet"

The wind howled across the icy plains, carrying with it the scent of the sea and the salt of distant lands. Niviarsiang stood at the edge of the cliff, staring out into the vast emptiness, the freezing air biting at her skin. She had lived her life by her own rules, refusing all suitors, determined to remain free from the constraints of marriage. She was known throughout the village as *Uinigumissuitung*—the woman who wouldn't take a husband.

But all of that had changed when she met Ijirqang.

At first, he seemed no different from the other dogs that roamed the village, loyal and strong, with his red and white spots gleaming against the snowy backdrop. But something in his eyes—something that no one else could see—called to Niviarsiang. It was not love, not in the human sense, but an undeniable connection that went beyond the ordinary. So, she did the unthinkable: she married him.

In time, Niviarsiang bore ten children. Five were fully dogs, and the others were Adlet—creatures born of both human and animal. They were strange and wild, their dog-like lower halves moving with a grace that matched their father's, but their upper halves were human, full of curiosity and intelligence. They grew quickly, hungry and loud, and as the years passed, Niviarsiang's once-peaceful life became a cacophony of demands.

Ijirqang, her husband, did not hunt. His time was spent quietly at her side, offering nothing to ease the burden of feeding their large family. It was her father, Savirqong, who had to provide, hunting the animals to keep them fed. But there was only so much he could do, and the strain began to show.

One day, in desperation, Savirqong took the family—his daughter, her strange children, and Ijirqang—and placed them in a boat. "I will carry you to a small island," he said, "where you will live. Tell Ijirqang to come for meat every day."

Niviarsiang Mother of The Adlet Dog Men

Niviarsiang agreed, though she had little choice. She hung a pair of boots around Ijirqang's neck to guide him, and he swam after them, his tail cutting through the cold water. But Savirqong had a plan, one born of years of frustration. Instead of giving Ijirqang meat, he filled the boots with stones. The dog-husband sank to the depths of the sea, drowning as Savirqong watched, a quiet satisfaction filling him.

Niviarsiang wept for her lost husband, but the pain in her heart was soon replaced by fury. With a voice full of anger, she sent the young dogs after her father, commanding them to gnaw off his feet and hands. Savirqong, enraged, retaliated by kicking his daughter overboard as she clung to the side of the boat. When she grasped at the gunwale, he severed her fingers, and as they fell into the sea, they turned into whales and seals.

But Niviarsiang's anger had not yet been sated. She feared for her children, the Adlet, and their eventual fate at the hands of her vengeful father. So, she sent them inland, where they would breed and multiply into a people of their own. As for the young dogs, she sent them across the sea, where they arrived in the lands beyond and became the ancestors of the Scandinavians.

In the end, the Adlet and the young dogs found their places in the world, their fates forever tied to the actions of Niviarsiang. But her story was one of vengeance and survival—a tale that would echo through the ages, carried by the wind across the icy lands of Greenland, into the hearts of distant ancestors.

The Adlet Dog Men

4.

Skin-Walker – The Witch of Transformation

Navajo Folklore

The **Skin-walker** is one of the most feared and mysterious creatures in Native American folklore, particularly among the Navajo people. Known as *yee naaldlooshii* in their language, meaning "by means of it, it goes on all fours," the Skin-walker is a malevolent witch capable of transforming into any animal at will. While some stories describe Skin-walkers as shapeshifters who wear the skins of the creatures they transform into, others emphasize the idea that they possess the power to morph their very bodies into animal forms.

The Skin-Walker

Often depicted as sinister beings who engage in harmful and malevolent acts, Skin-walkers are believed to possess both dark magic and a deep connection to the spirit world. In many traditions, they are associated with evil sorcery, and their abilities to shapeshift are seen as a form of power that is used for nefarious purposes—typically for personal gain or vengeance. The

Skin-walker myth serves as a cautionary tale against dabbling in forbidden knowledge and the dark arts.

> **First Sightings:**
>
> While the Skin-walker legend is primarily associated with the Navajo tribe, the concept of shapeshifting witches appears in many Native American cultures across North America, albeit with regional variations. The Navajo, however, are the most well-known in telling stories of Skin-walkers. The first references to these witches date back to centuries ago, and their tales have been passed down through generations as both terrifying myths and a warning to respect the boundaries between the physical and spiritual realms.
>
> ## Habitat and Behavior:
>
> Skin-walkers are typically believed to live in remote areas, such as deep forests, caves, or abandoned buildings. Their primary behavior involves using their shape-shifting abilities to deceive, hunt, or harm others. When they transform into animals, they may take on the form of wolves, coyotes, bears, or other animals that are traditionally considered to be powerful or dangerous.
>
> They are also thought to use their powers to walk among humans undetected, taking on the guise of trusted individuals or familiar faces to gain the upper hand. This ability to blend into both human and animal societies makes them particularly elusive and terrifying.
>
> While the Skin-walker may appear as an ordinary animal, many Navajo people believe they can be identified by certain telltale signs, such as red or glowing eyes, unnatural movements, or a sense of unease or dread that accompanies their presence.

Physical Description:

- **Appearance:** The physical appearance of a Skin-walker can vary depending on the animal form they take, but their human form is often described as being unnaturally gaunt, with unsettling eyes and a twisted, menacing demeanor. In animal form, they appear just as any other creature, though they may possess certain unnatural qualities—glowing eyes, unusual size, or the ability to move in ways that defy natural behavior.
- **Size:** Skin-walkers are said to be of normal human size when in their human form, but when they transform into animals, they take on the size and proportions of the creature they become.
- **Abilities:** Skin-walkers can transform into almost any animal, and their shape-shifting ability

is often linked to the acquisition of powers through dark rituals. They are believed to possess great speed, strength, and cunning, often using these traits to manipulate others or exact revenge.
- **Weaknesses:** Skin-walkers are vulnerable to being detected by certain sacred symbols or rituals, such as the use of protective charms, or through the recognition of certain signs that betray their true nature. In some stories, they are said to be unable to transform back into their human form unless they are in complete solitude.

Mythical Significance:

The Skin-walker is not only a creature of terror but also represents the dangers of overstepping natural boundaries. In many Native American cultures, particularly the Navajo, the Skin-walker symbolizes the consequences of abusing spiritual knowledge and the consequences of seeking power at the expense of one's humanity. They are often depicted as individuals who have turned away from traditional values and embraced forbidden practices, gaining immense power but losing their humanity in the process.

> The Skin-walker's ability to shape-shift also reflects the fluidity and adaptability of the spirit world. They are intermediaries between the human and animal realms, operating outside of the accepted social order and often sowing chaos in their wake. This makes them powerful symbols of both fear and the potential for corruption.

Lomasi meets the skin walker

"The Skin-Walker's Shadow"

The sun had barely dipped behind the horizon, leaving the land bathed in an eerie twilight that made the shadows stretch long and restless. Lomasi walked down the narrow path that cut through the forest, her boots crunching the dry leaves beneath her feet. She had been walking for what felt like hours, the tall pines around her now too familiar to offer comfort. She was alone. And she had never been more certain of the danger that lurked within the darkening woods.

Lomasi had heard the stories. Everyone in her village knew the legends of the Skin-walker—the witch who could transform into an animal at will, the one who hunted the unwary and wore the skins of those it killed. They said that Skin-walkers could be anyone—your neighbor, the hunter who smiled at you from across the fire, the old woman who lived at the edge of the village. They said you couldn't trust anyone.

Still, Lomasi had been stubborn. She believed in the old tales, but she had always thought they were nothing more than superstition, passed down to keep children obedient. Until now. Until she had found herself in the forest at dusk, far from the safety of her village.

She had been trying to reach the neighboring settlement to deliver a message, but the path had grown treacherous as the light had begun to fail. The trees loomed larger now, and every rustling noise seemed to echo through the silent woods. As she rounded a bend in the trail, she froze.

A figure stood in the path ahead—a tall man with dark eyes that gleamed unnaturally in the fading light. At first, she thought it was a hunter, but something about the way he stood, unnervingly still, made her heart race. His gaze never wavered from her, and she instinctively reached for the knife at her belt.

"Who are you?" Lomasi called out, her voice trembling slightly despite her best efforts to stay calm.

The man did not respond. Instead, he stepped forward, his movements unnatural and jerky. He tilted his head, and in that moment, Lomasi's blood ran cold. The man's face shifted—morphing into something that could only be described as grotesque. The nose elongated into a snout, and fur began to sprout from his skin. His hands twisted into claws, and his eyes glowed an eerie red.

A Skin-walker.

The creature growled, low and guttural, the sound sending a ripple of fear through Lomasi. She didn't hesitate. She turned and ran, the wind whipping through her hair, the forest closing in around her. Her footsteps were heavy with dread, but she could hear it behind her—the Skin-walker was following, moving faster than any human should.

She could hear the animalistic snarl as the creature drew closer, its claws scraping against the forest floor. Lomasi's heart hammered in her chest, but she knew she had no choice but to keep running. She had learned enough of the old ways to know that she couldn't let the Skin-walker get too close.

A blur of motion flashed past her—something large, something faster than anything that should belong to the forest. The Skin-walker had transformed, shifting seamlessly into a black wolf with glowing eyes, and it was closing the distance between them.

With every ounce of strength left in her, Lomasi leaped over a fallen log and veered left, her breath coming in ragged gasps. She had no plan. No escape. Just the desperate need to survive.

Then, just as she stumbled onto an open clearing, she saw it—the old stone circle that marked the boundary of the sacred grounds. In a desperate bid, she bolted for it, the Skin-walker's growl echoing behind her.

Lomasi reached the circle, gasping as she stepped inside its perimeter. The creature halted, its red eyes flickering with frustration and hunger. For a long moment, it circled the boundary, snarling, but it did not cross. It couldn't.

The Skin-walker could not enter the sacred space, for the symbols carved into the stones held the power to banish it.

Lomasi's chest heaved as she crouched behind the stones, watching the creature's glowing eyes fade into the shadows. The night was silent again, save for her ragged breath. But she knew, deep down, that the Skin-walker had not gone far. It never truly left.

And from that night on, she would always wonder—who else in the village was a Skin-walker? And could she ever truly trust anyone again?

34 | The Skin Walker

5.

Squawkowtemus – The Swamp Siren

Abenaki Folklore

The Squawkowtemus is a haunting figure in folklore, particularly among Indigenous peoples the Abenaki, though its myth extends across various swampy regions. Known as a female spirit, Squawkowtemus resides in the deepest, most fog-covered parts of swamps and marshes.

Squawkowtemus – The Swamp Siren

Her cries, eerie and unsettling, serve as a deadly lure to any who wander too close to her domain. Once drawn in by the sound of her voice, the unfortunate soul who approaches her is doomed, for the moment the Squawkowtemus touches them, their life is snuffed out in an instant.

The creature's origins and motivations are shrouded in mystery, but her presence in the swamps is a terrifying reminder of the dangers hidden in nature's most treacherous places.

First Sightings:

Squawkowtemus has been mentioned in oral traditions passed down through many generations. Her tale is most commonly told to warn children and travelers from venturing too deeply into swamps or marshy areas, especially at night or in the mist. The first accounts of the Squawkowtemus are believed to date back to the early days of European settlers encountering Native American communities. These settlers often heard whispers of the spirit but could never find any proof of her existence, further adding to the legend's chilling appeal.

Habitat and Behavior:

Squawkowtemus is said to haunt the deepest swamps, where the fog rolls thick and the water is stagnant. The air in these places is often heavy with decay and moisture, and it's easy to become disoriented, especially during the twilight hours. The creature is most active when the sun is setting or when the fog is thick, concealing her appearance.

Her primary method of hunting is through her voice. The cries of Squawkowtemus are described as haunting and sorrowful, resembling the sounds of a woman in pain or distress. These calls echo through the swamp, reaching the ears of unsuspecting travelers. The cries lure them closer, like a siren song, until they get too close to the spirit's reach. Once a person is within her grasp, the Squawkowtemus will strike. Her touch, often described as cold and unnaturally still, drains the life from her victim, leaving them lifeless at her feet.

While the Squawkowtemus does not often show herself in full form, her presence is often signaled by the chilling sound of her cries, which seem to come from all directions at once. In some accounts, the spirit is said to appear as a pale, semi-transparent figure, barely visible in the mist, her arms outstretched as she reaches for her prey.

Physical Description:

- **Appearance:** The Squawkowtemus is often described as a pale, ethereal figure, with long, flowing hair that blends into the mist around her. Her form is ghostly, almost translucent, making it difficult for observers to discern her true shape. Her eyes, when visible, are said to glow faintly, but it's the coldness of her touch that is most terrifying.

- **Size:** Similar in size to an average human woman, but she can appear both larger and smaller depending on how close her victim is to her.
- **Abilities:** Squawkowtemus possesses the ability to lure people in with her cries, manipulating the environment around her to disorient travelers. Her touch is the ultimate weapon; once she lays a hand on her victim, their life force is drained away, and they die instantly.
- **Weaknesses:** There are few known weaknesses to the Squawkowtemus. The only method of avoiding her is to stay away from the swamps or to be vigilant in recognizing the false cries that call out from the fog. In some stories, the Squawkowtemus can be repelled by certain herbs or charms, though these are rarely mentioned in the most traditional tellings.

> **Mythical Significance:** The Squawkowtemus embodies the dangers of the natural world that cannot always be understood or controlled. She represents the unknown and the lethal forces that can be found in swamps, an environment that has long been viewed with both awe and fear. Her spirit is often seen as a warning against venturing into places where the land is untamed and where nature can turn hostile.

Her cries, which are both sorrowful and deadly, are symbolic of the deceptive nature of beauty and danger. Much like the call of the sirens in ancient mythology, the Squawkowtemus' voice represents the allure of the unknown—at first enchanting, but ultimately fatal. The Squawkowtemus also highlights themes of isolation and desolation, as she exists in the deep, lonely parts of the world where few dare to tread.

"The Lure of Squawkowtemus"

The sun had set hours ago, and the sky had faded into an inky blackness. Abornazine had been walking for what felt like days through the swamp, the thick fog swirling around him and making it impossible to tell where the ground ended and the water began. His map had long since become useless, the landmarks lost in the labyrinth of towering trees and dense underbrush. He'd been promised that the shortcut through the swamp would save him time, but now, he was beginning to regret his decision.

The swamp was silent, save for the occasional croak of a distant frog or the rustle of something unseen moving in the brush. The air hung heavy and damp, the scent of moss and decay thick in his nostrils. He'd been walking alone for hours now, his only companion the sound of his boots squelching through the mud.

And then, he heard it.

At first, it was a faint cry—like the sobs of a woman in pain. It seemed to come from all around him, floating on the mist like a distant echo. Abornazine paused, his heart skipping a beat. The cry was unmistakable, and despite the chill running down his spine, he felt an unnatural pull toward it. The swamp had a way of playing tricks on the mind, but this felt different. It felt real.

The cry came again, louder this time, sharp with anguish and longing. It seemed to call to him, beckoning him forward.

"Hello?" Abornazine called into the fog, his voice trembling. "Is someone there?"

The cry echoed again, this time clearer and closer. It was a woman's voice, soft and sorrowful, as though she was in desperate need of help. Without thinking, Abornazine moved toward the sound, his feet sinking deeper into the muck with each step. The fog swirled around him, thickening, suffocating. His heart raced as the voice called again, now unmistakably close.

He pushed through a tangle of vines, and there, just ahead of him, he saw a figure. A pale shape, barely visible through the mist, stood in the clearing. It was a woman, her long hair flowing around her, her arms outstretched as if reaching for him. Her figure shimmered, almost transparent, the glow of her eyes faint but haunting in the dark.

"Please," the woman whispered, her voice trembling. "Please"

Abornazine's pulse quickened. There was something wrong about her—something he couldn't quite place—but the voice, so full of despair, made him step closer, despite the warning bells ringing in his mind.

Just as he neared her, the woman's head snapped up, her eyes glowing red, and a cold wind surged through the swamp. The figure's smile twisted into something inhuman, and her voice no longer sounded desperate, but sinister.

"You should never have come," she crooned, her hand reaching toward him.

The moment her cold fingers brushed his arm, a sharp pain shot through him, and his vision blurred. He staggered back, gasping for breath, but the world around him spun wildly. The swamp seemed to close in around him, the mist thickening, pressing against his chest like an invisible weight.

Abornazine's knees buckled, and he collapsed to the ground. His body felt numb, lifeless, as the woman's figure loomed over him, her form now fully visible, a spectral beauty with eyes like burning embers.

"Now you belong to me," she whispered, her voice the last thing he heard before everything went black.

The swamp fell silent once again, the fog rolling back as if nothing had ever happened. But if one listened closely, they could still hear the faint echo of a woman's sorrowful cry drifting on the wind.

And anyone who dared enter the swamp after dark would know—they too might hear the call of Squawkowtemus, and they too would never return.

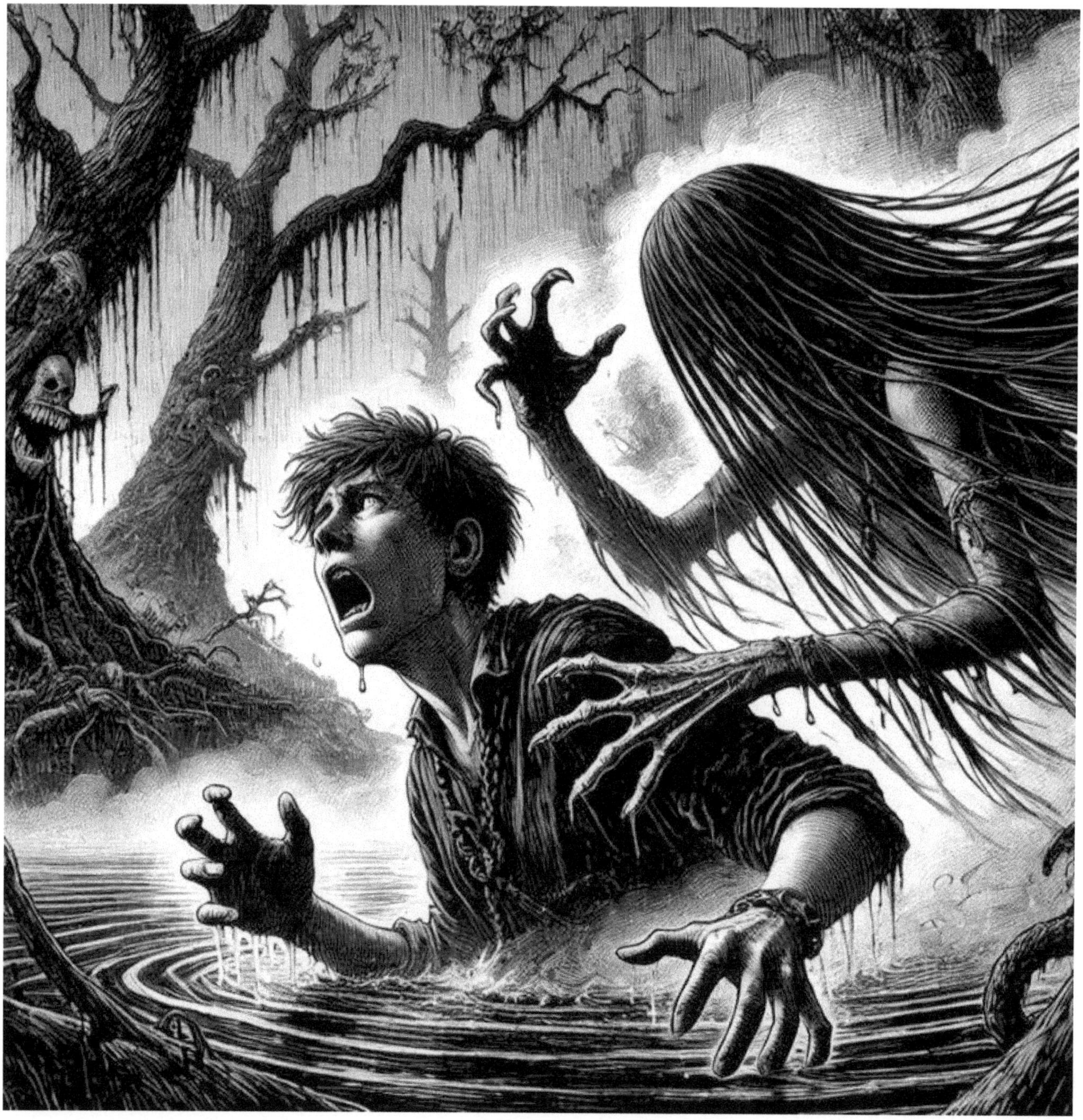

PART II
SHADOWS OF SOUTH EAST ASIA

The Myths of Southeast Asia

As we journey deeper into the heart of Asia, we now turn our attention to the rich and diverse folklore of Southeast Asia. From the dense jungles of the Philippines to the steamy swamps of Indonesia, the ancient myths of this region are filled with creatures both terrifying and fascinating, each steeped in centuries of tradition.

In the Philippines, the Aswang reigns as one of the most feared and multifaceted shape-shifters in folklore. Known for its ability to transform into a variety of monstrous forms—whether a blood-sucking vampire, a viscera-eating ghoul, or a carrion-devouring beast—the Aswang's many faces reflect the dark and mysterious forces that lurk just beyond the veil of the ordinary. But the Philippines is not alone in harboring such supernatural beings. To the south, Indonesia, Malaysia, Myanmar, and Thailand each possess their own unique creatures—spirits, demons, and monsters—that hold sway over the imaginations of their people.

In this section, we will explore these terrifying creatures, whose stories have been passed down through generations, from the beaches of Thailand to the rainforests of Indonesia. From shape-shifting vampires to vengeful spirits, these myths reveal the fears, hopes, and complex relationships between humans and the natural world.

The monsters of Southeast Asia are not mere figments of the imagination; they are deeply embedded in the cultural fabric of the region. They embody both ancient wisdom and the consequences of straying too far from the safety of community and tradition. As we delve into these stories, we will uncover not just the creatures themselves, but the rich traditions that have given rise to them.

So, step with us into the misty swamps of the Philippines, the shadowy forests of Thailand, and the winding rivers of Malaysia. Prepare to encounter the supernatural forces that continue to shape the landscapes and minds of those who call Southeast Asia home.

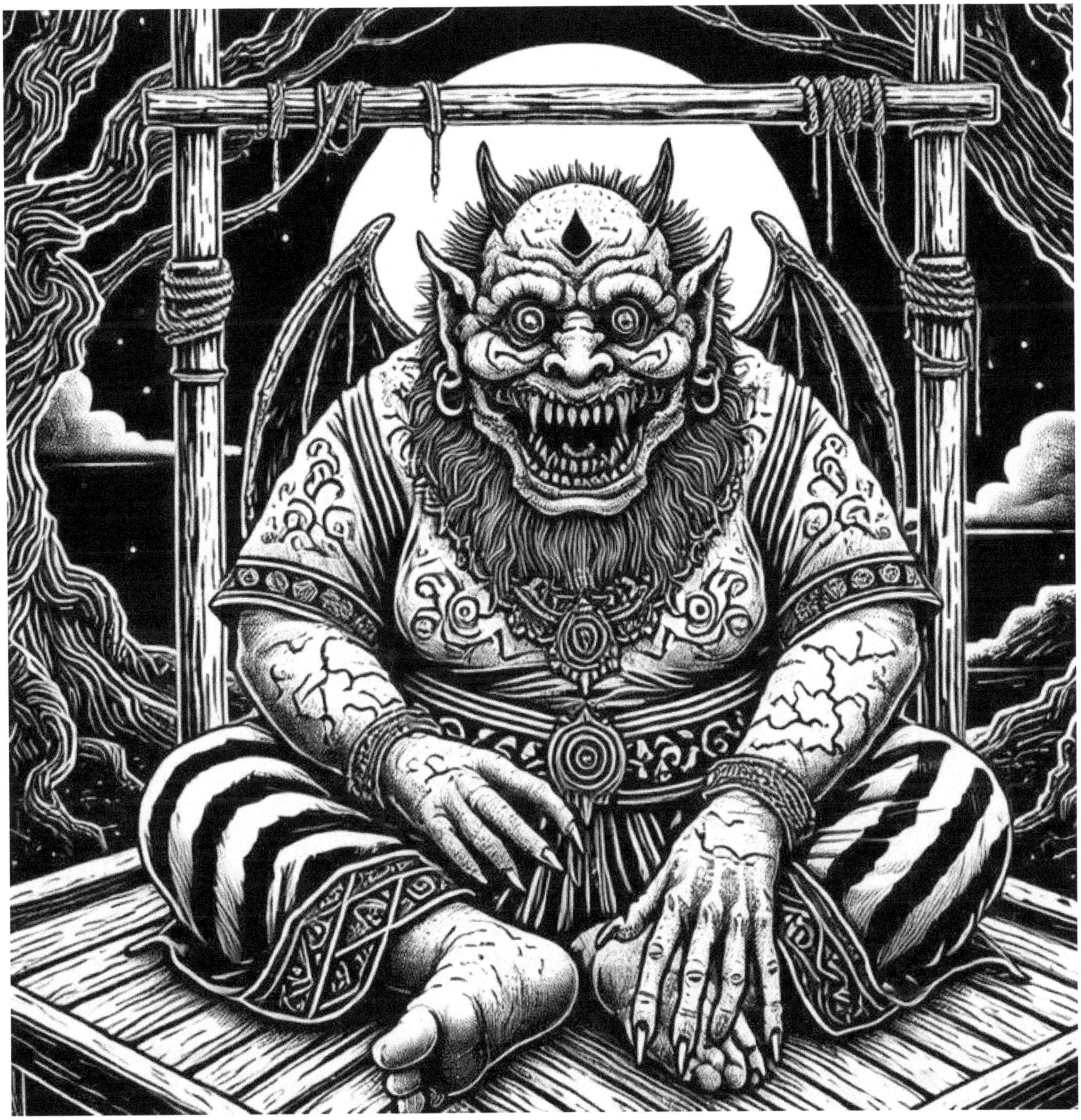

6.

The Aswang

Philippines Folklore

The Aswang is one of the most feared and versatile creatures in Filipino folklore. Known for its ability to shape-shift into a variety of terrifying forms, the Aswang is a creature that embodies a range of nightmarish qualities.

It can take the form of a blood-sucking vampire, a viscera-sucking monster, a man-eating weredog, a vindictive witch with the evil eye, or even a carrion-eating ghoul. The Aswang is often depicted as a malevolent being that thrives on fear and the suffering of its victims, and it is a common source of dread in rural Philippine communities.

Throughout the Philippines, the Aswang is used to explain unexplained deaths, illnesses, and misfortunes. It is also a warning to children and villagers to stay close to home at night, where the darkness hides not just dangers, but evil itself. The creature's many forms allow it to prey on people in different ways, making it an adaptable and ever-present threat.

Aswang – The Shape Shifting Monster of the Philippines

First Sightings:

The first recorded stories of the Aswang date back to the early Spanish colonial period in the Philippines, though tales of shape-shifting monsters and malevolent witches likely predate this. The Aswang was used by the Spanish colonizers as a way to explain mysterious deaths, especially those involving unexplainable illnesses or nocturnal predations. In rural areas, the Aswang is often believed to be the cause of illness or death that is otherwise unexplainable, and it serves as a central part of local superstition.

Habitat and Behavior:

The Aswang is primarily associated with rural areas, deep forests, and small villages, where it is said to thrive in the darkness. It is believed to be particularly active at night, when its various forms allow it to silently stalk and capture its prey. The Aswang is a shape-shifter, often taking on the form that best suits its needs—whether that be as a vampire hunting for blood, a viscera sucker consuming internal organs, a weredog attacking its victims with savage claws, or a ghoul scavenging for carrion.

While the Aswang is often depicted as a solitary creature, some stories suggest that it can be part of a coven of witches, or a family of creatures that work together to hunt and terrorize communities. Its attacks are often quick and ruthless, with victims succumbing to its bite, claws, or other means of predation before they can react.

Physical Description:

- **Vampire Form:** The Aswang in its vampire form is similar to a traditional vampire but with unique Filipino traits. It has sharp fangs and a predatory demeanor, often said to attack at night when its victim is most vulnerable. The Aswang is believed to suck the blood of infants or pregnant women, and in some stories, it can even drain a person's life force completely.
- **Viscera Sucker Form:** In this form, the Aswang is often depicted as a grotesque creature capable of detaching its upper body and leaving its lower half behind, allowing it to sneak

into homes through small openings. Once inside, it will prey on its victims by sucking out their internal organs, leaving them lifeless and drained of blood.

- **Weredog Form:** When in its weredog form, the Aswang resembles a monstrous dog or wolf, often described as larger than any natural animal. It is ferocious, with glowing eyes and the ability to move silently, stalking its prey through the woods before attacking.
- **Witch Form:** In its witch form, the Aswang can cast the evil eye, a powerful curse that brings misfortune, illness, or even death. It is often depicted as a vengeful, vindictive figure with supernatural powers that allow it to curse its enemies from afar.
- **Ghoul Form:** The Aswang's ghoul form is often seen scavenging the dead or the dying. It feasts on carrion, and its presence is a harbinger of death, especially in cases of unexplained mortality. It is often described as hideous and bloated, with glowing eyes and a hunger that cannot be satisfied.

Abilities:

- **Shape-shifting:** The Aswang's most terrifying ability is its shape-shifting. It can change into many forms, making it unpredictable and capable of attacking from multiple fronts. Its transformations are fluid, allowing it to adapt to different environments or situations.
- **Stealth and Speed:** In its various forms, the Aswang is incredibly stealthy. It can move quickly and silently, making it difficult to detect until it is too late. Its speed and agility make it a dangerous predator, able to strike before its prey even realizes it's in danger.
- **Supernatural Powers:** As a witch, the Aswang has the ability to cast curses and use other supernatural powers. It can curse individuals with illness or misfortune and, in some versions of the myth, even control the weather or the forces of nature to further its will.
- **Enhanced Senses:** The Aswang is said to have heightened senses, especially at night. It can hear the faintest sounds and track its prey over long distances, using its sharp senses to stay ahead of its victims.

Weaknesses: Despite its many forms and abilities, the Aswang has several weaknesses. Some traditional stories suggest that the Aswang is repelled by certain herbs or spices, such as garlic or salt, which can keep it at bay. It is also believed that the Aswang's human form is vulnerable to sharp objects or weapons, and it can be killed if its true form is revealed. In some legends, the Aswang can be destroyed by exposing it to sunlight or by using sacred charms or prayers.

The Aswang is always a creature of darkness. Legends describe the Aswang as a being that thrives on the fear of others and feeds off the vulnerability of its victims. The name itself is often used interchangeably with any of the various monstrous shapes it can assume, but at its core, the Aswang is a shapeshifter of extraordinary ability.

Its most common forms include the terrifying **vampire**, which hunts at night, thirsting for blood, often preying on pregnant women or infants; the **viscera sucker**, a grotesque figure capable of disassembling its body and sliding through narrow openings to feast on the internal organs of its victims; the **weredog**, a bloodthirsty predator that attacks under the guise of a large, ravenous dog; the **witch**, who possesses the power of the evil eye, capable of cursing those she desires with sickness or death from afar; and the **ghoul**, which is often seen scavenging on the dead or dying, feeding on flesh and carrion in dark corners of the world.

The Aswang's ability to shift between these forms makes it a uniquely unpredictable and dangerous entity. Its transformation is not just physical but often spiritual. In the eyes of those who believe in it, the Aswang embodies a kind of spiritual evil—one that does not just take life but corrupts the natural order, leaving a trail of destruction and fear in its wake.

What makes the Aswang truly horrifying, however, is not just its ability to transform but its tactics. It often strikes silently, only revealing its true nature in the most shocking ways. The Aswang can blend in with the human populace, using its cunning to gain the trust of those it will eventually feed upon. Whether as a friendly neighbor, a helpful stranger, or even a member of the family, the Aswang is always watching, always waiting.

Despite its terrifying power, there are ways to protect oneself from the Aswang. Certain rituals and sacred objects—garlic, salt, or even a betel leaf—are believed to ward off the creature. In some regions, folklore says that a certain kind of prayer can protect a person from the Aswang's curse. However, these protections only work if one is aware of the danger, and in many stories, the Aswang strikes without warning, leaving its victims little time to prepare or escape.

The Legend of the Aswang – "The Visitor in the Night"

The village of Pagsanjan had always been quiet, a place where the rhythms of daily life followed the sun and moon without interruption. But there were whispers—whispers that only the elders seemed to understand. It was said that the Aswang walked among them, hiding in plain sight, its true form obscured by shadows. The villagers spoke of it in hushed tones, warning their children to stay inside at nightfall, to lock their doors, and to never stray too far from the safety of the firelight.

Ana, a young woman from the village, had heard the stories her entire life. Her grandmother had told her of the creature's many forms, of the blood it drank and the lives it took. But Ana was different. She was skeptical of old wives' tales, her youthful spirit unconcerned by things that went bump in the night.

That was, until the night the visitor came.

Ana had been alone in her small house, preparing the evening meal, when the wind shifted. The air grew thick, heavy, as though something unseen was moving through it. She didn't think much of it at first—until she heard the knock.

It was a soft, rhythmic tap against the wooden door, almost melodic, like the gentle call of someone in need. Her heart skipped. No one ever knocked like that in Pagsanjan. Not at this hour.

"Who is it?" she called out, her voice betraying the unease she hadn't realized was there.

"Just a traveler," came the smooth reply, a voice both soothing and strange. "I seek shelter for the night."

Ana hesitated. It was late—too late for anyone to be wandering the woods. The village had its share of wanderers, but none ever came after dark.

"Please," the voice urged. "I've been walking for hours. I mean you no harm."

With a deep breath, Ana opened the door, peering into the darkness. A tall figure stood on her threshold, cloaked in shadow, its features hidden in the dim light of the hut.

"You must be tired," Ana said, stepping aside to allow the figure in. "Come inside. It's not safe out there."

The figure nodded, its movements fluid, almost unnatural. As it passed her, Ana felt a chill brush her skin, and a sense of unease settled over her like a weight. But she dismissed the feeling, her kindness and hospitality overriding the creeping doubt.

Once inside, the figure removed its cloak, revealing a woman with dark, hollow eyes and a pallid complexion. Her face was beautiful, almost too perfect, though there was something unsettling about it, something just out of place. The woman smiled, but the smile didn't quite reach her eyes.

"Thank you," the woman said, her voice soft, almost hypnotic. "I was worried I would not find refuge tonight."

Ana nodded, offering her a chair by the fire. She busied herself with setting out a simple meal, but as she worked, she noticed something odd. The woman's eyes never left her, even as she ate, the gaze intense, almost predatory. A shiver ran down Ana's spine, but she tried to push the thought away.

"Where are you from?" Ana asked, attempting to fill the silence with small talk.

The woman's smile faded, and she leaned forward, her gaze growing darker. "I come from far away," she replied, her voice taking on an edge of something ancient. "But I've been searching for something. Someone."

Ana felt a cold grip of fear tighten around her heart. The hairs on the back of her neck stood on end. Before she could respond, the woman stood suddenly, her movements swift and unnatural. She moved closer, and Ana instinctively backed away, the dread in her chest growing heavier.

Without warning, the woman's hand shot out, gripping Ana's wrist with unnatural strength. The room grew colder, and the air thickened with a presence that felt like death itself.

"You've invited me in, Ana," the woman whispered, her voice now a low, guttural growl. "And now, I take what's mine."

In a flash, the woman's form began to change. Her body twisted, contorting in ways that no human could. Her face elongated, her teeth growing sharp and vicious. In an instant, she was no longer a woman, but something far worse—an Aswang in its true form.

Ana screamed, but the creature's grip tightened, and the world around her spun. The Aswang's face loomed over hers, its eyes glowing with an eerie hunger. But just as quickly as it had attacked, the creature recoiled. A bright light pierced the darkness from the doorway, a figure stepping in—Ana's grandmother, holding an ancient carved bowl with the local holy herbs.

The Aswang hissed, recoiling from the light, its form shuddering before it melted into the shadows, disappearing without a trace.

Ana collapsed to the floor, her heart pounding in her chest, gasping for breath.

"Never invite strangers inside after dark, Ana," her grandmother said, her voice soft but full of authority. "The Aswang will take what it wants if you let it."

Ana nodded, too shaken to speak. The terror of that night would stay with her forever—the face of the Aswang, and the lesson she would never forget.

7.

Rangda – The Balinese Demon Queen of the Leyaks

Balinese Folklore

Rangda, the Balinese demon queen, is one of the most terrifying figures in Southeast Asian folklore. Known as the incarnation of **Calon Arang**, the legendary witch from ancient Java, Rangda is both a symbol of malevolent power and a representation of the eternal conflict between good and evil. As the leader of the **Leyaks**, a group of evil witches, Rangda embodies the darkest forces in Balinese mythology, particularly as a child-eating demon who thrives on fear, disease, and death.

Demon Queen, Rangda

The name **Rangda** itself is derived from the Old Javanese word for "widow," reflecting the tragic and vengeful nature of her character. In mythological tales, Rangda is not merely a spirit of chaos, but a powerful, wronged woman whose wrath and revenge shape the destiny of entire communities. Her very presence is believed to bring disease and misfortune, a living embodiment of suffering and destruction.

In the classic Balinese **Barong dance**, Rangda faces off against **Barong**, the spirit of good. This battle symbolizes the eternal clash between light and dark, chaos and order. The Barong, often represented as a lion or a large, mythical beast, is the protector of good, and its struggle against Rangda, who embodies evil, is a dance of life and death. As Barong and Rangda clash, they are often accompanied by dancers and a powerful chorus, creating a hypnotic and symbolic portrayal of the duality that governs the universe.

> **Rangda's appearance** is as fearsome as her reputation. She is typically depicted as an old, mostly naked woman, her body sagging with age yet brimming with malevolent power. Her unkempt hair is long and wild, symbolizing her chaotic and untamed nature. Her face is often shown as a grotesque mask with exaggerated features: sharp fangs, bulging, goggle-like eyes, and a long, protruding tongue that symbolizes her insatiable thirst for blood and vengeance. Her claws, long and sharp, further emphasize her monstrous nature and deadly capabilities.

As the queen of the **Leyaks**, Rangda has the ability to summon an army of witches, each capable of shapeshifting and performing dark magic. The Leyaks are known to practice black magic, causing harm to farmers' crops, spreading disease, and invoking chaos in the villages. Rangda's witches are feared for their power to cause misfortune, but also for their ability to manipulate the physical world and bring forth death and decay.

> Rangda is recognized as the Leyak queen, the reincarnation of Calon Arang, the infamous witch who caused chaos in ancient Java during Airlangga's reign in the late 10th century. Legend has it that Calon Arang was a widow skilled in the practice of black magic, often ruining farmers' harvests and spreading illness. She had a daughter named Ratna Manggali, who, despite her beauty, was unable to find a husband due to the fear surrounding her mother. Frustrated by her daughter's struggles, Calon Arang sought revenge by abducting a young girl. She took the girl to a Death temple to offer her as a sacrifice to the goddess Durga. The following day, a massive flood swept through the village, claiming many lives, and disease soon followed.

Physical Description:

Appearance: Rangda is often depicted as an old, emaciated woman with a grotesque and disturbing face. Her features include sharp fangs, goggle-like eyes, a long protruding tongue, and claws, which emphasize her monstrous form. Her body is sagging with age, but her presence radiates power and malevolence.

Size: Rangda is depicted as a towering figure, often larger than any human, with a body that defies natural proportions to create an imposing and terrifying silhouette.

Abilities: As the leader of the Leyaks, Rangda can summon and control an army of witches skilled in black magic. She is able to manipulate the elements, cause illness, and create fear and chaos. Her most fearsome ability is her power to consume the souls of children, further symbolizing her connection to death and destruction.

Weaknesses: Rangda's main vulnerability lies in the presence of **Barong** and the forces of good. In the Barong dance, the protective power of Barong is shown to counteract Rangda's malevolent magic. Additionally, sacred symbols and rituals are said to weaken her power.

The Legend of Rangda – "The Curse of Calon Arang"

The village of **Sukawati** was always peaceful, nestled beneath the towering volcanoes of Bali. But in the early hours of one fateful evening, a dark presence descended upon the land. It came first as a whisper in the wind—a voice, low and filled with rage, carried by the night air.

Kirana, a young woman of the village, had heard stories of Rangda, the dreaded demon queen. Her grandmother had told her tales of Calon Arang, the wicked widow who had once cursed the land with disease, and of Rangda, her darker, more terrifying incarnation. Yet, Kirana had always dismissed the stories as superstition, something to frighten children into obedience.

But on this night, Kirana would come to understand the full weight of those stories.

The village had been suffering for weeks. Crops had failed, the rivers had dried up, and sickness spread through the people like wildfire. It seemed as though the earth itself had turned against them. The elders whispered in fear that the curse of Calon Arang had returned, but Kirana, driven by her desire to help, sought out the truth.

That night, the village square was unusually silent. Kirana had walked outside to fetch water from the well when she heard a soft, haunting laugh on the breeze. It echoed in the distance, a sound that sent a chill through her bones.

Kirana turned, and there, standing in the moonlight, was an old woman, her face obscured by a wild mass of hair. Her skin was pale, her body bloated with age and hunger.

The woman's eyes gleamed in the darkness, bulging grotesquely, and her mouth hung open, revealing sharp, jagged teeth. The woman's outstretched hand was covered in claws, long and wicked, gleaming in the light of the crescent moon.

"You have been warned, child," the woman's voice rasped, sending an icy shiver down Kirana's spine. "I am Rangda, and you have broken the laws of this land."

Kirana's heart raced. The stories were real. This was no mere old woman, but the demon queen herself. Rangda was here, and she had come to finish what Calon Arang had started.

With a scream, Kirana ran, but the demon's laughter filled the air, mocking her flight. Her feet seemed to grow heavier with every step, as though the earth itself was trying to hold her back. The village square grew dark, and the weight of Rangda's curse seemed to press in from all sides.

In a desperate bid, Kirana turned to face the beast, clutching a necklace of sacred beads that her grandmother had given her. With trembling hands, she began to chant the incantations her grandmother had taught her, the words meant to banish evil and break curses.

Rangda paused, her goggle eyes narrowing, and for a moment, there was silence. The demon queen's power seemed to falter, and then, with a shriek of fury, she lunged forward, her massive claws reaching for Kirana's heart.

But just as the claws neared, a burst of light filled the air—Barong, the protector, appeared, its massive panther-like form standing between Kirana and Rangda. The clash was deafening as Barong roared, pushing Rangda back into the darkness. The battle raged, a dance of light and shadow, good and evil.

When the dust settled, Rangda had vanished, her power broken for the moment. Kirana, breathless and trembling, collapsed to the ground. She had been saved, but the victory came at a price. She knew that Rangda would one day return, and when she did, the battle between good and evil would begin again.

But for now, Sukawati was safe. The curse had been lifted—for the time being.

As the village began to heal, Kirana understood the true weight of the legends. Rangda, the embodiment of vengeance and death, was not a story to be dismissed. She was real, and as long as the cycle of hatred and suffering continued, she would always return.

And so, the eternal battle raged on.

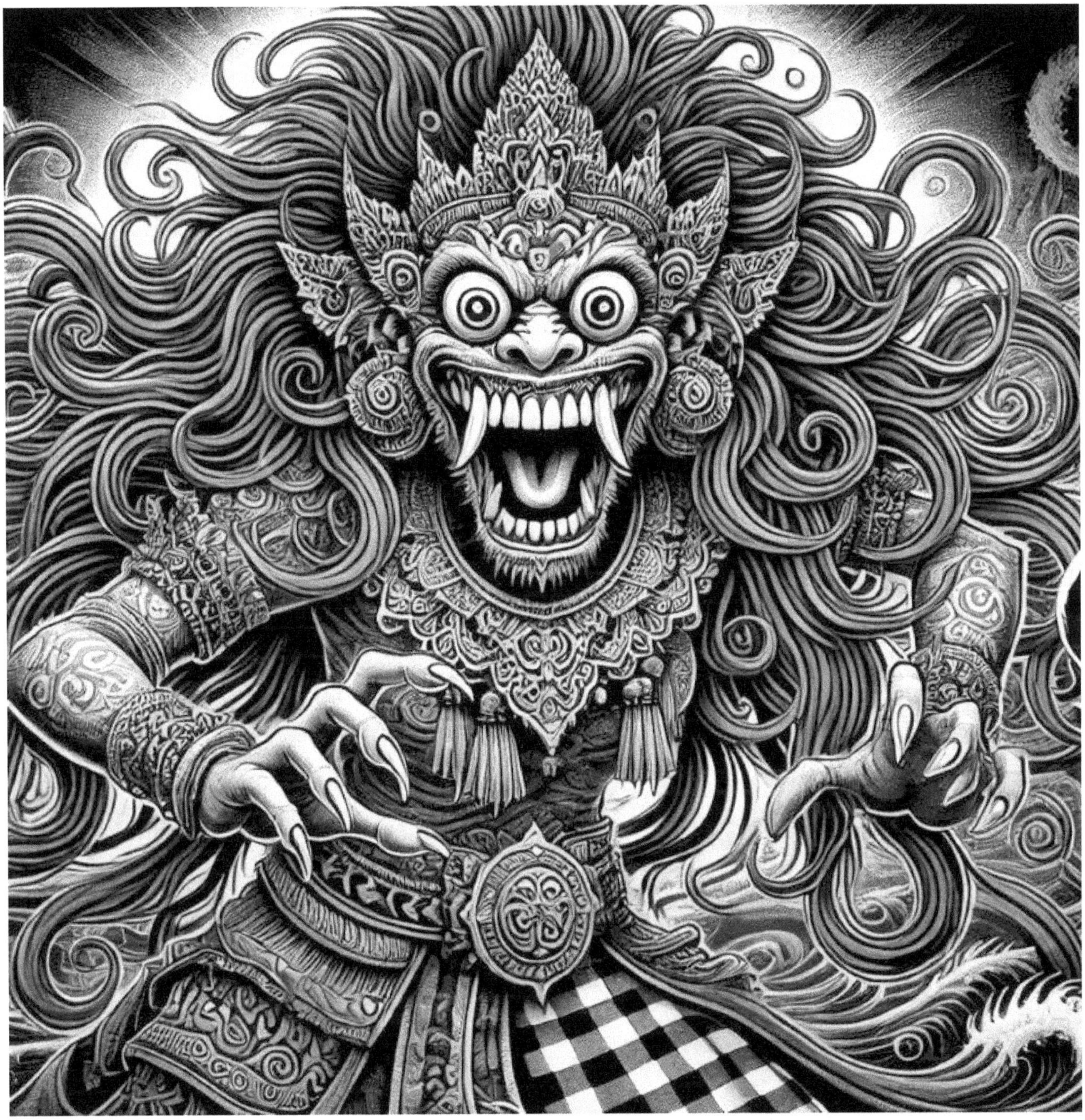

8.

BatiBat – The Obese Hag Demon.

Philippine Folklore

The **Batibat** is a wrathful demon from Ilocano folklore, while in Tagalog folklore, it is referred to as **Bangungot**. This creature appears as an ancient, grotesquely overweight female spirit that resides in trees. They typically encounter humans when their trees are chopped down, leaving them homeless, particularly if their tree is turned into a support post for a house.

This leads them to migrate and occupy the remnants of their former tree. The Batibat prohibits humans from sleeping near its post. If someone does rest close to it, the batibat reveals its true form and attacks by suffocating its victim and invading their dreams, resulting in sleep paralysis and terrifying nightmares. This phenomenon relates to the Ilocano term for nightmare, "batíbat" (or bangungot in Tagalog).

BatiBat – Obese Hag Demon.

The BatiBat is known for its insatiable appetite, which is symbolized by its monstrous size. Its hunger is not just physical but spiritual, feeding off the fear and pain of its victims. The demon's appearance varies, but it is often depicted as a massive, bloated woman with sagging skin and a hideous face, marked by a twisted smile that reveals sharp, jagged teeth. Her eyes are said to gleam with malice, and her movements are often slow and deliberate, creating a sense of impending doom.

What makes the BatiBat particularly terrifying is its ability to induce sleep paralysis in its victims. This demon is believed to enter the homes of its prey at night, typically after they've committed a sin or broken a taboo. Once inside, the BatiBat uses its power to paralyze the victim while they sleep, making them completely vulnerable to its presence. It is said that the BatiBat will then sit upon its victim's chest, suffocating them with its immense weight or feeding on their life force, until it has had its fill.

The BatiBat's connection to the supernatural realm is strong, and it is often thought to be a manifestation of repressed anger or vengeance. In some versions of the tale, the BatiBat is a spirit of a woman who was wronged in life, perhaps a victim of injustice or betrayal. Now, as a demon, she seeks to exact her revenge on those who cross her path, often using sleep paralysis as a means of taking control of her victim's body and mind.

To fend off the Batibat, someone should bite the victims thumb or pinch and wiggle their toes, which can help the person awaken from the nightmare caused by the Batibat.

Physical Description:

The BatiBat appears as a grotesque, obese hag with sagging flesh, bloated skin, and an unnaturally large mouth full of jagged teeth. Her eyes gleam with an evil, knowing gleam, and she is often depicted sitting or looming over her victim while they sleep.

The BatiBat is enormous, often described as massive and suffocating. Her size is a direct manifestation of her overwhelming hunger and thirst for power.

Abilities:

The BatiBat is capable of inducing sleep paralysis in its victims, rendering them completely immobile and helpless. Once paralyzed, the BatiBat sits on their chest or feeds off their life force. She can also manipulate shadows and darkness to her advantage, often using the night to hide her movements.

Weaknesses:

The BatiBat can be repelled with certain charms or rituals, particularly those involving light, salt, or sacred objects. In some stories, the demon is also vulnerable to offerings made to appease it, though these solutions are not always guaranteed to work.

Habitat and Behavior:

The BatiBat is primarily active at night, lurking in the shadows of villages, waiting for an opportunity to strike. She is particularly drawn to those who have committed transgressions, whether minor or major, as a way of punishing them for their perceived wrongs. The BatiBat's hunger is insatiable—no matter how much she feeds, she is always searching for more. This relentless drive makes her a terrifying and unpredictable entity, capable of appearing in the most unexpected places.

Though it is often said that the BatiBat cannot be seen during the day, its presence can be felt through an overwhelming sense of dread. The very air around it seems to grow heavy with despair, and its chilling laughter can sometimes be heard in the distance, a haunting reminder that it is always watching, waiting for the next victim.

The Legend of the BatiBat – "The Weight of Fear"

Lia had always known that the village elders held strange superstitions. They spoke of creatures and spirits that roamed the night, warning her to be cautious and to follow the rules. But she was young and reckless, certain that such stories were nothing more than scare tactics to keep children obedient.

That was until the night the BatiBat came.

It began subtly, a sense of unease that crept over Lia as she prepared for bed. She had spent the day walking in the fields, and carving her name into an old tree, defying her parents' warnings to stay close to the village. They had cautioned her about the dangers that lurked in the woods at night, particularly about the BatiBat, but Lia had dismissed their fears as nothing more than an old tale, one told to frighten children.

As night fell, the wind picked up, and a strange quiet settled over the village. The usual sounds of crickets and animals were absent, replaced by an eerie stillness. Lia lay in her bed, trying to sleep, but the darkness felt oppressive, as if something were watching her from the shadows.

The first sign came as she drifted into slumber—a faint whispering in the air, a soft, ghostly laugh that seemed to echo through the room. She stirred, her eyes flicking open. The room was dark, save for the faintest sliver of moonlight filtering through the window.

At first, she thought it was a dream, but then she felt it—the heavy weight pressing down on her chest. Her breathing became shallow, and panic gripped her as she realized she couldn't move. Her arms and legs were paralyzed, her body frozen in place as if an invisible force held her captive.

From the darkness, a figure began to emerge—a massive, bloated form that loomed over her, its shadow filling the room. The stench of decay and rot filled the air, and Lia's heart pounded in her chest as the figure drew closer.

Her eyes locked with the creature's, and she could see the twisted, grotesque face of the BatiBat, its mouth opening in a grotesque smile, revealing jagged teeth. The demon's eyes gleamed with malice, its presence suffocating. Lia struggled, trying to scream, but no sound escaped her lips.

"You broke the rules," the BatiBat whispered, its voice like a soft hiss, "And now you will pay. I will carve my name into you!"

Lia's mind raced—what had she done wrong? She remembered the tree, and then felt the BatiBat's nails digging, carving, into her skin. The BatiBat's crushing weight pressed against her, and she felt the demon's cold fingers tearing her skin, siphoning the life force from her body. The air around her grew colder, darker, as though the world itself was dying.

Then, just as the terror reached its peak, a sound broke through the suffocating silence. A door creaked open, and Lia's father, the village elder, rushed in, his face pale with fear. He had been watching over her, knowing that the BatiBat would come for those who defied the ancient warnings.

With a cry, he raised a bundle of herbs and salt, casting them in the air. And then he bit Lia on her thumb and pinched her toes. The BatiBat screeched, its form shuddering as if in pain. The dark weight on Lia's chest lifted, and her body slowly regained control. The BatiBat, its power broken by Lia being broken out of her sleep paralysis, hissed in fury before vanishing into the night.

Lia gasped for air, her body trembling, her heart racing. She was free, but the terror of what had just happened would stay with her forever. As would the letters B a T i... carved into her skin.

Her father knelt beside her, his face etched with both relief and sorrow. "Never again, Lia. Never again should you disregard the old ways. The BatiBat is real, and it feeds on the fear of those who stray from the path."

Lia nodded, her eyes wide with understanding. The weight of fear had almost been her undoing. And from that night on, she would never forget the price of defying the rules.

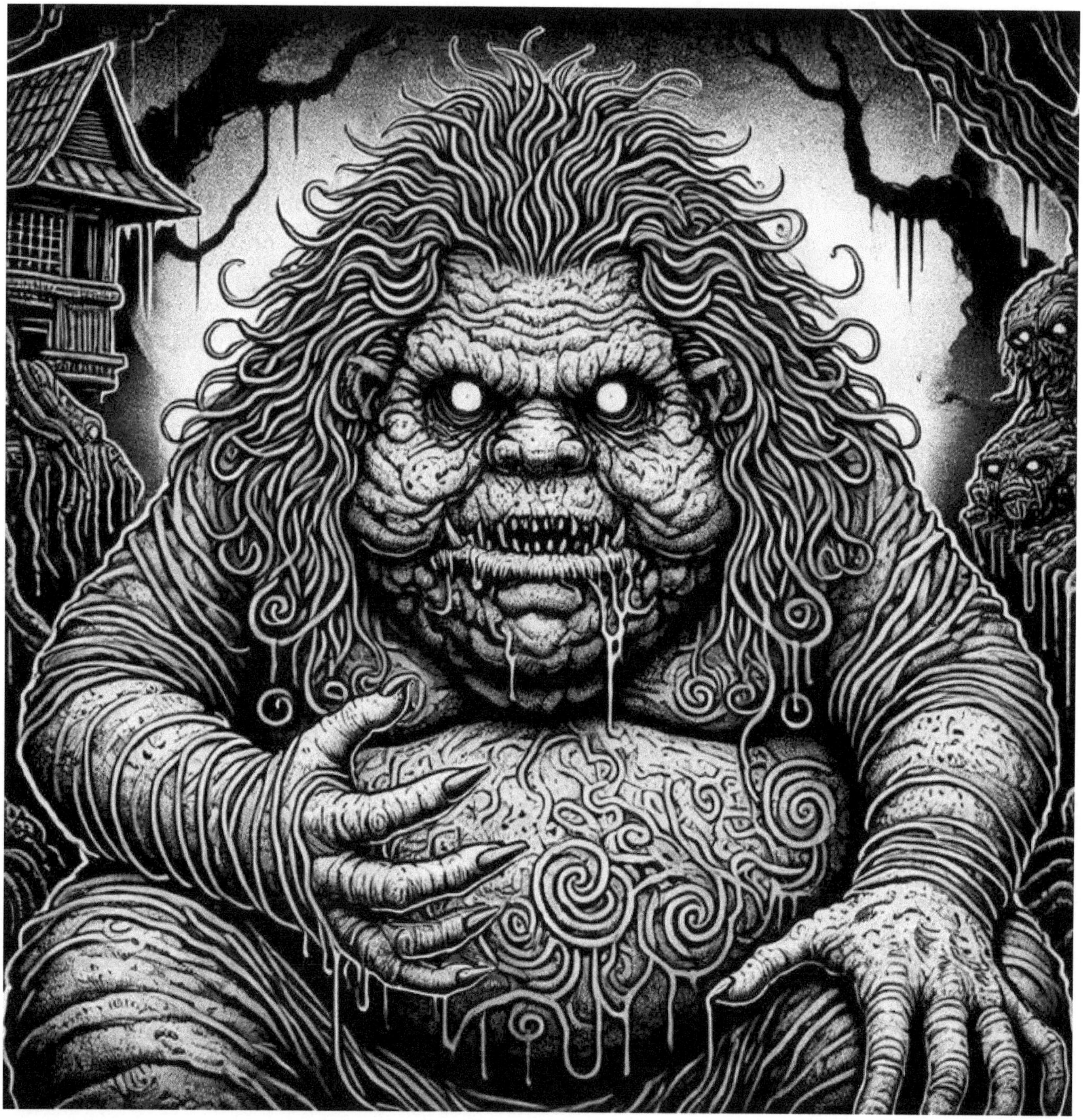

9.

The Malay Penanggalan

Malay Folklore

The **Penanggalan** is one of the most fearsome and disturbing entities in Southeast Asian folklore, especially in Malay culture. Known for its vampiric nature and horrifying physical form, the Penanggalan is a floating, disembodied woman's head with her organs and entrails trailing from her neck. This grotesque apparition hunts at night, preying on pregnant women and young children, drawing their blood with its long, sinister tongue.

Penanggalan – The Floating Head of the Malay Ghost Myths

The name *Penanggalan* is derived from the word *tanggal*, which means "to remove or take off," perfectly describing the creature's ability to detach its head from its body and float freely in search of victims.

From afar, the Penanggalan appears like a small ball of flame, similar to the *will-o'-the-wisp* phenomenon, drawing unsuspecting people closer with its eerie glow. As it gets nearer, however, the true horror of its form is revealed—its head and trailing entrails, glowing and grotesque in the night.

> The Penanggalan is part of a broader mythological tradition in Southeast Asia, with similar creatures found under different names across the region. In Cambodia, it is known as the **Ahp**, in Thailand as the **Krasue**, and in Laos as the **Kasu**, among others. While each regional variation has its own particular details, all share the same chilling features: a disembodied head with dangling organs.

Unlike other supernatural beings, the Penanggalan is not considered an undead creature, but rather a living woman who practices black magic. The process of becoming a Penanggalan involves a witch undergoing a ritual bath in vinegar, a substance that allows her body to shrink while her head remains detached and free to fly. This ritual bath is said to take place while the woman meditates, becoming one with the magic and transforming her body into a monstrous, night-haunting entity.

By day, the Penanggalan is indistinguishable from an ordinary woman, seamlessly reintegrating her head and body. However, at night, she must perform rituals to shrink her organs in order to detach her head once more. The Penanggalan carries with her the scent of vinegar, which serves as one of the few ways to identify her before her transformation. Though she may be an otherwise normal woman during the day, her supernatural nature becomes obvious by the pungent odor that clings to her wherever she goes.

Penanggalans are often depicted as using their floating, disembodied head to sneak into the homes of pregnant women, where they feed on the blood of both the mother and child. The Penanggalan's tongue is often described as long and serpentine, perfect for lapping up blood or sucking life force. In addition to her predatory nature, the Penanggalan is also associated with disease and suffering, leaving behind painful, festering wounds in her wake.

Protection from The Pananggalan.

To protect oneself from the Penanggalan, certain precautions can be taken. In Malay folklore, the plant **mengkuang**, with its sharp thorny leaves, is used to ensnare the Penanggalan's trailing organs as she flies in search of prey. The use of scissors or betel nut cutters is also said to ward off the creature, as it fears these objects. One of the most effective ways to stop a Penanggalan from returning to her body is to pour broken glass into her neck cavity before dawn, permanently preventing her from reattaching her head.

Physical Description:

Appearance:

The Penanggalan is a horrifying sight—an ethereal woman's head with glowing eyes, a long protruding tongue, and organs and entrails dangling from her neck. Her appearance is almost always depicted as grotesque and repulsive, emphasizing her vampiric and diseased nature.

Size:

The Penanggalan's head appears to float independently of her body, and although her body remains grounded during the day, her head can float freely at night. The size of her body is usually average, but her disembodied head gives her a spectral presence.

Abilities:

The Penanggalan is capable of floating, detaching her head from her body, and using her long tongue to feed on the blood of pregnant women and children. She is also associated with dark magic, capable of invoking disease and decay.

Weaknesses:

The Penanggalan can be repelled by sharp, thorny plants or items like scissors, and her head can be permanently destroyed by sealing her neck with broken glass or preventing her from reattaching her head by sunrise.

The Legend of the Penanggalan – "The Curse of the Vinegar Bath"

It was the height of the rainy season when Salma first noticed the strange odor that clung to her neighbor. A pungent scent, sharp and sour like vinegar, that wafted through the cracks of their small village in northern Malaysia. She had thought it odd at first, but dismissed it as a result of the

The Penanggalan | 71

swampy air. However, as the days passed, Salma began to see her neighbor's behavior shift—her movements became erratic, her eyes unnaturally wide, and her posture was hunched, as though she were hiding something beneath her skin.

It wasn't until one night, as the moon rose high above the misty village, that Salma's curiosity got the better of her. The scent of vinegar grew unbearable, thick in the air as she approached the house. She had heard the older women whispering in hushed tones about the Penanggalan, but the legends had always seemed too far-fetched, even for someone like her. Now, in the dead of night, those whispers seemed less like stories and more like warnings.

The door of the house creaked open, and Salma stepped quietly into the darkened interior. What she saw would haunt her for the rest of her life.

Her neighbor, a young woman named Khatijah, sat in the center of the room, her body still but her head hanging at an unnatural angle. Slowly, the woman's head twisted around—completely detached from her body, floating eerily in the air. The long, trailing entrails of Khatijah's body dangled beneath her, and the putrid odor of vinegar wafted from the decaying organs. Salma gasped, stumbling backward, as the Penanggalan's glowing eyes locked onto hers.

Khatijah—no, the creature that had once been Khatijah—smiled a twisted, gruesome grin. Its voice, soft and velvety, floated through the air. "You shouldn't have come."

Before Salma could scream, the Penanggalan lunged. Its tongue lashed out, wrapping around her arm as it dragged her closer. The long, sticky appendage left a trail of sharp, burning pain wherever it touched, drawing blood as the creature fed. Salma could feel the life draining from her body, her strength ebbing as her heart raced in terror.

In a final act of desperation, Salma reached for the betel nut cutter that lay on the floor beside her. The Penanggalan hesitated, its form recoiling at the sight of the scissors. In that instant, Salma managed to break free, but not without a parting gift—the curse of the Penanggalan lingered in the form of painful, festering sores that began to appear on her skin.

Salma fled the house, her body trembling, her mind reeling. She had seen the horrors of the Penanggalan firsthand—an embodiment of black magic, a woman whose thirst for blood and vengeance knew no bounds.

The next morning, Salma's body was covered in blisters, her skin burned by the creature's touch. She knew the village would need to act quickly to protect themselves from the Penanggalan's return. The people gathered, their elders reciting ancient prayers while others scattered thorny branches of mengkuang around their homes.

But Salma understood one truth now: the Penanggalan could not be escaped by mere protection or superstition. Its hunger was unrelenting, and it was only a matter of time before it would return—this time, perhaps, for all of them.

As the sun set that evening, Salma could not shake the feeling that the creature was watching, waiting to strike again.

10.

Hipag, the Vengeful Spirit

Filipino Mythology

The **Hipag** is a vengeful spirit from Filipino folklore, a type of **aswang** or supernatural being, who is most notorious for her malicious and violent tendencies. She is often portrayed as a ghostly woman who seeks retribution on those who have wronged her, particularly through acts of betrayal.

Hipag (Filipino)

Physical Appearance:

The Hipag is typically depicted as a tall, shadowy figure dressed in tattered clothing. Her appearance is often associated with darkness, and she is rarely seen in her full form. When she is visible, she may appear as a beautiful woman who, upon closer inspection, reveals a disfigured or horrifying face.

Abilities and Powers:

The Hipag has the power to manipulate shadows and darkness. She is known to inflict harm on those who cross her path, using her ability to control elements of fear and death. Her powers include curses, manipulation of dreams, and even the ability to curse the food or drink of her victims, causing illness or death.

Habitat and Behavior:

The Hipag dwells in the dark, typically in remote areas such as forests or hidden valleys. She is drawn to places where people live in sin or commit acts of betrayal. Her behavior is that of a wandering avenger, constantly seeking those who have caused her harm or violated the moral laws of society.

Mythological Context:

Origin Story: The Hipag is said to be a woman who was wronged in life, often due to the actions of an unfaithful lover or spouse. After her death, she becomes a spirit of vengeance, driven by the need to punish those who commit similar wrongs.

Symbolic Meaning: The Hipag symbolizes the destructive nature of vengeance and the consequences of betrayal. She is a representation of how unresolved anger and rage can haunt the living, disrupting the peace of those who live in sin.

Notable Legends and Tales: The Hipag's most well-known myth is her revenge on a cheating spouse, where she curses the offending party and causes them to become deathly ill, bringing them to their knees.

Cultural Variations: The Hipag is similar to other spirits of vengeance in Filipino culture, like the **Aswang**, who also embodies death and destruction as a form of punishment for wrongdoers.

Te Hipang

PART III
SHADOWS OF SOUTH AMERICA

Introduction to South American Creatures

South America is home to a rich tapestry of folklore, where myths and legends are passed down through generations. These stories are deeply tied to the diverse landscapes of the continent, from the thick, humid jungles of the Amazon to the towering Andes mountains. Each creature in South American folklore has its own unique characteristics and symbolism, offering insights into the cultures and traditions of the indigenous peoples. The creatures discussed in this section are emblematic of South American mythology, and they reveal much about the fears, hopes, and wisdom of the regions they hail from.

Among these legends, we find the **Capelobo**, a mysterious and terrifying creature that lurks in the forests of Brazil, the **Kayeri**, a plant-like cryptid that roams the floodplains of Colombia and Venezuela, the **Cu Bird**, a bird from Mexican folklore obsessed with its own vanity, and the **Monster of Lake Tota**, a giant creature haunting a deep lake in Colombia. Each of these beings has its own story to tell, shaped by the environment, the people, and the challenges they faced.

These legends are not just stories—they reflect a deep connection with nature, the supernatural, and the eternal battle between good and evil. In many ways, they serve as cautionary tales, teaching respect for nature, humility, and the importance of community. As we explore these creatures, we step into the heart of South America's mythical world, where the lines between reality and legend are often blurred, and where the powerful forces of nature still rule the land.

The Muki, a small, impish creature that lives in the highlands of Bolivia.

II.

The Kayeri, Humanoid Plant Cryptid

Cryptid of Colombia and Venezuela

The **Kayeri** is a cryptid from the folklore of the **Cuiba people**, indigenous to the border regions of **Colombia** and **Venezuela**. This mysterious being is described as a **giant, plant-like humanoid** with physical characteristics that blend botanic and humanoid traits. The Kayeri's appearance is often compared to that of a **giant with a large mushroom-like hat** or a **ficus tree**, and its physiology is primarily **cryptobotanic** in nature. There are various visual descriptors for this being, ranging from an appearance akin to a **fungus** to a tree-like humanoid with limbs resembling **roots** or **branches**.

The Kayeri – Giant Plant-like Humanoid Cryptid

The most striking feature of the Kayeri is its ability to blend seamlessly with the forest environment. It is said that after significant rainfall, the Kayeri appears at the base of trees, mimicking the appearance of large **mushrooms**, and much like fungi, the Kayeri is often dormant during periods of intense sunshine. Its **mushroom-like hat** may vary in size, sometimes growing to an enormous size, which only adds to its mysterious and frightening nature. The Kayeri's physical form is closely tied to the forests in which it resides, and the local belief holds that **all the mushrooms** in the forest are, in fact, aspects of the Kayeri.

Diet and Behavior:

The Kayeri is known to have a **voracious appetite**, but its dietary habits are particularly disturbing to the Cuiba people. Unlike many cryptids or animals that feast on smaller creatures, the Kayeri is said to **consume only cattle**. Its strength is legendary, as it is believed to be capable of **carrying away entire cows** from the herds of the Cuiba people. This mysterious disappearance of cattle often leads to fear and superstition surrounding the Kayeri, with local farmers attributing the loss of livestock to this terrifying creature.

The Kayeri's behavior is largely nocturnal, and it is said to emerge from its **dormant state** after rainfall to search for food. The creature's **large, powerful limbs** allow it to drag the unsuspecting cattle back into the dense forest, where it is presumed to feast on the animals. Its plant-like nature allows it to remain **undetected** among the foliage, with its mushroom cap blending in with the natural surroundings, making it difficult to spot unless it is actively moving.

Weakness and Defeat:

According to the Cuiba, the most effective way to **kill** the Kayeri is by shooting it in the **kidney** with a **bone-tipped arrow**, a method that is said to strike at the heart of its plant-based biology. This knowledge has been passed down through generations, and the Cuiba believe that the **kidneys** are the **vulnerable spot** of the Kayeri, where its **life force** can be most effectively extinguished.

Cultural Significance:

In Cuiba mythology, the Kayeri is both a **mysterious and feared** entity. While the creature is often seen as an enforcer of the natural order, it also represents the deep-rooted fear of the **unseen** forces that lurk in the wilderness. The relationship between the Cuiba people and the Kayeri is one of both reverence and fear—reverence for its power and its connection to the land, and fear due to the creature's impact on their lives through the loss of cattle and its menacing presence.

The Kayeri is often spoken of in **whispers** around campfires, with the stories passed from generation to generation as a reminder of the power of nature and the importance of respect for the natural world. While the Kayeri may be considered a cryptid in modern terms, in the folklore of the Cuiba, it is an integral part of the mysterious **landscape** that shapes their everyday existence.

The Kayeri – Cryptid of Colombia and Venezuela

"The Harvest of Shadows"

The rain had come in torrents that night, the sky cracking with thunder and the wind howling through the trees. **Tuma**, a young Cuiba man, sat at the fire with his father, his eyes flicking to the dark woods that loomed beyond the firelight.

"The Kayeri is near," his father muttered, his voice low and tense. "The rains have woken it."

Tuma glanced out at the misty horizon, his heart pounding. The Kayeri was not something easily spoken of in their village, for it was a creature of **shadow** and **whispers**, a terror that stalked their herds after the rains. The strange disappearances of their cattle, the sudden silence in the fields, the feeling of being watched—it was always the Kayeri.

"You must remember, Tuma," his father continued, "the Kayeri's power comes from the earth itself. It is the forest's protector, and the protector of the rains. If we are to survive, we must respect the land, and we must be vigilant when the rains fall. They bring life… and death."

Tuma nodded, his fingers tightening around the bone-tipped arrow that was passed down to him. It was said that the arrow was the only weapon that could defeat the Kayeri, a tool of **ancient knowledge** that could strike at the very heart of the creature. His father had told him the stories, how the Kayeri could be slain only by a well-placed shot, right into its kidney, where its life force pulsed. But Tuma had never seen the creature, and now, as the storm raged, he wasn't sure he could believe in the old legends.

But when the first screams echoed through the village, Tuma didn't hesitate. He grabbed his bow and ran into the forest, his heart racing.

The night was alive with strange sounds. Tuma could hear the rustling of trees, the thundering crash of branches breaking under something heavy. He moved swiftly, following the cries, until he came upon the clearing. There, illuminated by the pale light of the moon, stood the Kayeri.

It was enormous, a **giant figure** whose massive body seemed to blend with the forest itself. Its head was **mushroom-like**, wide and covered in spores, and its **legs were thick like tree trunks**, carrying it with an eerie grace. Tuma could see the faint glow of its **eyes**, red and glowing like embers in the darkness. It was standing near a cow, its massive claws already wrapped around the creature's body.

Tuma swallowed hard, raising his bow.

With every ounce of courage, he drew the arrow and aimed at the creature's **kidney**, just as his father had taught him. The Kayeri turned, its eyes locking with his, and for a moment, time seemed to stop. Tuma's breath caught in his chest. It was not just a creature—it was a force, something ancient, something **alive** in the very fabric of the earth.

The arrow flew, and the world exploded into motion.

The Kayeri screeched, a sound like the rustling of leaves in a storm, and collapsed to the ground, its massive body thrashing. Tuma felt his heart pound in his chest, but he did not stop. He had done it.

The Kayeri was defeated, but at what cost? The forest had been altered, and Tuma could feel the earth tremble beneath his feet, as though the **spirit of the land** itself was mourning the loss of its guardian.

With the creature's final breath, the air grew still, and Tuma fell to his knees, his arrow still in hand.

The Kayeri was no more. In the distance, the thunder rolled again, and the rain began to fall.

The Kayeri is shot by Tuma

12.

The Monster of Lake Tota – "Diablo Ballena"

Colombian Cryptid

The **Monster of Lake Tota**, often referred to as **"Diablo Ballena"** or the **Devil Whale**, is one of the most mysterious and enigmatic creatures in Colombian folklore. Known to inhabit **Lake Tota**, the largest natural lake in Colombia, it is described as a **monstrous fish** with **a black head resembling an ox** and a body **larger than a whale**. Over the centuries, the creature has been linked to many cryptozoological cases similar to other legendary lake monsters, such as **Nessie** of Scotland and **Nahuelito** of Argentina. Despite various references, its true nature remains an enigma, blending myth, historical testimony, and folklore into one terrifying creature of the deep.

The Monster of Lake Tota – "Diablo Ballena" (Devil Whale)

The monster is said to appear from time to time in the **deep waters** of the lake, its large body partially visible before it disappears again into the depths. Descriptions vary across sources, but it is most commonly depicted as an enormous, **serpentine** or **whale-like** creature, with a head resembling that of an **ox** and sometimes even described as having features akin to a **dragon**. The **dark color** and **giant size** give it an imposing, malevolent presence, often described as **"the devil"** or a **divine animal archetype**, emphasizing its fearsome and mysterious nature.

Historical References:

The first **modern reference** to the Monster of Lake Tota appeared in 1676 in the writings of the **Spanish historian Lucas Fernández de Piedrahíta**, who detailed a report from **Gonzalo Jiménez de Quesada**, the conquistador who first documented the sightings. According to these early accounts, the creature was said to have been seen by trusted individuals in the region, with one specific sighting in **1652**, where a woman named **Doña Andrea Vargas** described encountering the massive fish with a **black ox-like head**, much larger than a whale.

In the **19th century**, **Gaspard Théodore Mollien**, a French explorer, visited the region and encountered local legends surrounding the lake. He noted that the people living around Lake Tota were filled with superstition and terror about the mysterious creature. Mollien's account of the lake being **"unsettling"**, with its **blueish, thick, and unpleasant water**, reflects the ominous nature of the area, where storms often stirred the waters and occasional sightings of the **"monstrous fish"** kept the locals on edge. He described the lake as **"enchanted"**, further cementing its place as a site of mystery and fear.

Further research has connected the creature's legend to the **Muisca culture**, the indigenous people who inhabited the Altiplano Cundiboyacense. For them, the lake and its surrounding lands were sacred, and the idea of a **lake monster** was a terrifying concept—an embodiment of the unknown forces of nature and divine intervention.

Physical Appearance and Behavior:

The **Devil Whale** is often depicted as having **a dark, monstrous form**, with descriptions ranging from a **giant fish with the head of an ox** to **a creature resembling a giant whale or dragon**. The creature is generally described as being **larger than life**, sometimes said to be **larger than a whale**, but with a **mysterious and terrifying presence** that hints at its supernatural origins. While sightings are rare, it is said to appear briefly, often near the center of the lake where the water is deep and murky.

The creature's **dark, aquatic nature** makes it a terrifying figure, often emerging during storms or at night. Its body is said to **thrive** in the thick, turbulent waters of the lake, moving with **swift and powerful strokes** that send waves crashing onto the shores.

Cultural Significance and Local Myths:

The **Monster of Lake Tota** is deeply embedded in the folklore of the region, particularly among the **Muisca people** and later, among the **local Colombian villagers**. The lake, surrounded by thick **mountains**, is considered a **sacred and dangerous place**. The monster is not only a symbol of the mysterious forces of nature but also represents a **spiritual and malevolent force**, often associated with the devil, as referenced by local myths.

Some accounts describe the creature as being **divine**, an entity created by the gods, while others suggest it is a **guardian** or **punisher**. The fear surrounding the creature was reinforced by the **devastating storms** and floods that occasionally plagued the region, with many locals attributing these events to the wrath of the monster. The **sightings** of the creature have been tied to **important cultural rituals** and **warnings**, with the creature often seen as an omen.

The **Kariba legend** from **Southern Africa** and **Nessie** from **Scotland** are often compared to the Tota Lake monster in cryptozoological circles, as they share similar traits in being associated with **large bodies of water** and feared as **supernatural creatures**.

The Devil Whale of Lake Tota"

The storm had been brewing for days. The wind howled over the **Altiplano**, stirring the waters of **Lake Tota** into a frothing rage. **Rafael**, a fisherman from the village near the lake, sat in the small boat he had inherited from his father, waiting for the storm to pass.

It had been weeks since the last sighting, but the stories still lingered in the old man's mind, as vivid as the day they were told. **The Devil Whale**, the **Diablo Ballena**, they called it. The massive creature that inhabited the dark depths of the lake, seen only by the brave or the foolish.

Rafael's father had often spoken of it, an ancient tale that still sent shivers down his spine. "Do not wander too far from the shore," his father had warned. "The monster of the lake is real, and it is not something you should challenge."

But Rafael had always been skeptical. Old men, with their stories and warnings—what did they know? The lake was no different from any other body of water, he thought. Until the night came when the creature would prove him wrong.

As he rowed deeper into the heart of the lake, the wind picked up, sending waves crashing against the side of the boat. The distant rumble of thunder echoed through the mountains, and the air grew heavy with the scent of rain.

Suddenly, the water in front of him began to churn. It was subtle at first—small ripples that seemed to appear out of nowhere. But then, as the storm raged on, the ripples grew larger, and Rafael's heart began to race. Something was moving beneath the surface.

Out of the murky water, a dark shape slowly emerged. It was huge, much larger than any fish he had ever seen. **A massive, black head** like that of an **ox**, its eyes glowed in the dark, red and menacing. The body, like a **giant whale**, stretched far beneath the surface, and Rafael realized that the lake was hiding something far more ancient and terrifying than he could ever imagine.

His hands shook as he gripped the oars. The **Devil Whale** had appeared, just as the old stories had foretold. It was real.

With a deafening roar, the creature lunged from the water, sending waves crashing against the boat. Rafael barely had time to react as the boat was overturned, tossing him into the cold, dark water.

The last thing Rafael saw was the massive, monstrous form of the Devil Whale, its **giant black body** slipping back into the abyss, leaving nothing behind but the roar of the storm.

And as the lake settled once more, the storm began to fade, and the **Devil Whale** disappeared into the depths, waiting for the next soul foolish enough to challenge the waters of Lake Tota.

Monster of Lake Tota, Cryptid of Colombia

13.

The Capelobo Cryptid

Brazilian Folklore

The **Capelobo** is a fearsome creature from Brazilian folklore, particularly common in the **states of Maranhão**, **Amazonas**, and **Pará**. Known for its terrifying nature and unique appearance, the Capelobo is often depicted with both animal and humanoid forms, each more horrifying than the last.

The Capelobo – The Mythical Creature of Brazilian Floodplains

In its **animal form**, the Capelobo resembles a **tapir** with dog-like characteristics, an odd mix of herbivorous and carnivorous features. The creature's large, rounded body is covered in hair, and it is said to be swift and agile, darting through the floodplains and forests, often near human settlements. This form is seen as the more passive of the two, primarily hunting smaller animals, especially newborn puppies and kittens.

However, in its **humanoid form**, the Capelobo is far more terrifying. It has the **head of a giant**

anteater, though some variations of the myth suggest it could have the head of a tapir or even a dog, depending on the regional retelling. Its body is that of a human, but with **rounded, bottle-shaped legs**, giving it an unnatural, otherworldly appearance. The Capelobo's body is covered in a thick coat of hair, and it is said to be as strong as it is menacing, capable of squeezing its victims to death with ease. This form is also marked by a fearsome **screech**, a blood-curdling scream that lures prey deeper into the forest while simultaneously scaring anyone nearby.

The Capelobo's primary **diet** consists of blood and brains, and it is particularly dangerous to humans. When it chooses to attack, it will squeeze its victim's body with incredible force before drinking their blood and consuming their brains. The most unsettling aspect of the creature's abilities is its supernatural nature, with some stories claiming that certain individuals, particularly the elderly, can transform into Capelobos as they age.

Etymology:

The name "Capelobo" is a fusion of two words: **"cape"**, which comes from an indigenous Brazilian term meaning "broken bone," and **"lobo"**, the Portuguese word for "wolf." The combination of these words suggests a creature that is as deadly and fierce as a wolf but with an eerie connection to brokenness and decay, highlighting its brutal and predatory nature.

Habitat and Behavior:

The Capelobo is most commonly found in the **floodplain regions** of Brazil, particularly in dense forests near human settlements. These areas provide the perfect environment for the creature to stalk its prey. The creature is highly active during the night, hunting in silence except for its terrifying scream, which serves both to attract and to paralyze its victims with fear.

In its humanoid form, the Capelobo is said to be incredibly stealthy, lurking in the woods and preying upon those unfortunate enough to wander into its domain. Its eerie call can be heard echoing through the forest at night, a harbinger of doom for anyone who might be drawn to investigate the sound. As it hunts, the Capelobo's scream is both a lure and a weapon, drawing prey in while scaring off potential threats.

Legends and Tales:

The Capelobo's myth is often tied to stories of **horror and retribution**. One of the most well-known tales is that of a village where the Capelobo terrorized the inhabitants, killing livestock and **capturing children**. In the legend, a group of brave villagers banded together to hunt down the creature, armed with **bone-tipped arrows** and powerful rifles. After a long and harrowing pursuit, they managed to corner the Capelobo, but not before it had claimed several lives.

The **screeching cry** of the Capelobo is central to many of its stories. It is said that the creature's scream, which can be heard from miles away, serves to paralyze its victims with fear, drawing them into its lair. Some accounts suggest that the only way to defeat the Capelobo is by shooting it in its **navel**, the supposed weak point of its otherwise invulnerable body.

In some regional variants of the myth, it is said that the Capelobo is not only a creature of terror but a **curse**. It is believed that when people grow old, they might transform into Capelobos, giving them the power to attack and consume others as part of a dark, supernatural cycle of revenge.

Defeating the Capelobo:

The **key to defeating the Capelobo** is a **well-placed shot in its navel**. In the myth, this is seen as the creature's most vulnerable area, and the only way to kill it before it can squeeze and devour its prey. This knowledge has been passed down among the **indigenous tribes** and local villagers, and the method of attack is widely known, though few are brave enough to confront the creature.

The Capelobo of Brazil

"The Call of the Capelobo"

The sun had set hours ago, and the dense forest of the **Amazon Basin** was alive with the sounds of the night. **Joaquim**, a young man from a nearby village, had heard the stories about the Capelobo for years, passed down through generations like a warning whispered on the wind. Tonight, however, the warnings felt different.

He had been out in the woods collecting firewood when the shrill, eerie **screech** pierced the air. It was a sound unlike any animal call he had ever heard—high-pitched and unnaturally sharp. He froze, the hairs on his neck standing on end. His heart raced in his chest, and he cursed under his breath. It was the call of the **Capelobo**.

His grandmother's voice echoed in his mind. "If you hear the screech, you must run, Joaquim. The Capelobo will call to you. It will lure you deeper into the forest, and before you know it, it will have you."

But Joaquim was no child, and he had never truly believed in the monster. It was just a tale, a story meant to scare the younger ones. Still, something inside him urged caution. He hesitated, looking toward the path home, but the screech came again—closer this time.

Something urged him forward, a deep-seated curiosity and perhaps a foolish sense of bravery. He turned and walked toward the sound, his feet crunching on the forest floor, every step feeling heavier than the last. The night grew colder, and the sound of the forest seemed to grow louder, almost oppressive.

Suddenly, he saw it. There, standing in the clearing, its **huge, misshapen body** bathed in moonlight, was the **Capelobo**. Its head, the size of a dog's, with the monstrous, **mushroom-like snout of an anteater**, loomed over him. It had **human legs**, but with a bizarre, twisted shape that made it look more like a **tree** than a creature. The beast's eyes glowed red, and its voice—more of a growl than a scream—vibrated through the very earth beneath his feet.

Joaquim took a step back, his instincts screaming for him to run. But before he could turn, the Capelobo screeched again, louder, the sound reverberating through his bones. It was too late. The creature lunged.

As it wrapped its enormous, hairy arms around him, Joaquim's mind raced. The legends were true. The creature's grip was like iron, and it smelled of decay and damp earth. He struggled, but it was futile. With its **single massive leg**, it pinned him to the ground.

His mind flashed to his grandmother's words. **Shoot it in the navel**.

His hands reached for his bow, still clutched tightly by his side. With the last ounce of strength he had, he aimed at the **soft spot**—the navel of the Capelobo. He let the **arrow fly**.

The creature howled in agony, its grip loosening. Joaquim's world spun as he scrambled away, feeling the creature's dying strength falter behind him.

The Capelobo fell, its enormous body crumpling onto the forest floor. The forest fell silent, save for the distant cries of the night.

Joaquim didn't look back as he ran, the **mournful screech** of the Capelobo echoing in his ears as he fled toward the safety of the village.

The Capelobo and Joaqium

14.

The Cu Bird – The Tale of Vanity and the Lost Voice

Mexican Mythology

The **Cu bird**, also known as **pájaro cu** or **cú** in Spanish, is a mythical creature from Mexican folklore, associated with vanity and the consequences of neglecting responsibilities. It is a **mysterious bird** that originally had no feathers, but through a **collective effort of other birds**, it was gifted with an array of feathers from various species, transforming it into a **beautiful creature**.

The Cu Bird

The Cu bird's most distinctive feature is its **iridescent plumage**, a blend of the feathers from the different birds that contributed. With its new attire, the Cu bird looked resplendent, yet it failed to realize the **responsibility** that came with its newfound beauty. Instead of fulfilling the role it had been entrusted with—**acting as the messenger for the bird council**—the Cu bird became enamored with its own reflection, spending all its time admiring itself rather than performing its task.

In a version of the story, the Cu bird's neglect leads to **the god of forests** taking away the birds' ability to speak, as a punishment for their quarrel and the disruption caused by the Cu bird's actions. In another version, after receiving its feathers, the Cu bird is cursed to **remain silent** during the day, as it can no longer speak due to its pride.

Habitat and Behavior:

The Cu bird is most commonly associated with **forests and lakes**, places where it would often look at its reflection in the water, distracted by the beauty of its feathers. It typically hides during the day, staying out of sight, and only comes out at night, when it **can no longer admire its plumage** in the sunlight.

The Cu bird is often described as a **beautiful** yet **vain creature**, whose inability to recognize the importance of duty over appearance leads to its **downfall**. It is now believed to be a creature of **the night**, a shadow in the forests, hidden from the world of sunlight, symbolic of the emptiness that vanity brings.

Legends and Myths:

The story of the Cu bird is often told to emphasize the consequences of **selfishness** and neglecting one's duties. According to the myth, the Cu bird's original form was that of a **plain, featherless** bird, without any special features. The other birds, seeing its plight, decided to help by gifting the Cu bird a feather each. In exchange for these feathers, the Cu bird agreed to become the **messenger of the bird council**, a position of responsibility and importance.

However, when the Cu bird received its magnificent new feathers, it became so **entranced** by its appearance that it **forgot its task**. One day, when the **eagle**, the head of the bird council, sent the Cu bird to call the other birds to a meeting, the Cu bird was so absorbed in its reflection that it completely missed the meeting, and the **birds were left waiting** in vain.

In a fit of rage, the eagle and the other birds began to argue over who was to blame for the failure. The noise and quarrels woke up the **god of the forests**, who, disturbed by the commotion, sent a silent bird to stop the bickering. However, because the bird was **silent**, the quarrelling birds ignored it, leading the god to become so enraged that he **took away their speech**.

As punishment, the birds blamed the **Cu bird** for neglecting its task and the **barn owl** for giving it the feathers in the first place. To teach them a lesson, they decreed that both the Cu bird and the owl would **no longer be seen during the day** and would only be able to exist in the dark, where their beauty and gifts were **no longer appreciated**.

Alternate Versions:

In another version of the story, the Cu bird had no feathers to begin with. The **barn owl** and the **hoot owl** organized the other birds to **donate a feather each** to the Cu bird, giving it the gift of beauty. However, instead of keeping its promise to remain loyal and fulfill its duty, the Cu bird, once adorned with its beautiful feathers, flew off to **better lands**, leaving the other birds behind. This betrayal led to the **hoot owl** being blamed for trusting the Cu bird, and now, the hoot owl calls to the Cu bird at night with a mournful cry: **"Ticú-ticú"**, a name that has become synonymous with the Cu bird's **absence from daylight**.

The Cu Bird of Mexico

"The Cu Bird's Vanity"

In the lush forests of **Mexico**, just as the day was breaking, a quiet council of birds had gathered by the banks of a still lake. The birds, all feathers bright and proud, had come together to discuss the matter of a young bird, the Cu bird, who had no feathers and was often ridiculed by the others.

The **barn owl**, wise beyond years, spoke up, proposing a solution. "Let us help the Cu bird," said the barn owl. "If we each give a feather, the Cu bird will be transformed into a creature of great beauty and strength, and in return, it will serve as our messenger, spreading our words."

The other birds agreed, eager to help, and one by one, they donated a feather. The **hummingbird**, the **parrot**, the **eagle**, and even the shy **woodpecker** gave their finest feathers. Soon, the Cu bird was adorned in a brilliant mix of colors, its plumage shimmering in the light.

"Now, go and fulfill your duty," the barn owl instructed, but the Cu bird, now so entranced by its new feathers, barely heard the words. It fluttered its wings and gazed at its reflection in the water, admiring the vibrancy of its new colors.

Days passed, and the Cu bird failed to appear at the council meetings. It became **lost in its own beauty**, oblivious to the world around it. Its duties as messenger were forgotten, and the birds began to worry.

Finally, the eagle, the head of the council, summoned the Cu bird to deliver an important message. But once again, the Cu bird was nowhere to be found. It was staring at its own reflection, its prideful heart too consumed with vanity to heed the call.

The eagle, furious, searched the skies, calling upon the other birds to help. But the quarrel grew loud, each bird blaming the other for the delay. The commotion reached the ears of the **god of the forests**, who could no longer tolerate the noise. In his wrath, he sent a silent bird to quiet them.

The silent bird fluttered through the trees, but the quarrelling birds ignored it. This angered the god, and in his fury, he took away the birds' ability to speak.

The Cu bird's neglect had cost the entire bird community their voices. Now, no longer able to speak, the birds knew they had been punished, and they turned their anger upon the Cu bird and the barn owl, blaming them for the disaster.

As a final lesson, the god decreed that the **Cu bird** and the **owl** would **no longer be seen in daylight**, relegated to the dark of night, where their beauty could no longer be admired.

And so, the Cu bird remains, hidden in the shadows, its dazzling feathers unseen by the world. Only the mournful call of the **hoot owl**, crying **"Ticú-ticú"**, reminds the birds of the Cu bird's **vanity** and the lesson it taught.

From that day on, the birds knew that beauty without purpose was a curse, and the gift of speech was not to be squandered in the pursuit of self-love.

The Cu Bird is gifted feathers by other birds

15.

Guide to South American Shadows

South American Mythology

South American Creature Guide

Amaru (Andean Folklore)

The Amaru is a powerful serpent-like creature in Andean mythology, often depicted as a giant snake with wings and the ability to fly. Its body is said to resemble a dragon, with scales shimmering in hues of gold and red. Its large, terrifying eyes are capable of seeing into the hearts of humans.

In the myths of the Inca civilization, the Amaru is seen as a guardian spirit that protects the underworld. It is also believed to hold knowledge of both the physical and spiritual realms. The Amaru is said to have a deep connection to water sources and is often associated with rivers and lakes.

Some versions of the myth suggest that the Amaru was defeated by the great hero Pachacuti, but its spirit still guards sacred places in the mountains, ensuring the safety of the people.

Amaru (Andean Folklore)

Coi Coi-Vilu (Chiloe, Chile)

A sea serpent and deity in the folklore of Chile, Coi Coi-Vilu is said to be a powerful being that

Creature Guide | 105

governs the oceans. It is often described as having the body of a giant snake with shimmering blue scales, and its head is adorned with long, flowing fins.

According to the myth, Coi Coi-Vilu battles the land deity, **Pillan**, in a struggle to control the world. The battle between the two causes earthquakes and floods. Eventually, Coi Coi-Vilu is defeated and drowned, but it is said to still influence the tides and weather.

The myth of Coi Coi-Vilu reflects the culture's reverence for both land and sea, as well as the belief in the cyclical nature of life and death.

Teju Jagua *(Paraguayan Folklore)*

A monstrous, multi-headed serpent or lizard, the **Teju Jagua** is said to have seven heads, each capable of breathing fire. Its scales are made of diamond-like material, and its tail is as long as a river.

The Teju Jagua is a guardian of treasure and often seen as a malevolent being, attacking anyone who dares to approach its lair. In some versions of the myth, it is a creature of the underworld, and its roar can be heard echoing in the depths of the earth.

In Paraguay, the Teju Jagua is sometimes said to guard ancient Mayan or Guarani treasures, adding an element of mystery to its legend.

Ten Ten-Vilu *(Chiloe, Chile)*

The Ten Ten-Vilu is a rival serpent to Coi Coi-Vilu, and it represents the **earth and land** in the mythological battle for dominance. It is often depicted as a giant, five-headed serpent with massive claws that can break through mountains.

According to the myth, the Ten Ten-Vilu and Coi Coi-Vilu battled for control of the world. While Coi Coi-Vilu was associated with the sea, Ten Ten-Vilu ruled over the land. The battle between them created the Chilean Archipelago, with the land serpent being buried deep beneath the earth after the war.

The Ten Ten-Vilu myth is tied to the creation of Chile's landscape, with the serpent's remains said to still cause tremors and land shifts today.

Ten Ten-Vilu (Chiloe, Chile)

Boiuna (Amazonian Mythology)

A massive, anaconda-like serpent said to live in the waters of the Amazon River. It is often described as a black, shimmering serpent that can grow to immense sizes, swallowing entire villages and people whole.

The Boiuna is said to be a malevolent entity, devouring anything in its path. In some myths, it is associated with the **underworld** and acts as a protector of the river's depths. It is said that the creature controls the flow of the river and can summon floods to drown those who anger it.

The Boiuna is often linked to ancient myths about the **creation of the Amazon River** and is thought to be one of the oldest beings in the region's folklore.

Curupira (Brazilian Folklore)

The Curupira is a forest spirit often depicted as a **small, red-skinned humanoid** with **backward feet**, making it impossible for anyone to track it. It has wild, flaming hair and a mischievous nature.

The Curupira is considered a protector of the forests and wildlife. It punishes anyone who harms the environment, leading travelers astray and causing them to get lost in the dense Brazilian forests.

Despite its trickster-like behavior, the Curupira is respected as a guardian spirit of nature, emphasizing the importance of maintaining harmony with the environment.

Alicanto (Chilean Mythology)

A **large, radiant bird** with **golden or silver feathers**, the Alicanto is said to live in the mountains of Chile. It is described as having glowing eyes and the ability to fly for long distances without tiring.

According to myth, the Alicanto feeds on gold and silver, leading miners to either riches or ruin. It is said that the Alicanto can lead treasure hunters to hidden caches of precious metals, but only if they are worthy.

The Alicanto's myth is often used as a metaphor for the dangers of greed and the unpredictable nature of fortune, making it a symbolic creature of Chilean folklore.

Chullachaki *(Amazonian Mythology)*

The Chullachaki is a **shape-shifting spirit** that inhabits the Amazonian rainforest. It is said to take the form of a human, but with one feature that is distorted—either a deformed leg, an oversized hand, or a grotesque face.

The Chullachaki lures unsuspecting travelers into the forest, where it can trap them in a state of disorientation. It is a trickster, preying on the weakness of human curiosity and the desire to explore the wilderness.

The Chullachaki is believed to be a protector of the forest, punishing those who disrespect nature. It also symbolizes the consequences of venturing into the unknown without respect for the environment.

Pishtaco *(Andean Folklore)*

A **vampiric creature** from the Andes, the Pishtaco is often depicted as a pale, menacing figure with the ability to drain fat from its victims, leaving them skeletal and lifeless.

The Pishtaco is said to prey on travelers or anyone who strays too far from civilization. The creature is said to use special tools to extract fat from its victims, which it consumes to gain strength.

The Pishtaco is deeply tied to **fear of outsiders** and the belief that foreign invaders (such as colonizers) sought to drain the life force from indigenous peoples. It also serves as a cautionary tale about the dangers of greed and exploitation.

Muki (Bolivian Mythology)

The Muki is a **small, impish creature** that lives in the highlands of Bolivia. It is described as having the body of a **deformed child**, with large, exaggerated features and a grotesque appearance.

The Muki is a mischievous spirit that lures children into the mountains, where it takes them to its lair. It is said to have the power to transform into different animals and can hide in the shadows.

The Muki is often used in stories to teach children about the dangers of wandering off alone, emphasizing the importance of staying close to home and being cautious in unfamiliar places.

Muki (Bolivian Mythology)

PART IV
SHADOWS OF OCEANIA

Oceania, a vast and diverse region encompassing the islands of the Pacific, the rugged terrains of Australia, and the mysterious highlands of New Guinea, is rich with folklore and mythological creatures that speak to the unique cultures and natural landscapes of these lands. From the dense jungles of Melanesia to the deserts of Australia and the coastal plains of New Zealand, the myths of Oceania feature creatures that embody the spirit of these landscapes—beings that are both protectors and punishers, creations of nature, and manifestations of ancestral spirits.

Creatures of Oceania: A Realm of Mystery and Myth

In this section, we explore the most fascinating and enigmatic creatures that roam the vast lands and oceans of Oceania. These include the wild, demoness of **Melanesia**, the captivating and often dangerous spirits of **New Zealand**, and the formidable creatures of the Australian **outback**, where the boundary between the natural and the supernatural is often blurred.

The creatures of **Melanesia** often reflect the region's close connection to the sea, the jungle, and the ancestral spirits that guide the people. In **New Zealand**, Māori mythology speaks of a land steeped in powerful gods and terrifying creatures, like the **Taniwha** are beings that are guardians and punishers of the land. In **Australia**, the **Rainbow Serpent** reigns supreme, a powerful, life-giving force that shapes the land and controls water, while other creatures like the **Bunyip** lurk in the dark, feared and revered.

The stories and creatures of Oceania are rich in symbolism, often representing powerful forces of nature, ancestral wisdom, and the fragile relationship between humans and the world around them. Each myth is a reflection of the landscape, and each creature plays a crucial role in the ecosystem of both the physical and spiritual realms. In this collection, we uncover the deeper meanings of these creatures, from the danger they present to the lessons they impart, and celebrate the rich traditions of Oceania's mythological heritage.

114 | Shadows of Oceania

# 16.

The Bunyip - A Devouring Water Spirit

Australian Aboriginal Folklore

Classification: Amphibious, Nocturnal, Reclusive

Habitat: Lakes, Rivers, Swamps, Billabongs, Creeks, Riverbeds, Waterholes

The Bunyip

The Bunyip is described as an amphibious creature, capable of swimming swiftly with fins or flippers. Its appearance is often shrouded in mystery, but it is believed to possess a large body, long neck, and webbed limbs.

Behavioral Traits:

The Bunyip is known to be a reclusive creature, preferring to inhabit isolated areas of its habitat. It is nocturnal, meaning it is most active at night, and is said to emit a loud, roaring call that can be heard for miles. This call serves as a warning to potential intruders, deterring them from approaching its territory.

Diet and Hunting Habits:

According to Aboriginal mythology, the Bunyip is a bloodthirsty predator, feeding on humans, particularly women and children. It is said to target individuals who venture into its territory uninvited, taking advantage of their vulnerability.

Mythological Significance:

In Ngarrindjeri dreaming, the Bunyip is referred to as the Mulyawonk, a water spirit tasked with maintaining balance and order in the waterways. However, when it becomes aggressive, it is said to punish those who overfish or threaten the safety of children near the water's edge.

Cultural Significance:

The Bunyip holds significant cultural importance among Aboriginal Australians, serving as a cautionary tale about respecting the power of nature and avoiding unfamiliar bodies of water. Its legend has been passed down through generations, ensuring the continued reverence for this fearsome water spirit.

The Bunyip from Australian Aboriginal Folklore

The Bunyip's Lair

The Australian outback is a place of harsh beauty and ancient secrets. The sun beats down on cracked earth, stretching endlessly into the horizon, while the wind whispers through the sparse trees. But beneath the surface, the land holds stories—stories that the land itself seems to breathe, stories told only by those brave enough to listen.

It was on one such day, when the sun hung low in the sky, that young William set out on his journey. He had heard the stories of the Bunyip all his life, stories from the elders, whispered warnings passed down through generations. The Bunyip, they said, lived in the dark, murky waters of the swamps and billabongs, a creature of terror with the body of a giant, with dark eyes that glowed like embers in the night, and a voice that could echo through the souls of the living. It was a creature that no man dared approach, for to do so would mean certain death.

William, however, was no ordinary boy. He had grown up on the edge of the vast wetlands of New South Wales, and he had always wondered whether the Bunyip was real, or simply a figment of the old storytellers' imagination. Armed with little more than his wits and a sharp hunting knife, he decided that he would venture into the swamp to find out for himself.

His grandmother had warned him. "The Bunyip does not welcome trespassers," she had said, her voice a low murmur as she stared into the fire. "It's the keeper of the water, and no man, no matter how brave, should go searching for it. Not even in the daylight."

But William was headstrong. The sun was beginning its descent behind the mountains, casting long shadows across the earth, and he knew he needed to be quick if he was to return before nightfall.

The swamp was still, save for the occasional croak of a distant frog. The air hung thick with humidity, and the ground was soft beneath his boots, the mud sucking at his steps. He made his way deeper into the waterlogged land, the trees around him growing taller and more twisted with every step, as though they were watching him.

As the light began to fade, William reached a clearing at the heart of the swamp. The water here was still and dark, like a mirror to the sky above. He crouched low beside the bank, his eyes scanning the depths, waiting. It wasn't long before he heard it—a distant, low growl, barely audible over the wind. The hairs on the back of his neck stood up. His heart raced.

He had been warned. But there was no turning back now.

The water rippled. Slowly, methodically, the surface of the swamp began to stir, as if something large was moving beneath the water. A shadow, dark and foreboding, emerged. It was enormous, a great mass that seemed to rise from the depths itself, its head shaped like a large, twisted hump. Its eyes gleamed, two pale orbs staring directly at William.

The Bunyip.

William's breath caught in his throat. The creature's body was massive, with skin that glistened like the murky water, slick and dark. It had the body of a gigantic animal, but its face was something far more terrifying, a mixture of both human and beast. Its jaws parted slightly, revealing sharp, glistening teeth.

For a moment, the two locked eyes.

Then, without warning, the Bunyip let out a horrific roar that shook the air itself. The sound was like the cry of a thousand souls, filled with rage and sorrow, as though the creature was mourning something lost, something ancient. William's heart pounded in his chest, and his legs felt as though they had turned to stone. The Bunyip rose further from the water, towering above him.

But then, as quickly as it had appeared, it retreated. The ripples in the water grew larger, and the shadow of the creature dissolved into the depths. It left William standing alone in the swamp, his breath ragged, his eyes wide.

The air around him was thick with the creature's presence, but there was no sign of it now. Just the stillness of the swamp.

William stood there for a long moment, his mind spinning. Had he truly seen the Bunyip, or had it been a trick of his imagination? But deep down, he knew what he had felt. The Bunyip was real. It was the guardian of these waters, an ancient being that protected the swamp from intrusion.

He turned to leave, his legs trembling, but before he could take a step, he heard the sound again. A low growl, distant but unmistakable. William's heart raced. The Bunyip had not gone far—it was still watching him, waiting.

With a final glance over his shoulder, William made his way back, faster now, his thoughts full of the ancient creature that had stalked him in the depths. The Bunyip was not a myth. It was a guardian, a creature of the swamp. And its legend, like the water itself, would never truly fade.

As he stepped out of the swamp, the air felt different. It was as though the Bunyip's presence lingered in the air, a reminder that some legends are best left untouched. And though William returned to the safety of his home, he knew that the swamp would always be there, holding its secrets, waiting for the next fool to venture too close to its waters.

The Bunyip and William

17.

Taniwha, Creatures of Deep Rivers, Caves and Oceans

Māori Mythology

In Māori mythology, **Taniwha** are large supernatural beings that inhabit deep pools in rivers, dark caves, or the sea, particularly in places where dangerous currents or deceptive breakers (giant waves) exist. Their appearances vary greatly—some taniwha resemble whale-like or shark-like creatures, while others are described as lizard-like with spiny backs. These creatures may be considered highly revered guardians, or feared predatory beings, depending on the context of the legend.

Taniwha

Taniwha are typically seen as protectors, known as **kaitiaki**, of specific tribal areas, ensuring the safety of their people. However, they also have a dark side—some are believed to be dangerous, capable of kidnapping women, or engaging in violent acts, especially against those outside their tribe.

Taniwha can be male or female, with some legends telling stories of taniwha that arrived with early voyaging canoes, taking on roles as guardians of the people who sailed with those canoes. These beings can be territorial and very protective, but are typically understood to be respectful as long as people adhere to local customs, particularly when dealing with their lairs or sacred spaces.

Taniwha possess a vast array of supernatural abilities, including the power to **manipulate water**, **cause storms**, and **create or destroy land formations**. Some taniwha have been credited with carving out harbors, such as **Te Whanganui-a-Tara** (Wellington Harbour), or causing landslides near lakes and rivers. Their size and strength are formidable, and they are often depicted as controlling the elements—whether water, earth, or wind—at their whim.

In certain stories, taniwha are also capable of transforming into different creatures. While some are said to resemble the shape of a whale or shark, others take on the form of a gigantic reptile, often with spiny backs or fins.

Cultural Significance:

Taniwha are deeply embedded in Māori culture, often viewed as guardians of waterways, land, and the people who inhabit those areas. Tribal leaders sometimes used taniwha to symbolize the power and protection of their people, and they were often invoked in ceremonies to ensure good harvests, health, and safety from enemies. The dual nature of taniwha—both protective and dangerous—symbolizes the complex relationship between humans and the natural world.

Many Māori communities have their own taniwha, with each group considering theirs a direct protector or ancestor spirit. The mythology surrounding taniwha varies by region, and they have played an integral part in shaping tribal identity. The concept of **tapu** (sacredness) also ties into the relationship between taniwha and humans, where any violation of a taniwha's sacred territory could lead to retribution.

Taniwha: A Short Story

The Taniwha of Kaipara

A long time ago, in the rugged landscape of the Kaipara district, three sisters set out to gather berries near the edge of the forest. The land was untouched by human hands, with dense trees and the constant hum of nature filling the air. They wandered further into the thick woods, unaware of the dangerous spirit lurking nearby.

One of the sisters, **Riria**, was known for her beauty, her hair like the dark ocean and her eyes shining like the full moon. Her two sisters, **Aroha** and **Māhina**, were just as beautiful, but it was Riria who caught the eye of the taniwha that haunted the region.

As the sisters made their way home, the wind shifted, carrying an unnatural chill that made the hairs on the back of their necks stand. From the deep waters of the river, a low rumble echoed, followed by a splash so powerful it seemed to shake the earth itself.

A great **taniwha**, its body rippling with muscle and covered in scales like a giant gecko, rose from the depths of the river. It was an ancient creature, one that had lived for centuries, and it had set its eyes upon Riria.

"Run!" cried Aroha, grabbing her sister's arm as they raced through the trees. But Riria was too slow—before they could reach the safety of the village, the taniwha had caught her, its massive claws wrapping around her waist.

"Let her go!" shouted Māhina, wielding a large spear, but her words fell on deaf ears.

With an eerie roar, the taniwha retreated into the cave by the river, Riria helpless in its grip. The sisters returned to the village, their hearts heavy with sorrow, and pleaded with their elders for help. The taniwha had taken Riria, and no one knew how to defeat such a creature.

Time passed, and the village was slowly consumed with dread, fearing that the taniwha would strike again. Riria remained captive, forced to live in the taniwha's lair, but she had not forgotten her people.

Years later, the villagers realized that Riria had borne the taniwha six sons. Three of them were like their father, monstrous and lizard-like, but the others were human—strong, wise, and capable. Riria had taught her human sons the art of war, how to craft weapons, and how to use them against the taniwha.

One fateful night, the sons—armed with weapons forged from stone and bone—approached the taniwha's lair. They fought valiantly, but their battle was not without sorrow. The three human sons defeated their monstrous brothers, cutting them down with great skill and precision. The taniwha, enraged by the loss of its offspring, roared a final, thunderous cry before it was slain.

In the aftermath of the battle, the villagers returned to their homes, their hearts heavy with grief. They had slain the taniwha, but Riria's pain was too great. She mourned the loss of her monstrous sons, and though the village rejoiced in their victory, there was a deep sense of loss in the air.

As the years passed, the story of the taniwha lived on in the hearts of the people. They would tell it to their children, the tale of the great guardian and the monstrous beast, and how even in death, the taniwha had brought them both tragedy and strength. And though the taniwha was gone, its memory remained in the deep waters of Kaipara, ever-present, a reminder of the dangers that lurked beneath the surface.

Taniwha, the large supernatural water beings from Māori mythology

18.

Ponaturi, Hostile, Goblin-like Creatures

Māori Mythology

The **Ponaturi** are a group of hostile, goblin-like creatures in Māori mythology, known for their malicious nature and their ties to the sea. These creatures dwell beneath the waves during the day, returning to shore each evening to sleep in their eerie, mysterious house, **Manawa-Tāne**. Their connection to the sea makes them particularly dangerous, as they can emerge from the water at night, hunting and wreaking havoc on those nearby.

Ponaturi (Māori Mythological Creatures)

The Ponaturi dread daylight, as the rays of the sun are fatal to them. This vulnerability is central to their downfall in various legends. By day, they remain hidden beneath the water's surface, but by night, they emerge, taking advantage of the cover of darkness to carry out their nefarious activities. Often described as grotesque, they have monstrous features and are typically seen as a great threat to humans.

The Ponaturi are described as monstrous, goblin-like creatures, with some versions of the myth portraying them as short, squat beings with elongated, grotesque features. Their eyes are often depicted as glowing in the dark, and their forms are repulsive, with large, gnarled hands. In some versions of the myth, the Ponaturi are associated with the sea and are said to have marine features, such as scales or fins. They are considered terrifying in appearance, causing dread wherever they go.

Abilities:

The Ponaturi possess a variety of supernatural powers, including the ability to manipulate the environment around them through magical incantations. They have the ability to steal human bodies, take prisoners, and carry out cruel deeds in the darkness. However, they are most vulnerable when exposed to sunlight, which is fatal to them. Their connection to the sea grants them strength in the dark, but they are entirely dependent on the cover of night for their survival. They also practice dark magic, and their priests are capable of using powerful spells to harm others.

Cultural Significance:

The Ponaturi are typically viewed as dangerous and disruptive forces in Māori mythology, serving as a warning against venturing too far into the unknown or engaging in certain taboo activities. They symbolize the darkness and chaos that can invade the world when the natural order is disrupted. As creatures that hide during the day and are active by night, they represent the primal forces of nature that operate in the unseen and dangerous hours.

Their interactions with heroes like **Tāwhaki** and **Rātā** reflect the theme of overcoming seemingly insurmountable evil through cunning and bravery. The Ponaturi's vulnerability to sunlight and their eventual destruction by human ingenuity are recurring motifs that emphasize the triumph of knowledge, light, and courage over darkness and evil.

Ponaturi: A Short Story

The Revenge of Tāwhaki

The wind howled through the trees as **Tāwhaki** gazed out over the sea, his heart heavy with grief. His father, **Hemā**, had been taken from him by the **Ponaturi**, those monstrous beings who lived in the depths of the sea. It was their custom to steal from the land, abducting the innocent under the cover of darkness, and to Tāwhaki, they were nothing more than thieves and murderers.

His mother, **Urutonga**, had also been captured and forced to serve as the doorkeeper in their lair, **Manawa-Tāne**. No one could enter or leave their domain without her permission, and she had been helpless to do anything but watch as her husband was taken and their home invaded.

But Tāwhaki would not let this go unpunished. With a heart full of resolve, he set out to confront the Ponaturi and take back what they had stolen. Armed with his knowledge of their weakness—sunlight—and his quick wit, Tāwhaki devised a cunning plan to outsmart the creatures and bring an end to their reign of terror.

He journeyed with his mother to their home above the water, **Manawa-Tāne**, a place of dark magic and dreadful mystery. As they approached, Tāwhaki gave his mother a special tool—a stone he had carved from the heart of a mountain. This stone was key to his plan: a way to block all the holes in the Ponaturi's house and make them believe that it was still night.

Urutonga, with the stone in hand, began sealing up the openings of the Ponaturi's lair. They worked swiftly, sealing every crack and gap, until the house was completely shut off from the outside world. The Ponaturi, believing it was still the safety of night, did not notice the sunlight creeping in, filtering through the cracks.

When the moment came, Tāwhaki's voice rang out, a powerful chant that pierced the stillness. The stones fell away from the windows and doors, and rays of the sun flooded the house, turning the night into the dreaded day. As the Ponaturi writhed in pain, their monstrous forms dissolving in the sunlight, Tāwhaki watched with a mixture of triumph and sorrow.

The Ponaturi—creatures of darkness and shadow—were no more.

But Tāwhaki knew that their death had come at a cost. His father, Hemā, was lost forever, his body stolen by the creatures, never to return. Yet, in their destruction, Tāwhaki found a sense of peace. He had avenged his father's death and freed his mother from the Ponaturi's grip.

The sunlight now gleamed on the sea, the waves crashing softly against the shore and the house where the Ponaturi had once been. And as Tāwhaki stood with his mother, he felt a connection to the world of light—the world that could no longer be overshadowed by the creatures of the deep.

The Ponaturi were gone, but the memory of their terror would never fade, a lesson to all that darkness, no matter how powerful, could never stand against the light of knowledge, courage, and the dawn of a new day.

The **Ponaturi** in this story serve as the embodiment of the dangerous, shadowy forces that lurk in the unknown, waiting to prey on the unsuspecting. However, with bravery, wisdom, and the power of light (symbolizing truth and clarity), they are defeated, reinforcing the eternal victory of light over darkness.

Ponaturi, the group of hostile goblin-like creatures from Māori mythology

19.

Rainbow Serpent of the Dreamtime

Australian Aboriginal Mythology

The **Rainbow Serpent** is one of the most powerful and revered figures in Australian Aboriginal mythology, known for its immense size and influence over the landscape. It is a highly complex and multifaceted being, sometimes represented as a serpent, sometimes a snake, and in some versions, a great, undulating, rainbow-colored creature. The Rainbow Serpent is closely associated with the **Dreamtime** or **Tjukurrpa**, the Aboriginal creation myth, and is considered the ultimate creator or deity responsible for shaping the land, creating waterholes, rivers, and even entire mountain ranges.

Rainbow Serpent (Australian Aboriginal Mythology)

The Rainbow Serpent can inhabit deep waterholes, springs, and other sources of life-giving water, which are often seen as the Serpent's physical manifestation. In addition, the **Rainbow Serpent** is tied to the cycle of rain and floods, which are essential to the land's fertility. It is believed to control the life-giving waters and ensures that the natural world remains balanced. Its presence in the landscape is often signaled by rainbows, the colors of which are said to be the Serpent's colors.

Physical Appearance:

The Rainbow Serpent is described in many ways depending on the region and culture. Commonly, it is imagined as a massive serpent or snake, with iridescent scales that shimmer in all colors of the rainbow. In some stories, the Serpent's body is adorned with a crest or mane, and it can be depicted as both majestic and fearsome. Its long, flowing body is symbolic of both creation and destruction, as it can form vast rivers or deep gorges with a mere movement.

In certain Aboriginal cultures, the Rainbow Serpent is depicted as androgynous or bi-gender, emphasizing its creative force, which includes both masculine and feminine qualities. Its appearance is fluid and mystical, capable of shifting forms to suit its needs as both a creator and a punisher.

Abilities:

The Rainbow Serpent's most significant ability is its control over water, making it a vital part of the water cycle in Aboriginal cosmology. It is said that without the Serpent, no rain would fall, and the earth would dry up. When the Serpent is angered, powerful storms, cyclones, and lightning are unleashed. Conversely, when calm, the Serpent brings water, sustenance, and fertility to the land.

The Serpent is also a creator of landscapes, forming gullies, mountains, and rivers as it travels across the earth. It shapes the physical environment with its massive body, carving out the land and creating sacred sites. Some stories attribute to the Serpent the creation of human life and its role in transitioning individuals from adolescence to adulthood.

Cultural Significance:

The Rainbow Serpent is one of the most significant deities in Aboriginal culture. It is a symbol of creation, destruction, and renewal. The Serpent's power over water makes it an essential figure in fertility and sustenance, representing the balance between life and death. It is both revered and feared for its ability to control life-giving water and its capacity for destruction.

In many Aboriginal myths, the Rainbow Serpent is also associated with fertility rites and rites of passage, especially those related to adulthood and the cycles of nature. It is a symbol of both protection and punishment, enforcing the laws of nature and ensuring that the natural order is maintained. The Rainbow Serpent's vast influence extends over creation, life, death, and the sacred, connecting the spiritual world with the physical one.

The Awakening of the Rainbow Serpent

In the time before time, the world was barren, with no rivers, no mountains, and no creatures. The earth was a flat expanse, stretching out endlessly in all directions, devoid of life. The air was still, and the sun had not yet been introduced to the sky. But deep within the earth, a force stirred, its power unknown, its shape a mystery.

From the blackened soil, the great **Rainbow Serpent** began to emerge, its body coiling and uncoiling like a river of color. It moved silently at first, its vast body undulating across the ground, leaving behind a trail of iridescent light. The Serpent was the earth's pulse, the very breath of creation. As it moved, the land began to take shape: ridges rose up from the earth, rivers carved their way through the barren landscape, and deep gorges formed, their sides steep and jagged.

The Serpent's first task was to shape the waters. It slithered across the land, its body forming vast waterholes and springs wherever it touched the earth. These pools became the lifeblood of the land, feeding the earth with the water that would sustain all life. The Rainbow Serpent's colors began to reflect in the waters, shimmering with every hue of the rainbow.

But the Rainbow Serpent did not stop there. It could sense the void within the land, the emptiness that needed to be filled. From its body, the Serpent summoned the first animals—frogs, birds, and lizards—and gave them life. It molded the first humans from the clay, teaching them to walk, to speak, and to live in harmony with the land.

The Serpent's power over the waters was unmatched. When it slithered across the land, it would bring the rains, ensuring the land remained fertile. But the Rainbow Serpent was not just a creator; it was also a punisher. When the balance was disturbed, when the laws of nature were violated, the Serpent would rise in anger. Thunder and lightning would roar from the sky, and fierce storms would flood the land.

One such storm occurred when a group of people, in their ignorance, had disturbed the sacred waters where the Serpent dwelled. They had been warned, but they did not listen. The Serpent, enraged by their disrespect, rose from its resting place, its massive form coiling around the mountains. The winds howled, and the rains poured in torrents, flooding the earth and drowning those who had defied the Serpent's will.

As the storm raged, the people realized their mistake. They offered prayers to the Rainbow Serpent, pleading for forgiveness. But the Serpent, wise and patient, saw their remorse. The rain slowed, the winds ceased, and the clouds parted. The Serpent returned to its resting place beneath the earth, allowing the sun to shine through for the first time.

From that day on, the people understood the power and the importance of the Rainbow Serpent. They lived in harmony with the land, offering respect to the Serpent and its sacred waters. The Serpent, in turn, continued to shape the land, bringing rain and life, ensuring that the cycle of creation and renewal would never cease.

And so, the **Rainbow Serpent** became the eternal guardian of the land, the keeper of water, and the protector of all living things. Its colors would continue to reflect in the sky after every storm, a reminder of the Serpent's presence, power, and eternal watch over the earth.

The **Rainbow Serpent** remains a powerful figure in Aboriginal mythology, representing creation, fertility, destruction, and the balance of nature. Its stories reflect the intimate relationship between humans, the land, and the forces of nature that shape the world around them.

Rainbow Serpent of the Dreamtime, Australian Aboriginal Mythology

20.

Abere, the Fearsome Demoness

Melanesian Mythology

Abere is a fearsome demoness in Melanesian mythology, often depicted as a wild and captivating woman who dwells in the remote, mist-covered marshes. With her striking beauty, she lures unsuspecting victims to her domain, where she entraps them in a deadly snare. Abere is often accompanied by a retinue of young female servants, who assist her in carrying out her sinister deeds.

Abere (Melanesian Mythology)

Her beauty is the key to her power, drawing individuals—often travelers or curious souls—toward the dangerous marshlands. Once a victim is entranced by her allure and enters the marsh, Abere uses her control over nature to trap them. Reeds grow rapidly, ensnaring the victim and preventing any escape. This trap, a manifestation of her supernatural control over the environment, is both symbolic and literal: it reflects her ability to entangle, both physically and mentally, those who fall for her enchantments.

Abere is most commonly described as a beautiful woman, embodying the allure that makes her so dangerous. Her appearance is striking, often youthful and radiant, with long flowing hair and a figure that seems almost too perfect to be true. However, beneath this beauty lies her true monstrous nature. In some versions of the myth, her features shift once she captures her prey, revealing her true form: a wild, untamed creature with unnatural features that reflect her demonic origins.

Accompanying her are often young female servants, who may appear similar to her in beauty and are complicit in her acts of entrapment and devouring. These figures are often portrayed as both helpers and followers, operating under Abere's enchantment or out of fear.

Abilities:

Abere's primary power lies in her ability to control the natural environment around her, especially the marshes. She can cause the reeds and vegetation to grow rapidly, creating an impenetrable barrier that traps her victims. This magical control over nature is central to her ability to capture those who are lured by her beauty. Once ensnared, the victims are unable to escape, and Abere can feast upon them at her leisure.

In some stories, Abere is said to possess the ability to enchant with her voice or gaze, further ensnaring those who encounter her. She is also associated with the marshlands' dangerous and deceptive nature, a place where the boundary between the physical world and the spirit world is blurred. Her power lies not only in her control over the land but also in her ability to ensnare the minds of those who venture too close to her domain.

Cultural Significance:

Abere is a figure that embodies the dangers of temptation and the destructive consequences of falling prey to false appearances. In Melanesian cultures, her story serves as a cautionary tale about the perils of wandering into unknown, wild places and succumbing to the allure of beauty without regard for the dangers that lie beneath the surface.

The myth of Abere also reflects the importance of respecting natural boundaries and the sacredness of certain places. The marshes where she resides are often seen as liminal spaces, where the rules of the physical world are suspended, and where the supernatural realm is close. Abere's ability to entrap her victims highlights the power of the unseen forces that lurk in such places.

The concept of a beautiful woman leading others to their doom speaks to themes of power, control, and manipulation, with Abere representing the dangers of being deceived by outward appearances.

Abere, the demoness captures Kalo

Abere: The Marshes of Death

In the deep, mist-filled marshes of the highlands, the villagers told tales of **Abere**, the wild woman who lived in the heart of the wetlands. Her beauty was said to be unmatched—her face was like the first rays of dawn, and her laughter was like the soft rustling of reeds in the wind. It was said that she could make the water sparkle and the plants bloom with just a glance, but those who ventured too close soon found out that her beauty was but a mask for the deadly force beneath.

A young man named **Kalo** had heard these tales all his life. He had grown up in the village near the edge of the marsh, but the stories never ceased to intrigue him. He would listen to the elders speak of Abere, of how she would lure men with her enchanting beauty and then trap them in the reeds, never to be seen again. Some said she would eat them, others said she would imprison them forever. But the allure of the marsh—and the wild woman who lived there—pulled at Kalo's heart.

One afternoon, unable to resist any longer, Kalo set out toward the marsh. The mist was thick, and the air was heavy with the scent of damp earth and flowers. He walked deeper into the marshlands, feeling the soft earth beneath his feet, when he saw her—Abere, standing by a quiet pool of water, her long hair flowing around her like a veil.

She was more beautiful than the stories had ever described. Her eyes gleamed with an otherworldly light, and her smile was like the sun breaking through the clouds. Without a word, she gestured for Kalo to approach. Drawn in by her beauty, he moved forward, his heart racing. But as he stepped closer, he felt something strange—a creeping sensation, as if the very ground beneath him was shifting.

Before he could react, the reeds around him began to grow, their long, slender stalks wrapping around his legs, pulling him down. Panic surged through him as the marsh closed in, the once serene water now bubbling around his feet. He struggled, but the more he fought, the tighter the reeds pulled, until he was completely ensnared.

"Why do you come to my marsh?" Abere's voice was soft, almost like a whisper, but it echoed through his mind. She approached him, her eyes glowing with an eerie light.

"I wanted to see you," Kalo said, his voice trembling.

Abere's smile widened. "And now you will stay with me, forever."

With a wave of her hand, the reeds tightened further. Kalo felt his body grow cold as his strength began to drain away. The beauty that had drawn him in now felt like a cruel trick. Abere stepped closer, her face hovering near his, and whispered, "Do you regret it?"

Kalo struggled, his breath shallow. "I was foolish..."

Just then, a sharp crack broke the silence—a loud, splintering sound. A figure appeared from the mist, a woman who seemed to glide effortlessly across the marsh. It was **Raka**, Kalo's sister, who had been searching for him. She had heard the stories, too, and knew what to do.

Raka raised her hands high, calling out in a language that Kalo did not understand. The water rippled, and the reeds loosened, their grip faltering as the voice of the sacred chant filled the air. Abere hissed, her beauty warping into something monstrous as her servants—the young women who had served her for so long—appeared, their faces twisted in anguish.

"Leave him, Abere!" Raka's voice rang out. "The land is not yours to claim."

The wild woman recoiled, her eyes flashing with rage. With one final shriek, she vanished into the mist, her form dissolving like a wisp of smoke. The marsh fell silent once more, the water still and peaceful as the threat receded.

Kalo collapsed into his sister's arms, his breath returning. He had nearly fallen victim to the wild beauty of Abere, but his sister's knowledge of the old ways had saved him. As they walked back to the village, the marsh behind them seemed less ominous, the mist lifting as if in recognition of the balance being restored.

But Kalo knew, deep in his heart, that the stories of Abere would never lose their power—her beauty and her danger were forever entwined in the legends of the marsh.

The myth of **Abere**, the demoness of the marshes, serves as a powerful reminder of the duality of nature—its ability to both allure and destroy. Her beauty is a trap, and her domain is a place where life and death are inextricably linked. In this tale, her power is defeated by knowledge and ritual, reinforcing the importance of respect for the natural world and the ancient wisdom of the people.

Abere, Demoness from Melanesian mythology

PART V
SHADOWS OF EUROPEAN FOLKLORE

European folklore is rich with an expansive array of mythological creatures, each woven into the fabric of cultural traditions and belief systems. From the dark forests of Scandinavia to the misty hills of the British Isles, these creatures have been passed down through generations, their stories varying but often retaining their core elements of mystery, danger, and magic. Whether as agents of fear, guardians of the supernatural, or reflections of human nature, these creatures have captured the imaginations of those who dwell in the lands they haunt.

The Shadows of European Folklore

This section delves into the diverse creatures of European folklore, each uniquely tied to the customs and landscapes of their respective regions. From the ethereal **Wild Hunt** of northern Europe to the eerie ***changelings of Celtic origin***, these beings often embody the dangers of the natural world and the supernatural realm. Many are creatures of night and shadow, like vampires and werewolves, while others represent the eternal battle between good and evil, such as the notorious devilish figures and vengeful spirits.

These creatures not only reflect the fears and moral lessons of their time but also serve as powerful symbols in literature, art, and modern media. Their appearances have shifted and evolved over the centuries, yet they remain deeply embedded in European cultural identity.

Throughout this section, we will explore the origins, characteristics, and significance of these creatures, delving into their various forms and the mythological contexts in which they appear. From the ghastly *Wilde Jagd* (Wild Hunt) to the many forms of the white lady, the supernatural beings of European folklore offer a glimpse into a world where the line between the living and the dead is often blurred, and where the unknown is as feared as it is revered.

Prepare to encounter a host of creatures that range from mischievous sprites to terrifying monsters, each adding its own layer to the mythic tapestry of Europe.

Shadows of European Folklore

21.

Androktasiai (Greek Mythology)

Greek Mythology

The Androktasiai

The **Androktasiai**, also known as the "slayers of men," are violent, bloodthirsty personifications of war and destruction. These beings are female warriors, often depicted as terrifying and relentless in battle, fueled by an insatiable thirst for vengeance and bloodshed. Their names themselves are a reflection of their violent nature, as "Androktasiai" directly translates to "the slayers of men."

Physical Appearance:

The Androktasiai are generally portrayed as fierce, armored women with long, flowing hair, and their eyes gleam with an unearthly fury. They wear dark, battle-worn armor, decorated with symbols of death and carnage. Some depictions show them with wings or armored faces, making them appear otherworldly, and their bodies often seem to radiate an aura of death. Their weapons of choice are swords or spears, which they wield with precision, bringing swift death to their victims.

Abilities and Powers:

Androktasiai are imbued with the power of battle, capable of inciting bloodshed and destruction wherever they go. Their presence on the battlefield is enough to turn the tide of war, filling the hearts of warriors with a primal rage. They are also known for their resilience, impervious to most forms of attack, embodying the unrelenting nature of war itself.

Habitat and Behavior:

These vengeful spirits do not dwell in a specific place but appear on battlefields, where violence and death are rampant. They are attracted to chaos, embodying the violence that unfolds during war. Their behavior is one of pure destruction, and they delight in causing pain and suffering. They interact with other violent spirits like the Erinyes and the Keres, feeding off the rage and agony of war.

Mythological Context:

Origin Story: The Androktasiai are believed to have emerged as manifestations of the destructive aspects of war. They were born from the very chaos and bloodshed that war brings, created as embodiments of vengeance and rage.

Symbolic Meaning: In Greek mythology, the Androktasiai symbolize the uncontrollable fury and bloodlust that war can unleash. They represent the dark side of human conflict—the personal vengeance that drives soldiers to commit atrocities.

Notable Legends and Tales: Though they are often seen alongside other deities like Ares and Athena during battles, they don't play central roles in most myths. However, their presence is ever-looming on battlefields, and they are often mentioned in the context of large-scale wars where death reigns.

Cultural Variations: The Androktasiai are uniquely Greek, but similar concepts exist in other cultures. In Roman mythology, their counterparts would be the "Furies" or "Erinyes," who are also female figures that bring vengeance and punishment.

The Androktasiai

22.

Erinyes, Embodiment of Vengeance

Greek Mythology

The **Erinyes**, or Furies, are the embodiment of vengeance, tasked with punishing crimes, particularly those involving familial betrayal, such as matricide and patricide. They are known for their relentless pursuit of justice through torment, and they bring severe punishment to those who defy divine law.

Erinyes (Greek) and Furies (Roman)

Physical Appearance:

The Erinyes are depicted as terrifying, winged women with serpents entwined in their hair, their eyes burning with rage. Their bodies are often shown in dark, flowing robes that flutter menacingly as they fly. The Erinyes are armed with whips or snakes, which they use to lash their victims into madness or to execute their revenge.

Abilities and Powers:

The Erinyes possess the power to incite guilt and insanity in their victims, driving them to madness with their relentless pursuit. They are also capable of torturing the souls of the guilty, dragging them to the underworld for judgment. Their mere presence is enough to make any wrongdoer tremble with fear.

Habitat and Behavior:

They are often found in the underworld, where they reside and wait for the moment to rise from the depths of the earth and pursue wrongdoers. They are also present in mythological stories where individuals have committed heinous acts of betrayal. They do not rest until justice is served, and their behavior is marked by merciless persistence.

Mythological Context:

Origin Story: The Erinyes are born from the blood of Uranus when his son, Cronus, castrates him. The blood of Uranus falls onto Gaia, and from this, the Erinyes are created. They are vengeful spirits who exact retribution on those who commit crimes against natural law.

Symbolic Meaning: The Erinyes are symbols of divine retribution, particularly focused on punishing those who betray family ties. Their anger is seen as a necessary force for maintaining balance and justice in the world.

Notable Legends and Tales: The Erinyes play a prominent role in the myth of Orestes, who is pursued by them for avenging his mother's murder. The Erinyes' role is central to the themes of justice, vengeance, and moral retribution.

Cultural Variations: Similar entities in other mythologies include the **Furies** in Roman culture and the **Fates** in Greek myth, who also serve as forces of retribution but are more connected to destiny than personal vengeance.

152 | The Erinyes

23.

The Demogorgon

European Folklore

The Demogorgon – Origin and Etymology

The Demogorgon is a deity or demon that has captivated scholars and mythologists for centuries. While its origins remain somewhat ambiguous, the most commonly accepted theory is that the name "Demogorgon" stems from a misreading of the Greek word **δημιουργόν** (*dēmiourgón*), meaning "demiurge" or "creator," as mentioned in the commentary by Lactantius Placidus on Statius's *Thebaid*.

This early manuscript reference, dating from around 350-400 AD, marks the first known appearance of Demogorgon in written form. Scholars have since speculated that the name was a corruption of "demiurge," the philosophical concept of a cosmic creator that arises from the work of Plato, who described the demiurge as a being responsible for shaping the material world.

Despite its Greek roots, the term "Demogorgon" was later attributed to various mythological beings, including a demon and a supreme god, often linked to the **underworld** and the primordial forces of chaos. The name itself, influenced by the earlier term *daimon* (spirit) and *gorgós* (terrifying), conveys a sense of terror and divine power. Over time, Demogorgon became a fixture in **Renaissance mythography**, with Boccaccio and later scholars referring to it as an elemental force of nature, "the God of the Earth" or "Terror-Demon."

Description

The Demogorgon is often depicted as a **primordial being**, more of an abstract concept than a detailed physical entity. In some interpretations, it is visualized as a **giant**, part demon and part god, often characterized by a terrifying and indescribable appearance. It is said to reside in the **underworld**, where it presides over the forces of darkness and creation. In medieval texts, Demogorgon was considered the **father of all gods** or the **supreme deity** whose name was forbidden to know, reinforcing the mysterious and enigmatic nature surrounding its existence.

The most common physical depictions in later literature present Demogorgon as an embodiment of **primordial chaos**, often a shapeless force or a demonic figure with countless heads, an ever-shifting form, or boundless power that defies mortal comprehension. Its role as the "God of the Earth" and "Demon of Terror" makes it a symbol of the unknown and ungovernable forces that lay beyond human understanding.

Mythological Context

While the Demogorgon appears in Greek and Roman texts, it became more firmly entrenched in **medieval and Renaissance thought**. In these periods, it was often considered an element of the **cosmological hierarchy**, with some thinking of it as a **primordial deity** responsible for the earth's creation. In this context, it was seen as a creator-god with dominion over the physical world but shrouded in mystery, suggesting a force too powerful to be named or fully understood.

Legends

One of the most famous legends surrounding Demogorgon is the belief that it was the source of all the gods, emerging from the chaos before creation itself. The creature is sometimes linked with **Hades** or **Pluto**, the ruler of the underworld, and considered an equal or even a superior to these figures. It was thought that Demogorgon's influence could **bring destruction or creation**, depending on the needs of the universe. Its mere presence could induce chaos, and as such, it was feared as a deity who could alter the very fabric of reality.

Another significant legend involves its role in the **Renaissance**, where it became a prominent figure in occult and esoteric traditions. The concept of Demogorgon often appeared in the writings of **alchemists** and **philosophers**, with some linking the name to **transmutation** and the creation of life. This idea links Demogorgon with the alchemical tradition of the **philosopher's stone**, which represented the ability to transcend material existence and create eternal life.

Cultural Significance

The Demogorgon is significant not just as a figure of myth, but also as a symbol of **mystery, creation, and destruction**. In later occult and esoteric traditions, it is sometimes seen as a symbol of **transformation**, representing the cyclical nature of life and death. Its link to **primordial chaos** makes it a figure of immense power, embodying both the **fear of the unknown** and the forces that shape the universe in ways that cannot be understood by mortals.

"The Awakening of Demogorgon"

The night was unusually still, the moon casting an eerie glow over the barren landscape. Far beneath the earth, deep within the caverns of forgotten realms, something stirred. It had been millennia since it had last awakened, and the earth trembled in anticipation of its return.

In the city of Alexandria, in the year 320 BC, a group of scholars gathered in the grand library, debating over ancient scrolls and the secrets they contained. The air was thick with the scent of ink and parchment, the flickering candlelight casting shadows that seemed to dance in tune with their frantic discussions. At the center of the table was an ancient manuscript—one that none of them had dared to fully read.

One scholar, **Alexander**, a young and ambitious philosopher, was transfixed by a particular passage. It spoke of a being, a force, too powerful to be named, a god of creation and destruction that had existed before time itself. The text referred to the **Demogorgon**, a name that carried both fear and reverence. No mortal had ever dared speak it aloud, but the more Alexander read, the more he felt drawn to it. He understood the words on a deeper level, as if the being had been calling to him through the ages.

The library fell silent as he finished reading. His breath caught in his throat as he raised his head. "The Demogorgon…" he whispered. The other scholars leaned in, their curiosity piqued.

Before Alexander could explain, the ground began to shake. The air grew thick, heavy with an unseen presence. The candles flickered violently, casting grotesque shadows against the walls. In that moment, Alexander knew—he had opened the gateway. The **Demogorgon**, the ancient force that had been dormant for eons, was awakening.

Outside, the city of Alexandria felt the tremors. People rushed to the streets, looking up at the sky, where dark clouds began to gather. In the distance, the mountains trembled, and the sea began to churn. A wave of terror spread through the city, for it was clear that something ancient, something beyond comprehension, was coming.

In the library, Alexander's mind raced. He had unearthed a force too powerful to understand, a force that would change the course of history forever. As the darkness began to consume the room, he realized the price of knowledge.

The Demogorgon had returned.

This story explores the terrifying implications of awakening such an ancient power, encapsulating the essence of Demogorgon as a being of primordial chaos—capable of both **creation** and **destruction**, and forever bound to the very fabric of existence.

The Demogorgon, a timeless deity or demon of the underworld

24.

The Changeling

European Mythology

The Changeling – Origin and Etymology

The concept of the **changeling** appears in a wide array of European folklore, particularly in regions like Ireland, Scotland, Scandinavia, and parts of Eastern Europe. The word "changeling" likely comes from the Old French word *changer*, meaning "to change" or "to exchange." In folklore, a changeling is a creature that replaces a human, most often a child, who is taken by a supernatural being—commonly fairies, demons, trolls, or other mythological entities. The changeling itself is often a magical being, crafted to resemble the stolen human, and it is believed to have been left behind in the place of the abducted individual.

The changeling myth is not just confined to children, as in some stories, adults, particularly newlyweds or young mothers, were also stolen by fairies, replacing them with either a log or a lifeless object enchanted to appear like the person. This folklore is thought to illustrate the hardships of family life in pre-industrial Europe, where the survival of families often depended on the labor of each member. The changeling was a symbol of loss, misfortune, and the mysterious forces that might be at work in a world where life was fragile and difficult.

Physical Description

Changeling appearances can vary significantly depending on the culture and the type of supernatural being involved.

- **In Irish and Scottish folklore**, changelings often had distinct physical characteristics that set them apart from normal children. They might appear sickly, with pale skin, an abnormal growth rate, or unusual features like long teeth or even a beard. The changeling could also display intelligence well beyond its years, often behaving strangely when alone, such as singing, dancing, or playing an instrument.
- **In Scandinavian folklore**, changelings might appear somewhat like the kidnapped human but with a slight aura of otherworldliness—more often, these changelings had a strange, unearthly appearance, often exhibiting traits like excessive appetite or a disturbing presence.
- **In some cases**, changelings were said to have animalistic features, such as sharp claws, hooves, or a wild demeanor that separated them from their human counterparts.

The general behavior of a changeling often revolves around a deep sense of **otherness**. It might be excessively hungry, displaying a seemingly insatiable appetite, or it might act in strange and unpredictable ways. In some stories, changelings are able to use magic or display abilities far beyond what is considered normal for a child of their age.

> ### Legends and Myths
>
> Changelings are primarily associated with **fairy lore**. The fairies would steal human children and replace them with one of their own kind for various reasons: to gain a servant, to act as a companion for their children, or sometimes out of malice. However, there are also stories where elderly or sickly fairies are swapped for human children, allowing the older fairy to enjoy the comforts of human life.
>
> One of the most prominent legends involving changelings is that of **Bridget Cleary**, an Irish woman who was thought to be a changeling by her husband. In the 19th century, Cleary's husband, convinced that his wife was a fairy imposter, murdered her in an attempt to force the fairies to return his "real" wife. This tragic

> incident illustrates how deeply ingrained the changeling myth was in rural communities, where supernatural beliefs sometimes crossed into dangerous reality.
>
> In **Scotland**, the myth of the changeling often involved a ritual to "unmask" the changeling. It was believed that certain actions, such as the use of iron or chanting specific incantations, could reveal the changeling's true nature. One common method involved placing the changeling near a fire to see if it would display any unusual behavior, such as abnormal strength or resistance to the heat.

Cultural Significance

The changeling myth carries powerful symbolic meanings. In many cases, it was used to explain difficult and tragic occurrences, such as the death of a child, mental or physical disabilities, or the disappearance of a family member. In a world where infant mortality was high, a sickly or abnormal child might be seen as a changeling—an imposter sent by malicious spirits, rather than a child born with physical or mental limitations. These beliefs gave a supernatural explanation to tragedies that were otherwise difficult to understand.

The changeling also highlights the societal importance of **family structure** and **individual survival**. In cultures where resources were scarce, the changeling myth served as a way to explain the consequences of loss—whether the loss of a child, a spouse, or an important family member—and the anxiety that came from not knowing whether one's loved ones had been taken by malevolent forces.

"The Changeling's Shadow"

In the quiet village of **Ballaghmore**, nestled in the misty hills of Ireland, the arrival of a newborn was always a cause for celebration. However, for **Ellen O'Connor**, the joy was tempered by an unsettling feeling that grew each day her son, **Ciarán**, seemed to grow weaker. He had been a strong child at birth, but now, as the days turned to weeks, his face was pale, his eyes hollow, and his cries barely a whisper.

One cold evening, Ellen sat by the hearth, gazing at her son, his tiny form swaddled in the woolen blankets. Something wasn't right. The room was filled with shadows as the fire crackled, casting eerie, shifting shapes across the walls. Ciarán had stopped eating properly, and the few times he did manage to latch onto her breast, it was as if he drained her energy rather than gaining strength.

"You're not my Ciarán," Ellen whispered to him one night. His wide, knowing eyes stared back at her, but there was something in them that terrified her—an intelligence far beyond his age, a coldness that chilled her to the bone.

Her husband, **Seamus**, had been distant, dismissing her fears as simple superstition. But Ellen could not shake the feeling that something was terribly wrong. The stories of changelings haunted her thoughts—tales passed down by her grandmother, tales of faeries that stole human children and replaced them with their own.

The next morning, she went to the woods to seek help from the village **wise woman**, **Maebh**, who was rumored to have knowledge of the old ways. Maebh listened quietly, her old eyes narrowing as Ellen recounted her fears. After a long pause, Maebh spoke softly.

"A changeling, ye say?" Maebh muttered under her breath. "The fairies are not kind, child. They take when they please. But we can test him."

With that, Maebh took Ellen to a clearing in the woods, where the sun filtered through the trees in thin, golden rays. She took an iron nail from her pocket, holding it before Ellen's son. The moment the nail touched the changeling's skin, Ciarán's eyes widened, his lips curling into a snarl. The air grew colder, and his tiny hands gripped the blanket with unnatural strength.

"I knew it," Ellen gasped, stepping back. "He's not my son."

Maebh muttered an incantation, then turned to Ellen. "We must act quickly. The fairies won't give him up so easily."

As they began the ritual to reclaim Ellen's true son, the ground beneath them began to shake, the forest around them twisting and writhing as if it were alive. In a final desperate plea, the changeling's form began to shift, morphing into an unsettling creature—half-child, half-beast—before it was pulled back into the shadows of the forest, leaving only the faint scent of lavender behind.

Ellen, trembling, looked down at the bundle in her arms. She felt the warmth of her true son once again, his cries full of life and strength. But as she walked back home, the forest seemed to watch her, its eyes hidden in the darkness. She knew that she had narrowly escaped the fairy world's grasp, but the changeling's shadow would haunt her forever.

The Changeling, mythology shared among European cultures.

25.

The Goblin, Grotesque Humanoid

European Folklore

The Goblin – Etymology and Origins

The term "goblin" has long been associated with small, grotesque, humanoid creatures found in the folklore of multiple European cultures. First recorded in the 14th century, the word "goblin" is believed to derive from the Anglo-Norman *gobelin*, which appears to be linked to the Medieval Latin *gobelinus*. The origin of the word is also connected to the term *kobalos* from Ancient Greek, meaning "rogue," "knave," or "imp." Goblins are often depicted as mischievous or malicious creatures, with the word likely derived from the notion of these creatures as troublesome beings.

The mythology surrounding goblins is vast and complex, with differing characteristics and roles depending on the region and specific legend. In some stories, goblins are seen as mischievous household spirits, while in others, they are malicious thieves or monsters with a taste for cruelty and destruction. While the word "goblin" is most commonly used in Western folklore, similar beings exist in other cultures, such as the *pukwudgie* in Native American folklore, the *dokkaebi* in Korean mythology, and the *ifrit* in Islamic traditions.

Physical Description

Goblins are often depicted as small, grotesque, and monstrous humanoids. Their appearance can vary widely depending on the story and the cultural origin. However, common traits among goblins include their diminutive size, which is often described as ranging from the size of a small child to that of a dwarf. They are typically described as having exaggerated, monstrous features such as large, pointed ears, sharp teeth, and wild, unkempt hair. Their skin may be green, grey, or yellowish, with a rough or scaly texture.

Some goblins are also depicted as having animal-like characteristics such as claws, fangs, or bat-like wings, and may be portrayed with hunched backs or long, gangly limbs. Their eyes are often described as glowing or red, adding to their otherworldly and menacing appearance.

Goblins are frequently described as possessing magical abilities, such as shapeshifting or invisibility. These powers allow them to cause trouble or escape from situations when necessary. While many stories depict goblins as malicious and dangerous, others portray them as mischievous tricksters, playing pranks on humans, or performing tasks for their own gain.

Legends and Behaviors

Goblins appear in various forms across European folklore, ranging from household spirits to forest-dwelling monsters. Some cultures view goblins as nature spirits who dwell in caves, forests, or under bridges, while others associate them with the supernatural underworld or as servants of larger, more powerful deities.

- **English Folklore**: In England, goblins were often seen as mischievous household spirits, sometimes equated with imps or brownies. These goblins would live in the nooks and crannies of human dwellings, performing small tasks like cleaning or stealing food, and they were known for their pranks. However, if not properly treated or respected, they could turn malicious, damaging property or causing mischief.
- **Germanic and Scandinavian Folklore**: In Germanic traditions, goblins, often referred to as *kobolds*, were believed to inhabit mines and caves, sometimes aiding miners but also tricking them or leading them to their doom. *Kobolds* were also said to shape-shift into various forms,

including that of animals or even inanimate objects like logs or stones, to confuse humans and gain advantage over them. In some Scandinavian stories, goblins were considered spirits of the earth, with their dwelling places being caves or dark corners of forests.
- **Celtic Folklore**: In Celtic traditions, particularly in Irish and Scottish folklore, goblins were often associated with the fairy world. These goblins, known for their cunning and trickery, were said to lurk in the shadows, performing tricks on travelers or families. In some stories, goblins would steal children and replace them with a changeling or spirit in disguise.
- **French Folklore**: The goblin's role in French folklore often portrays them as mischievous but dangerous creatures, who would haunt villages, steal livestock, or even engage in petty theft from households. Some tales even tell of goblins taking over villages during the night and then retreating back to their caves by dawn.

Goblins are often depicted as solitary creatures but occasionally form groups or families. In some myths, they are said to live in large underground cities or caverns, where they hoard treasure or guard hidden knowledge. In others, they are more like wild animals, roaming the forests and hills in search of food or mischief.

Cultural Significance

The goblin myth serves a variety of functions across cultures. In some traditions, they represent the darker aspects of human nature—greed, malice, and trickery—while in others, they symbolize nature's unruly, untamed forces. Their ability to shapeshift, perform magic, or steal children or livestock reflects a fear of the unknown and the unpredictable aspects of nature.

Historically, goblins have also been associated with the fear of death and the supernatural, representing malevolent beings from the afterlife or other realms that could invade the human world. The goblin's deceptive nature and association with both physical and spiritual worlds have made it a central figure in stories about boundaries—between the known and the unknown, the natural and the supernatural.

The Goblin of European Folklore

"The Goblin's Bargain"

In the village of **Greystone**, nestled at the edge of an ancient, gnarled forest, strange things had begun happening. Livestock went missing, food stores were disturbed, and the villagers spoke of eerie, shrill laughter in the night. It was the work of the goblin, or so the elders said. For generations, the people of Greystone had known that the goblin lived in the woods—an ancient spirit, cursed to wander between worlds, causing mischief wherever it roamed.

No one had seen the goblin, not for years, but everyone knew its ways. It had come to their village once before, years ago, when a young woman named **Eliza** had made a bargain with the creature. Desperate to save her family's farm, Eliza had gone to the edge of the woods, where the goblin was said to live, to strike a deal.

The goblin had appeared in the form of a small, hunched man, with sharp teeth and glowing yellow eyes. His skin was dark, almost like bark, and his fingers were twisted and clawed. "What do you seek, mortal?" he had asked in a voice that was both sweet and menacing.

Eliza, trembling, had explained her plight—the crops had failed, and the farm was near ruin. "I will do anything," she had said, her voice almost breaking. "Please, help us."

The goblin had smiled, revealing his sharp, crooked teeth. "Anything, you say?" he had asked. "Then we have a bargain." He had promised her wealth beyond her wildest dreams in exchange for her agreement to give him something precious when the time came. Eliza had hesitated, but desperation had clouded her judgment. She had agreed.

The next day, the rains had come, and the crops had flourished. The farm had prospered, and Eliza's family was saved. But as the years passed, the price of the goblin's bargain became clear. Livestock began to disappear, and strange events plagued the village once more. Eliza knew the time had come to fulfill her part of the deal.

Late one moonless night, Eliza ventured once more into the woods, where the goblin awaited her. She found him near the same dark tree, his form hunched and shadowed, his glowing eyes fixed upon her. "I am here," Eliza said, swallowing her fear.

The goblin's lips twisted into a wicked grin. "You've come to pay the price."

Eliza's heart raced as she stepped forward, holding out a single, gleaming coin—her family's last treasure. "Take it," she said. "Take whatever you wish."

But the goblin merely laughed, his voice echoing through the trees like the wind. "You still don't understand, do you? The price is not a coin."

With that, he reached out and grasped her wrist, pulling her into the shadows. Her screams echoed in the night as the goblin's laughter faded, leaving only the sound of the wind rustling through the trees.

The villagers never saw Eliza again, but they knew the goblin had claimed his due. And from that night on, the goblin of Greystone remained a whisper in the wind, a creature of darkness, waiting for the next bargain to be struck.

The **goblin** remains a powerful symbol of the cost of desperation and the bargains we make with the unknown. Whether a trickster or a monster, the goblin is a reminder of the consequences that may come when we seek help from forces beyond our understanding.

The Goblin bargains with Eliza

26.

Rawhead and Bloody Bones

European Folklore

Bloody Bones – Origins and Etymology

The figure of *Bloody Bones*, also known as *Rawhead and Bloody Bones* or simply *Rawhead*, first appeared in English folklore around 1548. The name *Rawhead* was historically used to describe a terrifying specter, mentioned in various cautionary tales intended to frighten children into good behavior. Samuel Johnson, in his *Dictionary of the English Language* (1755), defined *Rawhead* as a "spectre, mentioned to fright children," reflecting the creature's role in folklore as a bogeyman.

Rawhead and Bloody Bones is thought to have emerged from early British tales, particularly in regions such as Lancashire and Yorkshire, before spreading to the United States. These figures were often invoked by parents or caregivers to encourage children to behave or to keep them away from dangerous places, such as ponds, rivers, and dangerous pits, reinforcing the social taboo against wandering or misbehaving.

Physical Description

The figure of Bloody Bones is depicted in various forms across different folklore traditions, but several consistent features emerge in most accounts. Bloody Bones is often portrayed as a gruesome, skeletal being, sometimes described as a monstrous, headless skeleton or a monstrous figure with raw, bleeding bones. The monster is said to inhabit dark and eerie places, such as the depths of water, marshes, or abandoned houses. His appearance can vary, but he is consistently described as grotesque and horrifying, with blood dripping from his face or body.

In some tales, *Rawhead* is portrayed as a decaying skull that bites its victims, while *Bloody Bones* is depicted as a skeletal figure that dances or moves, often headless. The combination of these two entities as one monstrous being – Rawhead (the skull) and Bloody Bones (the skeleton) – creates a chilling entity capable of terrifying children into good behavior.

Legends and Folklore

The figure of Bloody Bones is closely tied to the tradition of the bogeyman, and like many such figures, its role is to serve as a cautionary tale for children. Parents used stories of Bloody Bones to keep their children in line and discourage them from wandering or misbehaving. Bloody Bones was frequently said to lurk in dark, secluded areas, particularly in the water, much like the *grindylow* or *Jenny Greenteeth*, other malevolent water spirits from English folklore.

In some versions of the tale, Bloody Bones is said to dwell in deep ponds, marshes, or old marl pits, waiting to drag disobedient children into the depths. The warning cry, "keep away from the marl-pit or Rawhead and Bloody Bones will have you," was meant to keep children from straying too far or approaching dangerous water.

One famous version, recounted by folklorist Ruth Tongue in *Somerset Folklore*, describes Bloody Bones as living in a dark cupboard under the stairs. The creature was said to be waiting for children who misbehaved, crouched on a pile of bones belonging to those who had lied or spoken ill words. If a child dared to look through the crack or peep through a keyhole, the creature would seize them, adding a layer of dread to the tale.

In Cornwall, the creature was known as *Old Bloody Bones*, who was believed to have haunted Knockers Hole near Baldhu, a site of historical massacre. This interpretation casts Bloody Bones as not just a creature of folklore but as an embodiment of revenge or anger tied to violence or injustice.

In the Southern United States, Rawhead and Bloody Bones were sometimes seen as two separate entities, with Rawhead depicted as a skull stripped of skin and teeth, capable of biting its victims, and Bloody Bones as a dancing, headless skeleton. In one tale, a gossip is said to lose his head as punishment for his wicked tongue, aligning the creature with the concept of retribution.

As the stories spread to the United States, particularly within African-American folklore, Bloody Bones became an important figure in cautionary tales for children and was used to instill discipline and caution.

Cultural Impact

The *Rawhead and Bloody Bones* tale is an enduring one, deeply rooted in folklore and myth, reflecting humanity's fascination with fear, punishment, and morality. The duality of Rawhead and Bloody Bones, with one being a skull capable of biting and the other a skeletal figure, symbolizes the monstrous and the supernatural in a way that reinforces cultural norms and the consequences of bad behavior.

The influence of Bloody Bones extends beyond folklore and into modern culture, having appeared in various forms in literature, television, and other media. As a bogeyman figure, Bloody Bones continues to haunt the imagination, representing the shadow of childhood fears, the darker aspects of human nature, and the consequences of straying from societal rules.

"The Curse of Bloody Bones"

The village of **Hollowbrook** had always been a quiet, isolated place, tucked between thick forests and rolling hills. But for generations, the children of Hollowbrook had been told to fear one thing above all else: *Rawhead and Bloody Bones*. This ancient tale was passed down through families like a sacred warning, and the consequences of not heeding it were dire.

Tilly, the youngest of the Miller family, had heard the story countless times. Her mother would whisper it at night as she tucked Tilly into bed, the soft rustle of the wind outside only adding to the eeriness of the tale. "Don't go near the river," her mother would warn. "Stay away from the woods after dark. Or Rawhead and Bloody Bones will have you."

At first, Tilly had been terrified. But as the years passed, the stories began to lose their edge. She grew bolder, more curious about the world beyond the small cottage where she lived. One evening, as the sun began to set and the shadows lengthened, Tilly found herself walking near the edge of the woods, her feet crunching softly on the fallen leaves.

Suddenly, a strange noise broke the stillness. A low, rumbling sound that sent a chill down her spine. She froze, her heart pounding. Her eyes darted to the trees, but there was nothing there. Only the wind.

Tilly's thoughts returned to the tale her mother had told her. Was this the moment? Was Rawhead and Bloody Bones coming for her?

"No," she whispered to herself, "It's just the wind."

But then, out of the corner of her eye, she saw it—a shadow, moving swiftly between the trees. It was too fast to be human, too strange to be anything else.

Her breath caught in her throat. And there, standing at the edge of the forest, was the figure she had only heard about in stories. A large, monstrous skull with sharp teeth, stripped of skin, glowed in the dim light. Behind it, a skeletal body danced in the shadows, its movements jerky and unnatural.

Rawhead and Bloody Bones.

Tilly turned to run, but her legs felt like lead. The creature's laughter echoed through the woods, a deep, gravelly sound that made her blood run cold.

With one final scream, Tilly tried to escape, but the creature's claws reached out, pulling her back into the dark woods.

The villagers would say that Tilly's disappearance was just another tragedy. But the elders knew better. Rawhead and Bloody Bones had taken her, just as they had taken so many before. And so, the story would continue to haunt Hollowbrook for generations.

Rawhead (the skull) and Bloody Bones (the skeleton)

The legend of **Rawhead and Bloody Bones** lives on, its presence felt in the shadow of every dark corner and eerie breeze. A tale to frighten, a warning to those who dare stray too far from the safety of home.

27.

The White Lady

European Folklore

The White Lady: A Guide to the Global Legend

The *White Lady* is one of the most enduring and widespread figures in folklore, appearing in numerous cultures and across centuries. This mysterious and often tragic figure is typically described as a spectral woman dressed in white who haunts specific locations, such as roadsides, old homes, forests, and sometimes even specific landmarks. Often, the *White Lady* is associated with a story of lost love, betrayal, or death, and her haunting presence is marked by sadness or vengeance.

Etymology and General Description:

The concept of the *White Lady* is believed to stem from several traditions, including European, Latin American, and Asian folklore. The "White" in her name typically refers to her spectral, ghostly appearance, often dressed in a flowing white gown or wedding dress. Some versions of the legend portray her as a sorrowful figure, mourning the loss of her lover or family, while others depict her as an avenging spirit, seeking retribution for a wrong done to her.

The *White Lady* is often a symbol of unrequited love, the grief of untimely death, or a punishment for a past mistake. Her ghostly appearances tend to occur under the veil of darkness, and her sightings are often linked to tragic or mysterious events.

Famous White Ladies Around the World

1. La Llorona – Mexico & Latin America

In Latin American folklore, *La Llorona*, or "The Weeping Woman," is perhaps the most famous *White Lady* figure. According to the legend, she is a spirit of a woman who drowned her children in a fit of rage or despair and now wanders the waterways, mourning their loss. She is typically described as a pale woman in a flowing white gown, her face hidden by her long, dark hair. La Llorona's cries of grief and her ghostly figure are said to lure children to their deaths, urging them to join her in the watery depths.

2. The White Lady of Brazil

Known as Dama Branca or Mulher de Branco in Portuguese, the Brazilian Lady in White is believed to be the spirit of a young woman who perished during childbirth or under violent circumstances. Legend has it that she manifests as a fair-skinned female dressed in a flowing white gown or nightdress. While she is typically silent, there are moments when she shares her tragic stories.

The origins of this myth remain ambiguous. Luís da Câmara Cascudo's Dicionário do Folclore Brasileiro suggests that the ghost may be connected to the brutal murders of young white women by their fathers or husbands in acts deemed "honor" killings. Common motivations for these honor killings included adultery (real or suspected), refusal of intimacy, or maltreatment.

In his book Urupês, Monteiro Lobato depicts a young woman who was starved to death by her husband due to his suspicions of her affection for a black slave, as he only provided her with the stewed meat of his own corpse as sustenance.

The White Lady, Dama Branca

3. The White Lady of Avenel – Scotland

The *White Lady of Avenel* is a famous Scottish ghost story associated with Avenel Castle in the Scottish Borders. The tale tells of a lady who was imprisoned by her husband and starved to death in a dungeon. Her ghost, dressed in white, is said to haunt the area, walking the grounds near the castle in search of her lost love and seeking vengeance on those who betrayed her. Her apparition is often reported as a sorrowful figure, silently wandering the ruins of the castle at night.

4. The White Lady of Branxholm – England

The *White Lady of Branxholm* is another tragic ghost story from England. This apparition is said to be the spirit of a woman who died of a broken heart after her lover was killed in battle. She is said to appear dressed in white, drifting through the halls of Branxholm Castle, weeping for the man she could not save. The castle is located near the Scottish border, and it is said that her haunting presence is still felt today, with numerous sightings reported over the years.

5. The Witte Wiwer and Weiße Frauen

In northern Germany, White Ladies are referred to as Witte Wiwer, while in Standard German, they are known as Weiße Frauen. Legends of white lady apparitions are linked to the residential castles of the Hohenzollern family. Two women are believed to be the historical foundation of a haunting at the Plassenburg. According to legend, Countess Kunigunda of Orlamünde killed her two children, thinking it would allow her to marry Albert of Nuremberg, who instead wed Sophie von Henneberg († 1372). She later became a nun and passed away as the abbess of the Himmelskron monastery. Reports of a white lady ghost have surfaced in 1486, 1540, 1554, and 1677, often seen as an omen of bad luck. Another version of the story suggests that the white lady of the Plassenburg is the lamentable widow Bertha of Rosenberg from Bohemia, who was overthrown by the pagan Perchta.

6. The Kaperosa of the Philippines

In the Philippines, White Ladies, or kaperosa as they are locally known, are frequent subjects of ghost stories. These entities are often used to instill fear and intrigue in young listeners during storytelling sessions. Sightings of White Ladies are reported throughout the nation, with the most famous being the White Lady of Balete Drive in Quezon City. Legend has it that she is the spirit of a long-haired woman dressed in white who tragically perished in a car accident on Balete Drive. Many accounts of her have been shared by taxi drivers on the night shift, recounting experiences where, while crossing Balete Drive, a striking woman requests a ride. When the driver turns to look, he sees her face covered in blood and bruises, leading him to flee from his taxi in fright.

The Kaperosa of the Philippines

7. The White Lady of Thailand

In Thailand, a tale circulates about teenagers who ventured into an abandoned house in Thawi Watthana, a district of Bangkok, in search of ghosts, only to meet tragic accidents afterward. In every incident, there were reports of a woman dressed in white being seen at the location. A medium suggested that this was a vengeful spirit known as "Dao" or "Deuan," who was pursuing them and ultimately caused their deaths.

8. The White Lady of Charles Fort – Ireland

In Charles Fort, Ireland, there is a tale about a white lady, the spirit of a young woman who perished on her wedding night. Her tragic demise was a suicide that followed her husband's death at the hands of her father. She returned as a ghost in search of her father, and every year on the anniversary of her wedding, her screams can be heard. Additionally, people have reported seeing a woman referred to as "the woman in the white dress" or "an bhean bhán" (the white woman) in an abandoned house near the white river in Dunleer, County Louth.

9. The Suscon Screamer – USA

The "Suscon Screamer" is a female figure dressed in white, rumored to be seen and/or heard along Suscon Road in Pittston Township, Pennsylvania. This lengthy state route stretches for miles before becoming Thornhurst Road and Bear Lake Road. Many claim they have heard chilling screams emanating from the woods and observed a stationary bright light on the road.

Occasionally, a young woman in a white dress is said to appear. These occurrences generally take place near "the black bridge," an old railroad bridge that was taken down in the 1980s. Despite the bridge's demolition, strange sounds and sights continue to be reported. According to local legend, either a young bride took her own life nearby after her wedding or a girl was murdered following her prom night on the road.

This might explain why the woman is often seen in white to this day. She is frequently referred to as the Suscon Screamer. Many believe that if you honk your car horn three times at night near the old railroad bridge, you might hear her screams and possibly catch a glimpse of her.

The White Lady known as the Suscon Screamer

10. The White Lady in the Lake – USA

In Durand-Eastman Park in Rochester, New York, there is said to be a White Lady haunting the area. Also known as the Lady in the Lake, this 19th-century figure roams the park, desperately searching for her daughter's body, who was murdered by a boyfriend or a group of troublemakers, depending on the version of the tale. According to legend, the White Lady either succumbed to grief and took her own life or died alone and heartbroken.

11. *The White Lady of Avenel*

"The Lady in White" or "the White Lady of Avenel" is the most frequently reported ghost at Avenel in Bedford, Virginia. This apparition is believed to be Mary Frances "Fran" Burwell from the Burwell family of Virginia. Legend has it that she waited on the front porch for her husband to return from the Civil War, but he never came back, as stated by Adam Stupin, founder of SouthWest Virginia Ghost Hunters.

12. *The White Lady of Whopsy*

In Altoona, Pennsylvania, she is referred to as the White Lady of Whopsy. Her spirit is believed to haunt Wopsononock Mountain and Buckhorn Mountain in western Altoona. According to legend, she and her husband were involved in a tragic accident at a location known as Devil's Elbow as they entered the city, leading both to tumble over the mountain's edge. It is said she can be seen searching for her husband on foggy nights, has been picked up as a hitchhiker, and her reflection is absent from mirrors, yet she vanishes around Devil's Elbow.

The White Lady of Whopsy

13. The White Witch and Prom Dress Girl of California

Fremont, California has two variations of the White Lady Legend: one known as the White Witch and the other simply identified as the Prom Dress Girl. Both legends involve ghost sightings in the Niles Canyon area.

The **White Witch** narrative revolves around a woman named Lowerey, who was among the first fatalities from a horse carriage accident in the early 20th century. Sightings of her include appearances in a local cemetery accompanied by strange lights. Local lore suggests she can be seen walking along the ridge between the Niles Hollywood-style sign and the canyon. The **Prom Dress Girl** tale recounts a high school girl who died in a car accident on February 26 in the late 20th century. Witnesses report seeing her donning a white prom dress as she attempts to hitch rides from passing vehicles on Highway 84 between Fremont and Sunol.

14. The Lady of White Rock Lake.

In Dallas, Texas at White Rock Lake Park, there are reports of a twenty-year-old ghost known as "The Lady of White Rock Lake." Described as wearing a waterlogged evening dress from the 1930s, she typically appears at night along East Lawther Drive. Witnesses assert that this apparition asks for a ride home to Gaston Avenue in Dallas before vanishing from the car mid-journey, leaving behind a damp car seat. Legend has it that she was a drowning victim from a boating accident in the 1930s, with reports of her ghostly sightings appearing in Dallas-area newspapers during the 1960s.

15. The White Lady of Haapsalu Castle – Estonia

The most renowned white lady in Estonia is believed to inhabit Haapsalu Castle. As the tale goes, a canon fell for her, prompting her to conceal herself in the castle while posing as a choir boy. However, she was eventually uncovered during the visit of the Bishop of Ösel-Wiek to Haapsalu and was consequently walled up in the chapel for her transgression. Even now, it is said that she gazes out from the Baptistery's window, mourning for her lost love. Legend has it that she can be spotted on clear nights during the full moon in August.

16. The White Lady Perchta of Rožmberk – Czech Republic

The most famous White Lady in the Czech Republic is the spirit of Perchta of Rožmberk, who haunts Rožmberk Castle. Perchta of Rožmberk (circa 1429–1476) was the daughter of a prominent Bohemian nobleman, Oldřich II of Rožmberk. In 1449, she wed another noble, Jan of Lichtenštejn. Their marriage was rather unhappy, possibly because Perchta's father hesitated to provide the promised dowry. Throughout her married life, Perchta penned numerous letters to her father and brothers, vividly detailing her miserable domestic life and the mistreatment she endured from Jan of Lichtenštejn.

About 32 of these letters have survived over time. According to legend, as her husband lay on his deathbed, he sought her forgiveness for his behavior towards her. Perchta declined to forgive him, leading her husband to curse her. After her death, she returned as a ghost to her family's estate. Legends say that her apparition was most frequently seen in the areas of Rožmberk, Český Krumlov, Jindřichův Hradec, Třeboň, and Telč. The tale of the White Lady is also featured in the Ancient Bohemian Legends.

17. The White Lady Elizabeth Bathory – Hungary

In Hungarian folklore, a white lady is the spirit of a girl or young woman who met a violent end, typically those who took their own lives, were killed, or perished in captivity. This ghost is generally tied to a particular place and is frequently recognized as a certain individual, such as Elizabeth Báthory.

Countess Elizabeth Báthory of Ecsed was a Hungarian noblewoman and alleged serial killer from the powerful House of Báthory, who owned land in the Kingdom of Hungary. Báthory and four of her servants were accused of torturing and killing hundreds of girls and women from 1590 to 1610.

The White Lady Elizabeth Bathory

18. The White Lady of Blenkinsopp Castle – England

Thirteen stories from England indicate that the White Lady might be a victim of murder or suicide, having died without revealing the location of some concealed treasure. In 2019, a family occupied Blenkinsopp Castle in Northumberland. One night, the parents were awakened by their son shouting, "The White Lady!" By the time they reached his side, she had disappeared. The boy claimed she was angry and attempted to take him away after he declined to accompany her to a stash of gold hidden in the vaults below, stating that she could not find peace while it remained there. This same occurrence was reported for three consecutive nights. After the child began sleeping with his parents, the White Lady ceased to disturb him, but he never ventured through the castle alone again for fear of her presence.

19. The White Running Lady of Beeford Straight -England

The White Lady, also referred to as the "Running Lady," is known in Beeford, East Yorkshire, where she is said to appear on the "Beeford Straight," a road connecting Beeford and Brandesburton. Drivers have witnessed her spirit racing across the road toward the North Frodingham junction. There are also anecdotal accounts of a motorcyclist who picked up a female hitchhiker on this stretch of road, only to find she had vanished moments later when he turned around. In one tragic incident, a car collided with a tree, resulting in six fatalities, which is rumored to be linked to the curse of the White Lady.

20. The White Lady Of Portchester Castle – England

In another tale, a White Lady is said to retrace her steps after reportedly jumping from Portchester Castle while trying to save her fallen child. Her spirit is believed to haunt the castle.

21. The White Lady of Worstead Church – England

At Worstead Church in Norfolk, there are various accounts of a ghostly woman dressed in white. Her story varies; some view her as a benevolent spirit while others see her as an omen of death. Locally known as the "White Lady," her legends are said to date back to the 1830s, and she is often sighted on Christmas Eve. A notable incident occurred in 1975 when Peter Berthelot and his wife Diane sought refuge from the heat in a church. Peter captured a photo of Diane sitting in a pew, which revealed a faint image of a woman in old-fashioned white with a bonnet behind her. Following this event, Diane recovered from her illness.

22. The White Lady of Okehampton Castle – England

An old ballad tells of a ghost haunting Okehampton Castle: "My Ladye hath a sable coach, with horses two an four. My Ladye hath a gaunt blood-hound, that goeth before. My Ladye's coach hath nodding plumes, the driver hath no head. My Ladye is an ashen white – as one who is long dead." This lady is believed to be a Howard woman from the 17th century who has reportedly murdered several of her husbands and children. Her curse involves collecting grass blades in the castle ruins for eternity, with no historical events or figures found to match this tale.

23. The White Lady Matilda – England

The ghost of Matilda (also referred to as Margaret), a Pomeroy lady, is said to haunt Berry Pomeroy Castle near Totnes in Devon, acting as a harbinger of death for anyone who sees her in the dungeon of St. Margaret's tower. It is claimed that Matilda was starved to death by her sister in that dungeon. Edward Montague wrote a novel titled "The Castle of Berry Pomeroy."

24. The White Lady of Radford – England

In Radford, the White Lady of Radford is depicted as a young woman from the Harris family who wished to see a local young man from Oreston but was forbidden by her family. Despite this, she took a boat onto the lake one night while dressed in white. The boat allegedly capsized, leading to her disappearance beneath the water. Some say her lover was with her when it sank. Since then, many have reported seeing the White Lady beside the lake in ghostly form, resulting in a nearby street being named "White Lady Road."

The White Lady of Radford

25. Y Ladi Wen – Wales

In Welsh folklore, Y Ladi Wen (The White Lady) or Dynes Mewn Gwyn (Woman in White) frequently appears in Celtic mythology. Dressed in white and most commonly seen during Calan Gaeaf (Welsh Halloween), she was often invoked to caution children against misbehaving. Y

Ladi Wen is portrayed in various ways, ranging from a frightening ghost who may seek help if approached.

Y Ladi Wen is also linked to restless spirits guarding hidden treasures, with one of the most famous tales originating from Ogmore, Bridgend. This story includes many typical elements found in Celtic and Welsh folklore, such as hidden cauldrons, shifting physical forms, and moral lessons.

A spirit was said to wander the area until a man finally approached her. When he did so, she guided him to a treasure (a cauldron filled with gold) hidden under a heavy stone within Ogmore Castle's old tower and allowed him to keep half of it. However, after he returned for more treasure, she became enraged and attacked him as he made his way home, leading to his grave illness and eventual death only after confessing his greed. Consequently, an ailment known as Y Ladi Wen's revenge is said to afflict anyone who dies without revealing hidden treasure.

The White Lady – Y Ladi Wen

Conclusion

The figure of the *White Lady* is one that transcends national boundaries, appearing in many cultures with slight variations to her story. From the vengeful spirit of *La Llorona* in Latin America to the tragic figures of the *White Lady of Blanchardstown* in Ireland, the *White Lady* serves as a potent symbol of loss, heartbreak, and the mysteries of death. Whether she is a sorrowful mourner or a vengeful spirit, the White Lady remains one of the most enduring and haunting figures in folklore worldwide.

28.

The Wild Hunt

European Folklore

The *Wild Hunt* is a widely recognized motif in European folklore, particularly among Germanic, Celtic, and Slavic cultures, and it typically features a mythological leader at the head of a supernatural hunting party. This eerie procession is often associated with ghostly figures, spectral hounds, and otherworldly riders, traversing the sky or landscape in a frenzied chase.

The Wild Hunt

The hunt is most commonly seen as a premonition of impending doom, foretelling war, death, or natural disaster. The figures involved in the hunt vary from culture to culture, but are often beings associated with the afterlife, such as souls of the dead, fairies, gods, or demons.

Etymology and Conceptual Origins

The term "Wild Hunt" (*Wilde Jagd* in German) was popularized by Jacob Grimm in his 19th-century studies of Germanic mythology, though the concept itself predates his work. It likely has its roots in ancient *pagan rituals* related to the gods and nature, particularly the belief in a god or leader who led a group of supernatural hunters across the land. The term *Wild Hunt* refers to the frenzied, chaotic nature of the chase, while the *Host* (as it is also known in some traditions) refers to the ghostly or supernatural gathering of figures. The Hunt is generally seen as an omen, bringing misfortune to those who encounter it.

While the name *Wild Hunt* is associated primarily with Germanic traditions, the motif can be found throughout Europe, with varying names and attributes depending on the country. It is often linked to deities such as Odin in Norse mythology, but also to figures like Herod, the Devil, or legendary kings.

Cultural Variations

- **Germanic Traditions**: The *Wild Hunt* is most often associated with the god Odin, who is said to lead the hunt across the night sky, accompanied by spectral dogs and dead warriors. In Germany, the Hunt is sometimes referred to as *Wutendes Heer* (the "Raging Host"), with Odin leading his warriors in pursuit of souls. The hunt could appear as a storm or as a gathering of spirits.
- **Scandinavia**: Known as *Oskoreia* or *Odin's Hunt*, it features Odin as the leader, though sometimes a female figure like Freyja is mentioned. The *Wild Hunt* in Scandinavia is often seen as a storm, with riders crashing through the skies, and it was believed that thunder and lightning were signs of their approach.
- **Welsh Folklore**: The leader of the *Wild Hunt* in Wales is often *Gwyn ap Nudd*, the King of the Underworld, who leads a pack of white hounds, chasing the souls of the dead. The hounds are sometimes described as hellhounds, and the hunt is associated with the afterlife.
- **Slavic Traditions**: In Slavic cultures, the *Wild Hunt* is known as *Divoký Hon* in Czech, *Dziki Gon* in Polish, and *Divja Jaga* in Slovenian. It is often linked to the spirits of the dead and is believed to bring death or disaster to those who witness it.
- **French Traditions**: In French folklore, the *Wild Hunt* is called *La Chasse Sauvage* or *La Chasse Hellequin*, with Hellequin being a mythological figure who leads the hunt. In some versions, the hunt is said to be the souls of the damned, led by a demonic figure who punishes those who have died unjustly.

The Wild Hunt in the Hills

The wind howled through the trees, carrying with it an unnerving chill that set the hairs on Aric's neck standing on end. He had been warned of the *Wild Hunt* before, but he had never believed in the old tales. Not until now.

He had been traveling through the dense woods of northern Europe, a place shrouded in mist and mystery, when the storm had come. He had thought it would pass, but as the hours wore on, the storm only intensified, the wind screaming louder, the trees groaning as though they, too, were caught in the grip of some terrible force.

It was then that he heard it—the sound of hooves thundering through the earth, the creak of a wooden chariot drawn by something unseen, and the low growl of dogs. Aric's heart raced, his legs rooted to the spot in fear. He knew the stories—*Odin's Hunt*, they called it, a great chase led by the god of war himself, followed by dead warriors and ghostly hounds.

But this was not a story. This was real. He could feel it in the air, the palpable tension that crackled around him. The storm had ceased, and the world had grown still, unnaturally so. And then he saw them—figures emerging from the mist, their faces hidden by the shadows of their hoods. They rode upon skeletal horses, their eyes glowing like embers in the darkness.

At the head of the procession was a figure cloaked in shadow, taller than the rest, a crown of silver upon his brow, his eyes a fierce gleaming blue. Aric knew, somehow, that this was Odin himself. And with him were the warriors—men long dead, their armor tarnished and broken, their eyes empty but determined, chasing something only they could see.

The ghostly hounds ran beside the riders, their breath steaming in the cold air. They were silent, but their presence sent a shiver through Aric's bones. He stood frozen, barely breathing, as the hunt passed by him, the riders ignoring him as they focused on their quarry.

As quickly as they had come, they vanished into the mist, leaving Aric trembling in the wake of their passing. He had heard the stories, of course, but never had he imagined that they would come to life before his very eyes. He had been given a glimpse into the world of the dead, a world that had once been ruled by gods and monsters.

But now, the storm had cleared, and the world seemed to return to normal. The trees no longer groaned, the wind no longer howled. But Aric knew—he would never forget the *Wild Hunt*, or the fear that it brought with it.

As he turned to leave, he heard one final sound—the distant howling of the hounds, fading into the night.

And Aric knew, with a chill in his heart, that they would return again.

The Wild Hunt of European Folklore

PART VI
SHADOWS OF EAST ASIA

Creatures of East Asia: Spirits, Dragons, and Mythical Beasts

The vast and ancient cultures of **East Asia**—encompassing **China**, **Japan**, **Korea**, and **Vietnam**—are steeped in mythology and folklore, where the natural world and the supernatural intertwine in tales of gods, spirits, and creatures both awe-inspiring and terrifying. From the fiery breath of dragons to the eerie presence of restless spirits, the myths of East Asia offer a fascinating window into the values, fears, and beliefs of civilizations that have shaped the world for millennia.

In this section, we explore the rich and diverse tapestry of East Asian mythology, delving into the legendary creatures that have captured the imaginations of generations. Whether they are revered guardians, cunning tricksters, or terrifying beasts, the creatures of East Asia reflect the region's deep connection to nature, the spiritual world, and the eternal struggle between good and evil.

In **China**, the mythical creatures range from the **Azure Dragon**, a symbol of power and strength, to the **Jiangshi**, a hopping vampire that preys upon the living. The **Nian**, a terrifying beast tied to the Lunar New Year, and the **Bai Ze**, a monstrous cow-like creature with multiple heads, show the diverse nature of Chinese mythology and its complex relationship with both the human and supernatural realms.

Japan, with its centuries-old traditions, presents a host of spirits and monsters. From the **Tengu**—winged, human-bird hybrids—to the **Kappa**, water creatures that lurk in ponds and rivers, the creatures of Japanese folklore evoke both respect and fear. In the realm of ghosts, **Onryō**, vengeful spirits, and **Yokai**, mischievous creatures, stir up both horror and fascination, providing endless tales of retribution, love, and the unknown.

Korea's **Gumiho**, a fox spirit with a penchant for transforming into a beautiful woman to devour hearts, and the **Imugi**, a serpentine creature aspiring to become a dragon, are both symbols of the powerful, untamable forces of nature. Meanwhile, Vietnam's mythical creatures like the **Bạch Xà** (White Snake) carry themes of love, transformation, and vengeance that resonate deeply with the human experience.

Each of these legendary beings holds a specific place within East Asian cultures, reflecting not only ancient fears and desires but also the deep philosophical and spiritual foundations of these societies. These creatures transcend time and place, connecting past generations to the present, with stories that continue to shape the cultural fabric of the region.

In this collection, we journey through the most iconic and enigmatic creatures from East Asian folklore, uncovering their origins, powers, and the timeless lessons they impart. Whether they are protectors or predators, their stories continue to captivate and challenge us, reminding us of the ever-present forces of nature and spirit that shape our world and our destiny.

29.

Hanako-san: The Spirit of the School Lavatories

Japanese Urban Legend

Name: Hanako-san
Type: Yōkai/Yūrei (Spirit)
Habitat: School lavatories, particularly in Japan
First Sightings: Post-World War II era, particularly in schools

Toire no Hanako-san

Hanako-san, also known as *Toire no Hanako-san* (Toilet Hanako), is a prominent figure in Japanese urban legend, her tale both chilling and curious. This spirit is said to haunt the restrooms of schools, a place typically mundane but, in her case, fraught with mystery and terror. Hanako-san is a **yōkai**, or **supernatural being**, and sometimes classified as a **yūrei**, the restless spirit of a young girl trapped by tragic circumstances.

Hanako-san is often depicted as a little girl with a bobbed haircut, dressed in a red skirt or dress, and sometimes a white blouse. Her appearance is somewhat childlike, but there is something unsettling about her—a contradiction between innocence and the eerie aura she exudes. Her story, however, is far from innocent, as she is said to be the ghost of a girl who met a tragic, untimely end.

The specifics of Hanako-san's origins vary, but there are three common threads in the many versions of her story:

1. **World War II Version:** Hanako-san is said to have been a young girl caught in an air raid during World War II. She was hiding in the school lavatory when the bomb dropped, and her life was claimed by the devastating event. The horror of her death trapped her spirit within the confines of the restroom.
2. **Murder or Suicide Version:** In another variation, Hanako-san is the victim of a violent act. Some versions claim that she was murdered by a parent, a stranger, or a classmate in the school's restroom. Others believe that Hanako-san took her own life due to extreme bullying, unable to bear the torment anymore. Her spirit then lingers in the school, forever tied to the scene of her death.
3. **Vengeful Spirit:** In some renditions of the tale, Hanako-san is said to haunt not only the toilets but also the students who dare to challenge her. It's said that if a student attempts to summon her by knocking on the bathroom stall door three times, Hanako-san will appear, sometimes as a friendly but eerie presence, and sometimes as a vengeful spirit.

Interesting and Bizarre Facts:

- **The Ritual of Summoning:** Hanako-san's urban legend has become a rite of passage for schoolchildren. To summon her, one must go into a school restroom, knock three times on the third stall door, and ask, "Hanako-san, are you there?" If the legend is to be believed, Hanako-san may respond with a voice, often inviting the child to enter the stall. However, this summons often leads to terrifying results, with children disappearing or encountering a frightening, spirit-like manifestation.
- **The Three Stalls:** In some versions of the legend, there are specific rules about which stall is Hanako-san's. It's commonly believed that the third stall in a school's restroom is where she resides. This stall is either cursed or simply where her spirit is bound, creating an eerie association with this particular place.
- **The Male Version – Hanako-kun:** Some interpretations of the legend have adapted Hanako-san into a male counterpart, known as *Hanako-kun*. This male spirit has appeared in modern

depictions in manga, anime, and video games, often embodying similar characteristics but with variations to suit different storytelling purposes.
- **Modern Popularity:** Over time, Hanako-san has appeared in various media, from horror films to comic books, and even video games. While the story remains a cornerstone of Japanese urban legend, modern adaptations often reimagine her as a more complex character, perhaps even a misunderstood spirit seeking peace.

The Haunting of Hanako-san

"The Third Stall"

It was a day like any other, though a strange weight seemed to hang in the air as Yuki entered the restroom of her high school. The school, old and worn, had its share of rumors—whispers that echoed through the hallways like the wind that rattled the windows on stormy days. But none were as terrifying as the legend of Hanako-san.

She had heard the stories, of course. Every child did. Hanako-san, the little girl trapped forever in the school's lavatories, her spirit lingering in the darkness, waiting for the next curious soul to summon her. But Yuki never believed in such things. Ghost stories were for children, not for a high school senior like herself.

Still, something about that day felt different. The silence in the hallway, the muffled sounds of footsteps, the faintest creak of the school's aging plumbing—it all felt wrong. And when Yuki stepped into the restroom, she felt it again: that uncomfortable stillness. The kind of stillness that made the air heavy and oppressive.

There were three stalls. Yuki's eyes lingered on the middle one—the third stall—just as the legend said. It was the one where Hanako-san was supposed to reside. She knew the story well, having heard it countless times from younger students. Hanako-san, a ghost, bound to the third stall after dying tragically during World War II. Or maybe it was something else. No one truly knew.

The restroom was empty except for her. She took a deep breath, shaking off the unsettling feeling creeping up her spine. *It's just a story,* she thought. But the thought came back, nagging at her: *What if it's real?*

Compelled by an impulse she couldn't explain, Yuki walked over to the third stall. Her heart pounded in her chest as she raised her hand and knocked three times on the door.

"Hanako-san, are you there?" she whispered, the words leaving her mouth before she could stop them.

For a moment, nothing. Absolute silence.

Then, a voice. Faint, as if coming from far away. "Yes... I'm here."

Yuki froze. Her blood ran cold. The voice was so soft, so childlike. But there was something about it—something wrong. It was too soft, too... inviting.

She glanced over her shoulder nervously. The restroom felt smaller now, the walls pressing in on her as the silence thickened. She took a step back, ready to turn and leave. But then the door creaked open slowly.

Inside, the stall was dark, far darker than it should have been. The light above flickered. The air grew heavier with every passing second. Yuki's body screamed at her to leave, to run—but her feet remained rooted to the floor.

"Come in," the voice whispered again. "I'm lonely."

The door opened fully, and there she was. Hanako-san.

She was a small girl, no older than ten, with a bobbed haircut. Her face, however, was a blank—no eyes, no mouth, just an endless black void where her face should be. Her red skirt fluttered unnaturally, and the air grew colder around her. The absence of her eyes was suffocating, as if the darkness itself was consuming the light.

Yuki wanted to scream, but the sound was stuck in her throat. Her hands trembled, and her mind raced for an explanation, any explanation at all. But nothing could explain this.

Then, slowly, Hanako-san reached out a hand—claw-like fingers, eerily long and pale.

"Come play with me," she whispered, her voice like a soft wind, carrying with it the scent of something ancient and decayed. "Stay with me forever."

Yuki tried to turn and run, but her legs wouldn't move. She was frozen in place, the terror rendering her body useless. Hanako-san stepped forward, her ghostly form drawing nearer, the air growing colder with each step.

With a final scream, Yuki broke free, stumbling backward into the wall. She didn't look back as she sprinted out of the restroom, bursting through the door and into the hallway.

Her heart hammered in her chest as she gasped for breath. The restroom door was closed, the third stall hidden from view. And yet, she could feel it—the presence of something watching her from within.

She never returned to that restroom. And from that day on, she avoided the third stall, knowing that Hanako-san was still there, waiting for the next curious soul to enter her world. A world where escape was impossible.

30.

Baku: The Dream-Eating Beast

Japanese Folklore

Name: Baku
Type: Supernatural Creature
Habitat: Dreams, sleep realms, occasionally associated with shrines or sacred temples
First Sightings: Muromachi Period (14th–15th century, Japan)

The Baku

The **Baku** is a mystical creature deeply embedded in Japanese folklore, revered for its ability to devour nightmares. This supernatural being is said to consume the dark and disturbing dreams that plague people during sleep, allowing them to rest peacefully. Originally from **Chinese folklore** (where it is known as the Mo), the concept of the Baku was brought to Japan during the Muromachi period and slowly evolved into a widely recognized figure, particularly associated with sleep and dreams.

The appearance of the Baku is as fantastical as its nature. The Baku is a creature made by the Gods, using all the body parts and pieces they had left over after they had finished creating all other creatures. Traditionally, it is a chimera, combining the most powerful aspects of various animals. Early descriptions depict the creature with the trunk and tusks of an elephant, the ears of a rhinoceros, the body of a bear, the tail of a cow, and the paws of a tiger. This diverse mixture of animal features symbolizes its ability to overcome a wide variety of problems, both physical and spiritual. The Baku, in its early depiction, was a protective force, warding off pestilence and evil.

In later centuries, however, the Baku's role shifted more towards a creature specifically designed to consume nightmares. In this updated form, the Baku is often depicted with the head of an elephant, tusks and trunk, horns, and claws of a tiger, characteristics that define its modern appearance. The creature is often associated with good fortune and protection, but its abilities to devour nightmares are most cherished.

Abilities and Powers:

The Baku's primary power is the ability to **consume bad dreams**. In folklore, individuals who suffer from nightmares can call out to the Baku, asking it to devour the disturbing visions plaguing their sleep. This ability makes the Baku an important figure in dream-related folklore. If a person wakes up from a nightmare, it's said that they can call for the Baku three times by saying, "Baku-san, come eat my dream." The creature is believed to come into the room and, with its dream-devouring powers, cleanse the mind of the disturbing visions, allowing the sleeper to return to rest.

However, this gift comes with a cautionary tale. If the Baku is called too frequently, or if it remains hungry after consuming nightmares, it is believed that the creature will begin to devour not only the bad dreams but also the person's hopes and desires. This, in turn, could leave the individual hollow, living without ambition or joy.

Habitat and Behavior:

The Baku does not reside in a physical realm but instead inhabits the world of dreams. It is associated with the dreamscape, intervening in the minds of those who need its assistance during sleep. Some stories suggest that the Baku can be summoned by ritual, particularly through amulets or talismans that children would keep beside their beds to ensure protection from nightmares. In some traditions, it is said that before sleep, people can ask the Baku for protection from bad dreams, invoking it as a guardian of their dreams.

In its natural habitat—the realm of sleep—the Baku moves between the dream worlds, consuming nightmares and ensuring that only the peaceful slumber remains. It is depicted as a creature that moves silently through the night, intervening in the dreams of those who require its aid.

Mythological Context:

- **Origin Story:** The Baku's origins lie in ancient Chinese myth, where it was a powerful figure that could protect people from pestilence. Over time, this evolved in Japan, where it was adapted as a nightmare eater, a guardian spirit that could be called upon to safeguard sleep. The creature's evolution into a dream-devouring being likely stems from its symbolic nature—its combination of various animal traits represented its ability to overcome many different kinds of evil or malady.
- **Symbolic Meaning:** The Baku symbolizes both protection and danger. It is a dual-force creature, capable of offering relief from nightmares while also serving as a warning about overdependence. It represents the thin line between comfort and vulnerability, a reminder that there is a cost to every gift. The creature is deeply tied to the concept of balance—consuming only the bad and leaving the good behind. In Japanese culture, it also represents an element of control over one's dreams and subconscious.
- **Notable Legends and Tales:** In many Japanese folktales, the Baku is invoked by children who are terrified of their nightmares. In a specific story from the early 17th century, a child suffering from persistent nightmares calls the Baku to relieve her suffering. However, the child eventually falls into an emptiness of spirit after relying too heavily on the Baku, unable to find her own strength or hope after the creature devours all her desires. This cautionary tale is often told to children to prevent overuse of the Baku's powers.

Interesting Facts and Cultural Variations:

- **Baku and the Malayan Tapir:** In modern times, the name *Baku* is also used to refer to the **Malayan tapir**, a real-world animal known for its distinct black-and-white coloration. This

connection to the tapir has sparked some modern reinterpretations of the Baku, where it is depicted as a more gentle, tapir-like creature rather than the fearsome, nightmare-eating beast of tradition.
- **The Baku as a Talisman:** In the early 20th century, it was common for Japanese children to carry a Baku talisman in their pockets or keep one under their pillow. These talismans, often shaped as small figurines or carvings, were thought to protect them from bad dreams and nightmares, serving as a physical embodiment of the Baku's protective powers.
- **Baku in Popular Culture:** Today, the Baku appears in various forms of media, including anime, manga, and video games, often maintaining its association with dreams and nightmares. The creature has been depicted as a wise and helpful being, but its darker side is also explored in modern interpretations where it is seen as a more ominous figure who can consume more than just nightmares.

The Nightmare Feast

"The Call of the Baku"

It had been weeks since Yumi had slept through the night without waking up in a cold sweat, her heart racing, her mind trapped in the claws of nightmares. Every evening, as the shadows of night crept in, she would feel the terror of what awaited her the moment her eyes closed. Her dreams, once peaceful, had become battlegrounds, filled with phantoms, monsters, and menacing figures that chased her endlessly. Each night, she would wake up, gasping for air, her pulse a frantic drumbeat, only to fall back into the same torment.

Her mother had told her about the Baku. "Call to it when the nightmares return," her mother had said softly, "and it will come to you, like a guardian of your dreams."

At first, Yumi had laughed off the idea, thinking it just another one of her mother's superstitions. But the nightmares had not stopped, and desperation had led her to look for a talisman, something to protect her, something to end the nightly horrors.

She found a small carving in a dusty old shop in the corner of town. The figurine was an elephant-headed creature, with tiger claws and horns sprouting from its head. It was a Baku, the nightmare eater. Yumi wasn't sure whether it was a superstition or something more real, but she placed it under her pillow that night, whispering the words her mother had taught her.

"Baku-san, come eat my dream."

The room fell into an eerie silence as she waited. Minutes passed, and Yumi almost drifted into sleep, but then she heard it: a faint rustling, the soft padding of feet on the floor. When she opened her eyes, the Baku was standing at the foot of her bed. It towered over her, its elephant trunk swinging low, tusks gleaming in the moonlight, its body shrouded in a mist of dark energy. Its eyes glowed faintly, watching her with a silent understanding.

Yumi closed her eyes and whispered again, "Baku-san, come eat my dream."

The creature moved closer, and in the quiet darkness, it began to consume the nightmares that plagued her mind. Yumi felt the weight lift from her chest, the pressure in her head begin to fade. She could almost hear the crackling of the dreams dissolving into nothingness, leaving only peace behind.

But as she sank deeper into the calm, a strange unease began to creep into her soul. She felt the Baku lingering, its hunger still present. She had asked for its help—perhaps too eagerly, too often.

The creature turned its gaze toward her, and in that moment, Yumi realized something: the Baku was not just devouring nightmares. It was consuming more. Her desires. Her joy. Her hopes.

The room grew cold, and the silence was filled with a hollow emptiness. She felt claws in her skin, holding her down. With all the strength she could muster she managed to call out, "Baku-san Stop!" The Baku's head snapped back, eyes filled with hate, and then as if being woken from its own dream state, its eyes became solemn and filled with shame. Yumi could sense that it had stopped draining the life from her spirit. It was a lucky escape.

When morning came, Yumi woke up, and she wondered if she had dreamed it all and maybe nothing was real. Until she saw the talisman laying next to her, and small drops of blood leading to the unopen window...

The Baku Chasing Away Nightmares

31.

Nue: The Chimera of Nightmares

Japanese Mythology

Name: Nue
Type: Yōkai/Mononoke (Supernatural Creature)
Habitat: Japanese forests, mountainous areas, and the night sky
First Sightings: Late Heian Period, Japan

The Nue

The **Nue** is one of Japan's most terrifying and elusive yōkai, a creature of dark mythology that has haunted the annals of Japanese folklore for centuries. Often described as a chimera—a monstrous creature composed of the parts of various animals—the Nue is a formidable and unsettling being. Its very name invokes fear, as it is associated with dreadful, ill omens and dark forebodings.

In the *Tale of Heike*, one of the earliest accounts of the Nue, the creature is described as having the head of a monkey, the limbs of a tiger, the body of a Japanese raccoon dog (tanuki), and the tail of a snake. This hybrid form is meant to evoke both the fierce, predatory nature of its individual parts and the unnaturalness of their combination. Some interpretations, however, depict it with a torso resembling that of a tiger, reinforcing the creature's terrifying aspect.

What sets the Nue apart from other mythical creatures is its eerie cry—described as a "hyoo hyoo" sound, resembling that of a scaly thrush bird. The Nue's shriek is enough to send chills down the spine of anyone who hears it, and it is often said to signal impending disaster or misfortune. The phrase *"nights where the Nue cry are dreadful"* reflects the deep-rooted belief that the creature's cries portend calamity.

Abilities and Powers:

The Nue is a shapeshifter, one of its most dangerous attributes. When not in its terrifying physical form, it is said to transform into a large black cloud, which can fly through the night sky. Its shapeshifting nature allows it to avoid detection, making it an elusive and elusive figure. Some legends claim that its voice can cause illness, misfortune, and even death, amplifying its role as an omen of bad fortune.

The Nue's nocturnal nature is significant, as it is most often encountered at night, when its cries echo through the darkness, striking fear into the hearts of those who hear them. The creature's abilities extend beyond physical appearance; its very presence is said to warp the atmosphere around it, making the air feel heavy, ominous, and foreboding.

Habitat and Behavior:

The Nue's presence is often tied to natural settings such as forests or mountainous regions, where it remains hidden in the shadows of the night. It is believed to be a solitary creature, lurking in the wilderness, its cries echoing through the trees as a warning to those who are nearby. In many legends, the Nue is said to be an entity of misfortune and is most frequently associated with disaster.

Its behavior is described as malevolent and unpredictable. Though it is not a creature that attacks directly, the Nue's cries are enough to bring about terror and anxiety, especially in times of political or personal instability. Those who hear its cry are often led to pray for protection, especially during times of vulnerability, as it is believed that the Nue's wail signifies a time of impending tragedy.

Mythological Context:

Origin Story: The Nue is thought to have appeared in Japan during the late Heian period, a time of political instability. The creature is said to have emerged as an omen of bad fortune, likely influenced by earlier Chinese mythology, where it was described as a monstrous chimera. In the Japanese version, however, it became more than just a creature; it was a symbol of the unpredictable nature of fate and the sorrow that accompanies the loss of control. Its presence was often interpreted as a sign that something terrible was about to unfold.

Symbolic Meaning: The Nue is a representation of chaos, unpredictability, and the unexplainable aspects of the world. Its hybrid form reflects the fear of things that cannot be understood, things that transcend the normal laws of nature. The creature embodies the fear of the unknown, and its cries serve as a reminder that disaster can strike without warning, leaving the people it touches in a state of anxiety and unease.

Notable Legends and Tales: One of the most famous tales of the Nue is the story of Emperor Konoe, who heard the creature's cry in the night. His court was gripped by fear, and he ordered that prayers be made to protect the realm from whatever calamity the Nue's cry foreshadowed. In some versions, the creature is defeated by a warrior or a spiritual practitioner, who confronts it with sacred rituals or by calling upon divine powers.

Interesting Facts and Cultural Variations:

- **The Nue in the Sexagenary Cycle:** The creature's hybrid form may be a reflection of the Chinese *Sexagenary Cycle* of astrology, which associates animals with specific directions and elements. In this context, the Nue might be a representation of multiple, conflicting energies—combining the northeast Tiger, the southeast Snake, the southwest Monkey, and the northwest Qian (Dog/Wild Boar).
- **The Nue and the Japanese Imperial Court:** In Japan, the Nue's cries were believed to be linked to political disaster. Nobles and emperors would often take the Nue's cries as signs of ill fortune, and prayers or rituals would be performed to ward off its malevolent influence. Its cry was feared because it seemed to mark the beginning of an era of misfortune, not just for

individuals, but for entire political entities.
- **Modern Depictions:** In modern media, the Nue has been adapted into various forms, often reimagined as a more literal monster or used as a metaphor for uncontrollable forces. Its hybrid form is frequently featured in anime, manga, and video games, where it serves as a menacing or mysterious entity. In some depictions, the Nue retains its supernatural power, while in others, it is downplayed or reinterpreted.

The Cry of the Nue

"The Wail in the Darkness"

The wind howled through the mountains, carrying with it the faintest sound—a strange, eerie wail that seemed to hang in the air, chilling the bones of all who heard it. It was the sound of something ancient, something forgotten by time but not by fear. Yuki had heard stories about the Nue before, whispers of a creature that haunted the night with its cries. But she had never believed in it—until now.

Yuki and her companions had ventured far into the mountains, searching for a place where they could escape the stresses of city life. The tranquil beauty of the region had been a welcome respite, but tonight, as the fire flickered and cast shadows on the walls of their tent, the air had turned thick with unease. Something wasn't right.

Yuki was the first to hear it, the faintest sound carried on the wind. It was a cry—a strange, birdlike wail that echoed through the valley. The others didn't hear it at first, but as the night deepened, the cry grew louder, rising in pitch until it became a screech that seemed to tear through the fabric of the night itself.

"Do you hear that?" Yuki whispered, her voice tight with fear.

The others nodded, their faces pale. They knew the legend—the Nue. The creature whose cries foretold disaster. The cries were unmistakable, and yet, it was impossible to tell where they came from. It felt as though the very mountains were alive with the sound.

As the wail reached its peak, the wind shifted, and for a moment, there was silence. The group held their breath, waiting for something—anything. But the silence was too oppressive, too unnatural.

Then, as if from nowhere, a shadow appeared in the distance. At first, it was a small blur against the night sky, but then it grew larger, a cloud of darkness that seemed to hover just above the ground, drifting towards them.

Yuki's heart raced as the shadow took shape. It was the Nue, a chimera with the head of a monkey, the body of a raccoon dog, and the snake-like tail coiling behind it. The creature's eyes glowed with an eerie, otherworldly light, and its wail filled the air again, louder than before.

But something was wrong. The creature wasn't just crying—it was feeding. The ground beneath their feet seemed to tremble, and Yuki felt a sudden heaviness in her chest. The air grew thick with despair, and the sense of foreboding deepened.

Yuki tried to scream, but the sound was strangled, choked by the weight of the creature's presence. The Nue's cry, once distant, was now upon them. It didn't just foretell disaster—it consumed it, leaving nothing but emptiness in its wake.

As the shadow engulfed them, Yuki's vision blurred. The last thing she saw before darkness took over was the Nue's eyes, staring into hers with a chilling, unblinking gaze.

The Fearsome Nue

32.

Lake Tianchi Monster: The Mysterious Creature of Heaven Lake

Chinese Cryptid

Name: Lake Tianchi Monster
Type: Cryptid, Lake Monster
Habitat: Heaven Lake (Tianchi) in Baekdu Mountain, Jilin Province, China, and Ryanggang Province, North Korea
First Sightings: 1903, with more frequent reports from the 1960s and 2000s

---

Lake Tianchi Monster

The **Lake Tianchi Monster**, also known as the **Tianchi Monster**, is a mysterious cryptid that is said to inhabit **Heaven Lake (Tianchi)**, located at the peak of **Baekdu Mountain**, which straddles the border between **China** and **North Korea**. The lake, situated in the **Baekdu-daegan** and **Changbai Mountain ranges**, is a volcanic caldera lake, often associated with mystical and supernatural events in local folklore.

Sightings of the Lake Tianchi Monster date back to 1903, with a range of descriptions that have made this creature one of the most well-known lake monsters in Asia. The first reports of the creature suggested a large, buffalo-like being that allegedly attacked three people before retreating underwater. However, skepticism about its existence has persisted, as scientists argue that it is unlikely for a large creature to survive in the lake, particularly given its recent volcanic activity. Skeptics often dismiss the sightings as either exaggerated, misidentified floating volcanic rocks, or simply the product of local imagination.

Despite the doubts of the scientific community, there have been numerous reported sightings over the years, many of which describe the creature as an elusive, mysterious presence in the lake, occasionally surfacing or creating ripples in the water.

Physical Appearance:

The Lake Tianchi Monster is often described in varying forms, but common features include:

- **Large Size:** Descriptions suggest a creature of significant size, often likened to the size of a **buffalo** or a large sea serpent.
- **Neck:** A human-like head attached to a long, 1.5-meter (5 ft) neck is commonly reported in sightings, with some witnesses noting a **white ring around the base of the neck**.
- **Skin:** The body is typically described as **grey and smooth**, lacking the rough textures of many land animals.
- **Head and Features:** Some reports have described the monster's head as vaguely human-like, though these descriptions are often vague and inconsistent.
- **Fins/Wings:** One of the more peculiar descriptions includes reports of **long fins** or even **wings**, larger than the creature's body, allowing it to move swiftly through the water—similar to the way yachts travel at high speed. These appendages have been linked to the creature's ability to quickly dive and reappear on the surface.

Abilities and Powers:

High-Speed Swimming: The creature is often described as having the ability to move incredibly fast through the water, sometimes vanishing and reappearing with remarkable speed. The report of the creature's swimming speed being likened to a yacht is a notable point of intrigue.

Synchrony: One of the more mysterious aspects of the creature's behavior is its apparent coordination. In a 2007 report, a Chinese TV reporter, **Zhuo Yongsheng**, stated that he had filmed six of these creatures swimming in parallel, in perfect synchrony, as if they were acting under some kind of collective command or instruction.

Disappearance: The creatures reportedly disappear into the water, often at will, adding to the elusiveness and mystery surrounding their behavior.

Habitat and Behavior:

Heaven Lake (Tianchi), the home of the Lake Tianchi Monster, is a serene but eerie location, formed by volcanic activity. It is a remote, high-altitude lake nestled between mountains, often shrouded in fog and mystery. The cold, clear waters of the lake and the surrounding forests provide a perfect hiding spot for a creature that is rarely seen by humans.

Reports from locals and adventurers describe sightings of the monster emerging from the depths of the lake, usually during the evening or early morning. The creature is described as reclusive and elusive, often surfacing only for short periods of time before vanishing beneath the water's surface again.

Despite its scarcity, sightings persist, with the creature often being associated with eerie sounds, including its bloodcurdling shrieks that can resemble a woman's scream or other unsettling noises in the night. These sounds, combined with the monster's apparent synchrony and mysterious nature, contribute to the belief that it may be a supernatural or mythical creature, possibly connected to ancient folklore of the area.

Mythological Context:

The origins of the Lake Tianchi Monster are shrouded in mystery, with no definitive explanation for its existence. Some locals view the creature as a guardian spirit or a mystical being tied to the volcanic history of the region, while others believe it is a rare and undiscovered species of aquatic creature. Folklore suggests that the creature may be a spiritual entity or a relic of a forgotten era, with legends passed down through generations warning of its presence as an omen or a sign of impending death.

The Lake Tianchi Monster, like many cryptids, symbolizes the unknown and the unexplored aspects of nature. It embodies the fear of what lies beneath the surface, both literally in the waters of the lake and metaphorically in the mysteries of the natural world. It also reflects the awe and respect with which the people in the region view the mountains and lakes, seeing them as places where the natural world can harbor creatures beyond human comprehension.

Reports from 1962 describe two creatures chasing each other in the water, further solidifying the idea of the monster's presence. More recently, the 2007 sighting by Zhuo Yongsheng, who filmed six of the creatures in the lake, added modern evidence to the ongoing mystery.

Interesting Facts and Cultural Variations:

Cultural Significance: The Lake Tianchi Monster is sometimes likened to other legendary lake creatures, such as the Loch Ness Monster of Scotland or the Ogopogo of Canada. Its reputation as a harbinger of doom or a mysterious force of nature has made it a subject of fascination in both China and North Korea, where the lake is revered for its natural beauty and cultural significance.

Scientific Skepticism: While many cryptozoologists and enthusiasts continue to search for evidence of the Lake Tianchi Monster, scientists are skeptical. They argue that the lake, formed by volcanic activity, may not support the existence of a large creature, particularly given the lake's environmental conditions and its recent geological history. Skeptics suggest that sightings could be explained by optical illusions, floating rocks, or misidentified animals, such as large fish or birds, rather than a true cryptid.

The Lake Tianchi Monster remains one of the most intriguing and elusive cryptids in Asia. While no definitive proof of its existence has been found, the numerous reports of sightings and the eerie, bloodcurdling cries that emanate from the lake continue to captivate the imagination of cryptozoologists and locals alike. Whether it is a natural animal, a supernatural entity, or a figment of collective myth, the creature's place in the folklore of the region ensures that it will remain a mystery for years to come.

Lake Tianchi Monster – Chinese Cryptid

33.

Guide to Chinese Beasts: Legendary Creatures of Mythology

Chinese Mythology

1. Ao (The Flaming Tortoise)

Ao is a mythological tortoise with a burning shell and cheeks made of magma. Its appearance is fiery and terrifying, with intense heat emanating from its body. Ao is considered a symbol of endurance, strength, and longevity. The flames surrounding Ao's shell are often thought to represent the fierce protection it provides, as well as its connection to the earth's core. Ao's presence in Chinese mythology suggests resilience, as it can withstand immense pressure and heat without succumbing to destruction.

Ao's body is surrounded by molten magma, which makes it impervious to most forms of harm. Its flames can scorch anything that comes too close, acting as both a defensive mechanism and a weapon. Ao also has the ability to survive extreme conditions, making it a symbol of perseverance.

---

2. Ao Guang (Dragon King of the East Sea)

Ao Guang is one of the four Dragon Kings in Chinese mythology, ruling over the Eastern Sea. Ao Guang is a powerful and revered dragon who commands the waters and is responsible for the protection of the Eastern seas. He is depicted as a dragon with immense size, and his presence brings the balance of the ocean and the forces of nature.

As a Dragon King, Ao Guang has dominion over all water-related elements, including the seas, rivers, and storms. His power is vast, as he can summon rain, wind, and waves. His control over aquatic life allows him to govern vast stretches of the ocean.

Ao Guang, the Dragon King of the East Sea

3. Azure Dragon (Qinglong)

Qinglong, also known as the Azure Dragon, is one of the Four Symbols of Chinese constellations, representing the cardinal direction East and the season of Spring. It is a symbol of strength, power, and protection, often depicted as a majestic, long-bodied dragon with a serpent-like form and radiant scales. The Azure Dragon is the guardian of the East, embodying vitality and growth.

Qinglong has the ability to summon storms and control the winds of Spring. It is considered a protector of the East and is often associated with the rising sun and renewal. It is also a bringer of rain, which nurtures life in the East.

---

4. Bai Ze

Bai Ze is a strange and powerful creature, often depicted as a cow-like monster with a human head, six horns, and nine eyes. It is a rare and elusive beast that is said to possess immense wisdom and knowledge of supernatural events. Bai Ze is known for its ability to see through deception and reveal the true nature of all things.

Bai Ze's multiple eyes grant it the ability to see both the spiritual and material worlds clearly. It is said to have vast knowledge of demons and supernatural beings, making it a powerful force in ancient Chinese legends.

---

5. Baihu (White Tiger)

Baihu, also known as the White Tiger, is one of the Four Symbols of Chinese mythology, representing the cardinal direction West and the season of Autumn. Baihu is a powerful, mystical creature that embodies strength, courage, and protection. It is often depicted as a large, majestic white tiger with golden eyes, exuding both grace and ferocity.

Baihu is associated with both the physical and spiritual realms, symbolizing strength and protection from evil. It is believed to be a guardian against negative forces and is considered a protector of the West.

Baihu the White Tiger, one of the Four Symbols of Chinese mythology

6. Bai Suzhen (White Snake)

Bai Suzhen, also known as the White Snake, is a legendary figure in Chinese folklore. She is a beautiful and powerful snake spirit who transforms into a human woman, often depicted as a figure of both beauty and danger. Bai Suzhen's story is one of love, betrayal, and transformation, as she falls in love with a human man and faces trials and tribulations due to her supernatural nature.

Bai Suzhen has the ability to transform into a human form and possesses powerful snake-related abilities, such as controlling venom and manipulating nature. She is also able to harness magical powers, including healing and shape-shifting.

7. Bai long ma (White Dragon Mare)

The Bai long ma, or White Dragon Mare, is a mystical creature that is a blend of both horse and dragon traits. In mythology, it is often depicted as a beautiful white horse with dragon-like features, such as a long, sinuous tail and scales. The Bailongma is a symbol of freedom and power, riding through the clouds with unmatched grace.

The Bailongma has the ability to fly through the skies at incredible speeds, thanks to its dragon-like traits. It is also associated with the ability to bring rain and is considered a divine creature that can traverse both land and sky.

8. Bashe (Snake that Eats Elephants)

Bashe is a monstrous, python-like snake in Chinese mythology, renowned for its terrifying size and strength. It is said to be so large that it can consume entire elephants in a single gulp. Bashe represents the overwhelming power of nature and the danger of the wild.

The Bashe has the ability to constrict its prey with immense strength, capable of taking down even the largest of creatures, such as elephants. Its immense size and hunger make it one of the most feared mythical creatures in Chinese folklore.

Bashe, the Snake that Eats Elephants

9. Bifang (Crane-like Bird)

Bifang is a crane-like bird that is known for its one-footed nature and the strange fires that accompany it. It is said to be a rare and mystical creature, often appearing during significant events or changes in the natural world. The Bifang is associated with both the sky and the earth, and its presence is seen as a portent of great transformation.

Bifang has the ability to create and control fire, often seen with flames surrounding it as it flies. The one-footed nature of the creature adds to its mystique, with its fiery aura symbolizing purification and transformation.

10. Bixi (Dragon Tortoise)

Bixi is a dragon-like creature with the body of a tortoise, often depicted as a guardian and protector in Chinese folklore. It is one of the Four Sacred Creatures of Chinese mythology, symbolizing endurance, stability, and strength. Bixi is often shown as a turtle carrying a stone tablet on its back, representing the recording of history and wisdom.

Bixi is known for its strength and endurance, able to withstand immense pressure. It is also a protector of sacred sites, particularly those associated with history and wisdom. The Bixi's ability to endure and protect makes it a revered symbol in Chinese culture.

11. Black Tortoise (Xuanwu)

The Black Tortoise, also known as Xuanwu, is another of the Four Symbols of Chinese mythology, representing the cardinal direction North and the season of Winter. This creature is a combination of a tortoise and a snake, often depicted as a turtle with a serpent coiled around it. The Black Tortoise symbolizes protection, strength, and the enduring forces of winter.

Xuanwu is a powerful guardian of the North, often associated with defensive and protective qualities. It is also said to have the power to ward off evil spirits and balance the forces of nature. Its combination of a tortoise and snake gives it both strength and flexibility.

Xuanwu, the Black Tortoise

12. Bo Beast

The Bo Beast is a mythical creature that resembles a horse, but with a single horn on its forehead.

Mythical Beasts | 229

This powerful creature is said to be capable of defeating large predators, such as tigers and leopards, with ease. It symbolizes strength, speed, and purity.

The Bo Beast's strength is in its single horn, which is said to possess extraordinary power. It can charge through the forest, taking down larger animals, and is revered for its ability to protect weaker creatures.

---

13. Boyi (Nine-Tailed Sheep Beast)

The **Boyi** is a mythical, sheep-like creature from Chinese folklore, often described as a beast with nine tails and four ears, with eyes located on its back. This strange and fantastical creature is known for its uncanny appearance, with the multiple tails and sensory organs providing it with extraordinary abilities. The Boyi is a symbol of heightened awareness and strength, attributed to its enhanced vision and heightened senses.

The Boyi is believed to possess the ability to see threats or danger from all directions, thanks to the eyes on its back and its multiple ears. These extraordinary sensory powers grant it unparalleled awareness of its surroundings. In some versions of the myth, it is said that a person who wears the fur of the Boyi becomes immune to fear, a powerful attribute in the face of danger or adversity.

The Boyi represents awareness, vigilance, and the power to face fear head-on. The tale of the Boyi is often a metaphor for the importance of being prepared for the unknown and embracing strength in the face of challenges. The idea of wearing the fur of the Boyi and becoming fearless suggests a spiritual connection between the wearer and the divine protection that the Boyi offers.

---

14. Cánshén (Silkworm God)

Cánshén, also known as **Cánwáng** ("Silkworm Ruler"), is the deity associated with silkworms and the art of sericulture in Chinese religion. Cánshén is worshipped as the protector of silkworms, who are vital to Chinese agriculture, as they are the source of silk, an essential material in Chinese culture. Cánshén is a divine figure, revered for overseeing the production of silk and ensuring the prosperity of this valuable resource.

Cánshén is believed to have control over the silkworms and the silk-producing process. He ensures the growth, health, and productivity of the silkworms, blessing the people who work with them and promoting the prosperity of the silk industry. Those who honor Cánshén are thought to be blessed with abundant silk production and good harvests in sericulture.

Cánshén is a symbol of fertility, prosperity, and the balance between nature and agriculture. The worship of Cánshén is particularly important in regions where sericulture is central to local economies, as his blessings are thought to ensure a bountiful harvest of silk and good fortune for those who engage in silk production. The reverence for Cánshén highlights the importance of agriculture and craftsmanship in Chinese culture.

---

15. Cánmǔ (Silkworm Mother)

Cánmǔ, also known as **Cángū** ("Silkworm Maiden"), is the goddess of silkworms in Chinese mythology, often revered as the protector and nurturer of silkworms. She is also linked to **Houtu**, the Queen of the Earth, and the **Sanxiao** ("Three Skies") goddesses. Cánmǔ is sometimes identified as **Léizǔ**, the wife of **Huangdi**, the Yellow Emperor, who is considered the progenitor of Chinese civilization.

Cánmǔ is believed to have the power to guide and protect the silkworms, ensuring that they flourish and produce silk in abundance. Her role as the goddess of sericulture makes her a patron of farmers, particularly those engaged in the cultivation of silkworms. Cánmǔ's influence extends to the nurturing of nature and the earth, where she symbolizes fertility, growth, and the successful harvest of silk.

Cánmǔ is an important figure in regions where sericulture plays a central role in local economies. Her worship reflects the deep connection between people and the earth, as well as the reverence for the natural cycles that sustain life. The goddess embodies both the nurturing aspects of motherhood and the agricultural importance of silkworms. In some traditions, she is venerated as a fertility goddess, symbolizing both the reproductive powers of the earth and the prosperity brought by silk.

16. Chi (Mythological Hornless Dragon)

The Chi is a hornless dragon, often depicted as a long, sinuous creature with the ability to control water and weather. Unlike other dragons, the Chi lacks horns, giving it a more mysterious and ethereal appearance.

The Chi has control over natural elements, especially water and storms. It is known for its ability to bring rain to parched lands, making it a symbol of life-giving power in Chinese folklore.

Chi, the Mythological Hornless Dragon that can control the natural elements

17. Chinese Guardian Lions (Foo Dogs)

Chinese Guardian Lions, also known as **Foo Dogs** or **Fu Lions**, are mythical creatures traditionally placed in front of temples, palaces, and homes in Chinese architecture. These guardian statues are often carved in pairs, with one male and one female. The male lion typically holds a ball (symbolizing authority) while the female lion is shown with a cub under her paw (symbolizing nurturing and protection).

The primary purpose of the Chinese Guardian Lions is to act as protectors of a place or family, warding off evil spirits and negative energy. They are believed to have powerful spiritual abilities that ensure safety, prosperity, and harmony for those within the protected space. The male lion represents power and protection, while the female embodies balance and protection.

The Chinese Guardian Lions are symbols of strength, power, and vigilance. Their presence is intended to keep bad influences away, ensuring that only positive forces and energy enter a home or sacred space. In Chinese culture, they are often associated with good fortune and protection from harm, making them vital in Feng Shui practices.

---

18. Denglong (The Heavenly Messenger)

Denglong is a mythical creature that serves as the messenger between **Heaven** and **Earth**. Often depicted as a luminous, winged dragon or a dragon-like entity, Denglong is believed to carry divine messages from the celestial realm to the mortal world. It is considered a celestial being who can bridge the gap between humans and gods, guiding the flow of wisdom, prophecy, and fate.

Denglong possesses the ability to travel between worlds, delivering messages from the heavens to those chosen to receive them. With its swift wings, it can traverse great distances in a short time, carrying divine instructions, warnings, or blessings. Denglong is also associated with communication and divine knowledge, capable of imparting wisdom and guidance to those who seek it.

Denglong is revered as a sacred messenger, often invoked in times of crisis or when seeking divine intervention. Its role as an intermediary between the gods and humans underscores the belief in divine oversight and the sacred bond between the mortal and celestial realms.

19. Dilong (Earth Dragon)

Dilong, also known as the **Earth Dragon**, is a mythical creature in Chinese mythology that governs the underworld and the earth's soil. Unlike the traditional flying dragons, Dilong is depicted as a serpentine dragon that resides within the earth, controlling the forces beneath the ground.

Dilong's powers are centered around the earth itself. It is believed to control subterranean water sources, such as rivers and springs, and influences the growth of plants and crops. In ancient times, Dilong was also associated with controlling earthquakes and landslides. Its role is critical in maintaining the balance of the earth's natural forces, especially the cycles of life and death.

Dilong represents the unseen and vital forces of nature that sustain life. It is a guardian of the land's fertility and is often invoked for agricultural blessings, ensuring the prosperity of crops and the well-being of the earth itself.

Dilong, the Earth Dragon that governs the underworld and the earth's soil.

20. Feilian (God of the Wind)

Feilian is the god of wind in Chinese mythology, often depicted as a winged dragon with the head

Mythical Beasts | 235

of a deer and the tail of a snake. His appearance is a fusion of animalistic traits, representing the chaotic and powerful nature of wind and storms. Feilian is sometimes shown with large, sweeping wings and a serene but commanding presence.

Feilian controls the wind, harnessing its forces to shape the weather. He is believed to be able to stir up storms, summon gusts of wind, and bring both calm and chaos. His control over the wind allows him to influence the natural world, from gentle breezes to violent storms. Feilian is also a symbol of change and transformation, as the wind constantly shifts and moves.

Feilian embodies the untamed and unpredictable forces of nature. As the god of the wind, he is a powerful and revered figure in Chinese mythology. He is often invoked for guidance in times of change or upheaval, as well as for protection during storms.

---

21. Feilong (Flying Dragon)

Feilong, also known as the **Flying Dragon**, is a legendary creature in Chinese folklore, depicted as a dragon with wings that allow it to soar among the clouds. Unlike other dragons, which are often associated with water, Feilong is linked to the sky and the winds, embodying the celestial and free-spirited nature of the heavens.

Feilong possesses the ability to fly high in the sky, often depicted gliding through the clouds with graceful, sweeping movements. It controls the winds and can summon storms or create clear skies at will. Feilong is a symbol of freedom, ambition, and the boundless possibilities of the air, representing power and control over the skies.

Feilong is often associated with high aspirations and success, as its ability to fly freely in the heavens signifies unattainable goals and the pursuit of greatness. It is revered as a symbol of transformation and spiritual ascent, guiding those who seek higher knowledge and enlightenment.

Feilong, the flying dragon is linked to the sky and the winds

22. Fox Spirit (Huli Jing)

The **Fox Spirit**, also known as **Huli Jing**, **Huyao**, **Huxian**, or **Huzu**, is a shape-shifting, supernatural creature in Chinese mythology. The Fox Spirit is typically depicted as a beautiful woman who has the ability to transform from a fox into a human form. Fox Spirits are known for their cunning, seductive nature and their ability to manipulate others.

The Fox Spirit can change shape at will, transforming between a fox and a human, often appearing as a beautiful woman to seduce or deceive men. Fox Spirits are also believed to have magical powers, such as controlling the elements or influencing the emotions of others. They are often associated with love, lust, and trickery.

Fox Spirits embody both positive and negative qualities. On one hand, they are symbols of grace, beauty, and charm, but on the other, they are also seen as dangerous and deceitful entities. In Chinese folklore, Fox Spirits often serve as a reminder of the duality of nature and the importance of wisdom in discerning truth from illusion.

23. Hulijing (Chinese Fox Demon)

The **Hulijing** is a more malevolent form of the Fox Spirit, often depicted as a powerful and vengeful fox demon. Unlike the more playful Fox Spirits, Hulijing are known for their darker side, often associated with malicious behavior and harm. They are said to possess a deep understanding of the human soul and can be both seductive and destructive.

Hulijing possess the ability to enchant and manipulate people's minds. They can create illusions, control emotions, and even possess individuals. They are also known to have a deep connection with the supernatural, able to summon storms or cause misfortune to those who anger them.

Hulijing represent the darker aspects of the Fox Spirit mythology. They embody the power of seduction and manipulation, but also the consequences of vanity, pride, and unchecked desires. In Chinese culture, Hulijing serve as a warning against the dangers of falling for illusions and the importance of discernment.

24. Hong (Rainbow Dragon)

The **Hong** is a two-headed rainbow serpent in Chinese mythology, symbolizing the balance between light and dark, good and evil. Its bodies shimmer with all the colors of the rainbow, and its two heads represent the duality of existence. The Hong is a powerful and mystical creature, often seen as a symbol of transformation and cosmic balance.

The Hong possesses the ability to control the colors of the rainbow, bending them to its will. It can influence the weather, creating vibrant rainbows or chaotic storms. The two-headed nature of the Hong gives it a unique perspective on the world, allowing it to see both sides of any situation and bringing harmony or chaos as needed.

The Hong represents the balance of opposites—light and dark, good and evil, order and chaos. In Chinese culture, it is seen as a symbol of cosmic harmony and the interconnectedness of all things. Its dual nature encourages individuals to seek balance and unity in their own lives.

The Hong, a two-headed rainbow serpent from Chinese mythology, symbolizing balance and duality.

---

25. Huan Beast

The **Huan Beast** is a cat-like creature with only one eye and three tails, known for producing the sound of hundreds of animals chirping at once. It is a mysterious and rare creature that is said to possess otherworldly abilities, allowing it to create confusion and disarray through its cries.

The Huan Beast has the ability to mimic the sounds of many animals simultaneously, creating an overwhelming noise that can disorient and confuse those who hear it. Its strange appearance, with one eye and three tails, adds to its mystical and eerie reputation, making it a symbol of chaos and mystery in Chinese folklore.

The Huan Beast represents the overwhelming force of nature and the unknown. It is associated with confusion, chaos, and the unpredictable forces of the world. In Chinese mythology, creatures like the Huan Beast remind people of the complexities and unpredictability of life, as well as the importance of understanding the forces that govern nature.

---

26. Fuzhu (Four-Horned Deer)

The **Fuzhu** is a mystical Chinese deer with four horns, possessing a gentle countenance. It is often associated with periods of flood or disaster, symbolizing the need for harmony and balance during times of great change. The Fuzhu is a serene creature, often depicted with a peaceful expression and graceful movements.

The Fuzhu is known for its ability to appear during times of flooding or natural disaster, serving as a symbol of hope and renewal. Its four horns represent balance and the interconnectedness of the natural world. The Fuzhu is a calm and peaceful creature, often seen as a guide for those seeking tranquility during troubled times.

The Fuzhu symbolizes purity, renewal, and the restoration of harmony in times of disaster. It is a creature of grace and peace, often invoked during times of upheaval to bring balance and calm to those affected by natural disasters.

---

27. Jiangshi (Hopping Vampire)

The **Jiangshi**, often called the **Hopping Vampire**, is a reanimated corpse in Chinese folklore that feeds on the life force of the living. Unlike traditional vampires, the Jiangshi moves by hopping, as its limbs are stiff from rigor mortis. The Jiangshi is typically depicted as a pale, undead creature with outstretched arms and a terrifying face.

The Jiangshi has the ability to drain life energy from its victims by sucking their breath. It is usually nocturnal, emerging at night to hunt for the living. The Jiangshi's stiff limbs prevent it from walking normally, so it hops or lurches toward its prey. It is also known to be impervious to most physical attacks unless specific methods are used to neutralize it.

The Jiangshi represents fear of the dead returning to life and the dangers of unresolved spirits. It is a warning to respect the dead and the supernatural forces that govern life and death. In Chinese culture, the Jiangshi serves as a symbol of the consequences of improper burial and the boundaries between life and death.

28. Jiaolong (Hornless Scaled Dragon)

The **Jiaolong** is a hornless, scaled dragon from Chinese mythology, often associated with water and the forces of nature. Unlike the traditional dragons that are depicted with antler-like horns, the Jiaolong is smooth, serpentine in form, and without horns. Its body is typically long and covered in scales, with a powerful tail and an elegant head. The Jiaolong is often portrayed as living in rivers, lakes, or the deep seas, where it exerts dominion over aquatic realms.

The Jiaolong possesses the ability to control water, causing floods, storms, and surges of oceanic energy. It is a symbol of strength and power in the water, with the ability to influence the tides and currents. Its connection to the aquatic world also grants it the power to communicate with other water creatures, such as fish and sea spirits.

In Chinese culture, the Jiaolong is a symbol of power and chaos in nature. It represents the forces of water, which can be both life-giving and destructive. The Jiaolong is often seen as a precursor to greater, more powerful dragons, embodying the untamed and raw nature of the elemental world.

Jiaolong, the dragon of the elemental forces of water, symbolizing both creation and destruction.

29. Luan (Mythical Bird)

The **Luan** is a mythical bird in Chinese folklore, known for its ability to carry a shield and trample

Mythical Beasts | 243

upon snakes while wearing one on its breast. It is often described as a majestic and powerful creature, with a striking appearance, resembling a large bird of prey. The Luan is associated with noble qualities, such as protection, strength, and courage.

The Luan is a fierce protector, often depicted as trampling on snakes, which symbolize chaos and evil. Its powerful wings allow it to soar through the skies, and its talons are capable of crushing its enemies. The shield it carries symbolizes its defensive nature, while the shield on its breast signifies its power to protect those in need.

The Luan is revered as a symbol of protection and victory over evil. In Chinese mythology, it is often linked to the forces of righteousness and justice, guarding against the forces of darkness and malevolence. The Luan represents the balance between the natural world and the supernatural, embodying the divine ability to maintain harmony and order.

---

30. Jin Chan (Prosperity Frog)

The **Jin Chan**, or Prosperity Frog, is a mythical creature often depicted as a three-legged frog with a coin in its mouth. It is a symbol of wealth, good fortune, and prosperity in Chinese culture. The Jin Chan is typically shown with a large, bulging body, frog-like features, and a golden coin held between its teeth or resting on its tongue.

The Jin Chan is said to have the ability to bring wealth and financial success to those who honor it. It is often placed in homes and businesses as a symbol of prosperity. Its magical ability is thought to attract wealth, fortune, and good luck, while dispelling misfortune and financial struggles. In some depictions, the Jin Chan is said to hop forward to bring wealth, symbolizing progress and opportunity.

The Jin Chan is an important figure in Feng Shui and Chinese folklore. It is frequently used in spiritual practices and placed in homes or workplaces to encourage the flow of money and good fortune. Its image is often seen as a reminder to respect the cycles of nature and the prosperity that comes with positive energy and good karma.

Jin Chan, the prosperity frog

31. Kalaviṅka (Human-Headed Bird)

The **Kalaviṅka** is a mythological creature in South Asian and Chinese mythology, often depicted

Mythical Beasts | 245

as a fascinating hybrid with the head of a human and the torso of a bird. With a long, flowing tail and graceful wings, the Kalaviṅka embodies the connection between the earthly realm of humans and the ethereal world of birds. Its appearance is both majestic and eeric, symbolizing a divine or otherworldly entity that exists between two realms.

The Kalaviṅka's primary abilities are often linked to both the physical and spiritual realms. It is believed to have the ability to travel freely between the human world and the heavens, symbolizing a bridge between the two. Some stories attribute the Kalaviṅka with the power of flight, and it is often associated with the carrying of divine messages, offering wisdom and guidance to humans.

In some versions of the myth, the Kalaviṅka is thought to possess a musical voice or enchanting song, drawing upon the celestial and divine qualities of its bird form. Its song is said to possess healing or transformative powers, able to calm the minds of those who hear it.

In mythology, the Kalaviṅka is often seen as a symbol of beauty, grace, and divine wisdom. It embodies the union of two realms—human and animal—representing the idea of a connection between the earthly and the spiritual. The creature is frequently featured in stories that emphasize the importance of balance, transformation, and transcendence.

The Kalaviṅka is also associated with spiritual messengers or divine beings that guide humans toward enlightenment. Its image can be seen in ancient art, poetry, and literature as a representation of ideals such as purity, balance, and celestial influence.

The Kalaviṅka serves as a representation of beauty and harmony, with its blend of human intellect and the freedom of flight associated with birds. It also symbolizes the importance of communication between the divine and human realms, often portrayed as a messenger or intermediary between gods and mortals. The Kalaviṅka's graceful and harmonious nature serves as a reminder of the divine order of the universe and the importance of seeking wisdom and enlightenment.

31. Moon Rabbit

The **Moon Rabbit** is a mythical figure in Chinese folklore, often seen as a companion to the moon goddess, **Chang'E**. This rabbit is said to reside on the moon, where it pounds the Elixir of Life with a pestle, creating the immortality potion that Chang'E consumes. The Moon Rabbit is often depicted as a gentle, hardworking figure, busy with its task of preparing the Elixir under the serene moonlight.

The Moon Rabbit's main ability is to craft the Elixir of Life, a potion that grants immortality.

Through its tireless work, it ensures the continued flow of eternal life for those who are worthy. In some versions of the myth, the rabbit is also associated with the full moon, which brings enlightenment, wisdom, and reflection to those who look upon it.

The Moon Rabbit is a symbol of immortality, diligence, and sacrifice. It embodies the eternal cycle of life and death, and the tireless pursuit of wisdom and enlightenment. It is a central figure in the Mid-Autumn Festival, where it is often depicted alongside Chang'E, serving as a reminder of the pursuit of happiness, longevity, and cosmic harmony.

---

32. Nian (Chinese New Year Beast)

The **Nian** is a mythological beast that is most commonly associated with the Chinese New Year. It is a terrifying creature, often depicted as a large, monstrous beast with a fearsome appearance. According to legend, the Nian would come down from the mountains or the sea to terrorize villages, devouring crops, livestock, and people.

The Nian is known for its immense strength and ferocity, capable of causing destruction on a grand scale. However, it is said to be afraid of loud noises, bright lights, and the color red. These weaknesses became central to the tradition of using firecrackers, lanterns, and the color red during the Chinese New Year celebrations, all of which are believed to drive the Nian away.

The Nian is closely associated with the beginning of the Chinese New Year, symbolizing the cycle of renewal and the triumph of light and hope over darkness and fear. Its story has led to the custom of setting off firecrackers and hanging red decorations to ward off evil and ensure a prosperous and safe year.

The Nian, the Chinese New Year Beast

33. Panlong (Aquatic Dragon)

The **Panlong** is an aquatic dragon in Chinese mythology, often depicted as a powerful, serpentine creature that dwells in rivers, lakes, or oceans. The Panlong is sometimes seen as a smaller, more agile dragon compared to the great Dragon Kings of the seas but still possessing great power over water and the creatures within it.

The Panlong has control over the waters it inhabits, able to summon storms or calm the seas at will. It is also associated with the ability to influence the weather, particularly in the form of rain, which is crucial for agriculture in Chinese culture. As an aquatic dragon, it can navigate and control both freshwater and saltwater environments.

The Panlong is a symbol of the mystical and natural forces of water. It represents the connection between the elemental powers of water and the cycles of life that rely on rain and water. It is also a guardian of natural bodies of water, ensuring their balance and harmony.

34. Peng (Mystical Bird)

The **Peng** is a mystical, giant bird of the ocean, often depicted as a massive, majestic creature that soars through the clouds. In Chinese mythology, it is said to transform into a great bird that flies from the ocean to the sky. The Peng is sometimes compared to the Roc in other mythologies, representing immense size and strength.

The Peng's most notable ability is its power to transform from a small fish into a giant bird, symbolizing the potential for growth and change. It is said to have the strength to create massive storms and is capable of soaring vast distances. Its wings can whip up winds, and it is known for its ability to challenge the heavens, flying to the highest realms.

The Peng symbolizes boundless ambition, the ability to overcome obstacles, and the potential for transformation. It is often seen as a symbol of strength and courage, representing the pursuit of greatness and the challenge of reaching new heights.

35. Shenlong (Dragon of the Storms)

Shenlong is a dragon in Chinese mythology, often described as the master of storms and the bringer of rain. This powerful dragon controls both the winds and the rains, ensuring that the

Earth receives the nourishment it needs for growth. Shenlong is depicted as a magnificent dragon with cloud-like scales and eyes that command the heavens.

Shenlong controls the weather, bringing much-needed rain to the earth and ensuring the balance of nature. He is also said to summon storms, winds, and tempests, with the ability to alter the course of natural events. Shenlong is revered for his role in agriculture, as his rains are crucial for crop growth.

Shenlong represents the forces of nature that sustain life, symbolizing both power and benevolence. He is a guardian of agriculture and a bringer of prosperity, ensuring that the land remains fertile and the people thrive. Shenlong is also a symbol of the authority of the celestial realms over the Earth.

Shenlong, Dragon of the Storms and Rain

36. Zhenniao (Poisonous Bird)

Zhenniao is a legendary bird known for its poisonous feathers in Chinese mythology. It is often depicted as a fierce and dangerous creature, whose feathers can cause harm to those who come into contact with them. This bird is associated with both the mystical and harmful aspects of nature.

The primary ability of Zhenniao lies in its poisonous feathers, which can cause sickness or death to those who are struck by them. The bird is often seen as a symbol of danger and warning, with its venomous nature making it a creature to be feared.

Zhenniao represents the hidden dangers in nature, a reminder that not all creatures are benign. Its toxic nature is symbolic of the hazards that lie within the natural world, and it serves as a cautionary figure in Chinese mythology, warning people to respect the dangers that exist beyond the safety of civilization.

---

37. Zhulong (Solar Dragon)

Zhulong is a giant, red solar dragon and a god in Chinese mythology. Often depicted as a fiery red dragon, Zhulong is said to control the sun's path across the sky, representing the power of the sun and the cosmic balance. It is believed that Zhulong is responsible for maintaining the cycles of day and night.

Zhulong has control over the sun, ensuring that it rises and sets at the proper times. As a solar dragon, it is associated with the force of fire, warmth, and light, bringing life to the Earth. Its fiery breath and power over the sun symbolize the forces of creation and destruction.

Zhulong represents the vital force of the sun in Chinese mythology. It is a symbol of strength, vitality, and the cosmic balance between light and dark. Zhulong is often revered as a deity that ensures the natural order and the cycle of life, death, and rebirth.

---

38. Zhuque (Vermilion Bird)

Zhuque, also known as the **Vermilion Bird**, is one of the Four Symbols of Chinese mythology. It represents the cardinal direction **South** and the season of **Summer**. The Vermilion Bird is a fiery, red bird often depicted as a majestic phoenix or a red-feathered bird with striking plumage. It symbolizes beauty, vitality, and the warmth of the summer sun.

Zhuque controls the fire element, symbolizing passion, energy, and renewal. It is associated with the warmth of summer and the vitality that comes with it, playing a role in the growth of crops and the flourishing of life. Zhuque is a bringer of light and energy, both in the physical world and within the spiritual realm.

Zhuque embodies the power of the sun and the transformative energy of fire. It represents strength, beauty, and the rejuvenating force of summer. In Chinese culture, Zhuque is revered as a symbol of life and vitality, often associated with positive transformation and renewal.

Zhuque, the Vermilion Bird linked to the South and Summer

34.

Bạch Xà (White Snake)

Vietnamese Mythology

The **Bạch Xà**, or **White Snake**, is a legendary creature deeply embedded in Vietnamese mythology, often associated with themes of love, transformation, and vengeance. The story of the White Snake is famous throughout many parts of Southeast Asia, especially in Chinese and Vietnamese traditions, with slight variations in each culture. In Vietnam, the White Snake is often portrayed as a spirit who, over centuries of meditation, transforms from a serpent into a beautiful woman. She seeks love and, in some cases, faces tragic consequences as a result of human prejudices against her serpent nature.

Bạch Xà (White Snake) – Vietnamese Mythology

The Bạch Xà is typically depicted as a large, elegant white snake, with eyes that glimmer with a supernatural aura. Upon transforming into a human form, she is usually shown as a woman of exceptional beauty, radiant and ethereal, often dressed in white to reflect her original form. She embodies both the grace of a serpent and the mystery of a human heart.

When in her snake form, the Bạch Xà is a majestic white serpent, shimmering with a light that seems to radiate from within. Her body is long and sleek, with glistening scales that shine like polished pearls under the moonlight. Her eyes are hypnotic and captivating, reflecting the depths of her ancient wisdom and power. In her human form, she appears as a stunning woman, her hair often long and black, contrasting with her pale skin, and she is usually draped in flowing, white garments that mirror her serpent nature.

As a magical being, the Bạch Xà possesses several supernatural abilities. Most notably, she can transform from a serpent into a human woman, a power granted by centuries of meditation and spiritual discipline. She is skilled in magic, able to manipulate natural forces, heal the sick, and sometimes even control the elements around her. The Bạch Xà is often linked to water sources, such as rivers or lakes, where she is believed to have originated.

Despite her benevolent qualities, her true nature is feared by those who do not understand her powers. In some versions of the myth, the Bạch Xà can summon storms, or her anger can cause natural disasters. However, her abilities are typically used in the service of good, especially in matters of love and protection for those she cares for.

Cultural Significance:

The legend of the Bạch Xà is deeply woven into Vietnamese cultural values, particularly those involving love, sacrifice, and the tension between the spiritual and physical realms. The White Snake represents the eternal conflict between human perceptions of reality and the magical, unseen world that coexists with it. The myth underscores the idea of forbidden love—how love can transcend boundaries, be it between species, classes, or the natural and supernatural worlds.

In some retellings, the Bạch Xà's story emphasizes themes of redemption and tragedy, as her love for a human man often leads to betrayal and suffering. The Bạch Xà is also symbolic of transformation—the snake, an animal often associated with rebirth, change, and healing, transforms into a woman, embodying the complex interplay between nature, love, and human fear.

Notable Legends and Tales:

The most famous tale involving the Bạch Xà is her love story with **Hứa Tiên**, a kind-hearted and brave man. The Bạch Xà falls in love with him after transforming into a woman, and they marry, leading a blissful life. However, a Buddhist monk named **Fong Thiên** discovers her true identity as a snake and attempts to separate them, believing that love between humans and supernatural beings is unnatural and dangerous. The monk's intervention leads to a tragic conclusion, and in some versions of the myth, the Bạch Xà is forced back into her snake form, trapped in a temple or river for eternity, her love unfulfilled.

The Bạch Xà's tale reflects the tension between the desires of the heart and societal or spiritual laws, often ending in sorrow or separation but leaving a profound mark on the hearts of those who hear it.

"The Love of Bạch Xà"

In the quiet village by the river, a young man named **Hứa Tiên** lived a simple but content life. He worked as a farmer, tending to his crops and fishing in the river. Though he was kind and good-hearted, he often felt that something was missing—he longed for love, for a connection deeper than the land and water around him.

One evening, while walking by the river's edge, he heard a soft, melodic voice calling to him from the water. At first, he thought it was the wind, but the voice was clear, gentle, and full of sorrow.

"Who calls?" Hứa Tiên asked, his curiosity piqued.

From the river emerged a woman, her long black hair flowing like silk behind her, and her skin as pale as moonlight. She wore a flowing white dress that shimmered under the stars. Her beauty was otherworldly, as if she had risen from the very water she stood beside.

"I am **Bạch Xà**," the woman said softly. "I have waited for you."

Hứa Tiên's heart skipped a beat. There was something about her—her voice, her presence—that made him feel as though he had known her his entire life. He had heard tales of the **Bạch Xà**, the White Snake, the magical being who could transform into a human, but he had always dismissed them as mere folklore. Now, standing before him, she seemed as real as the moonlight that bathed the river.

As the days passed, Hứa Tiên and Bạch Xà grew closer. She would visit him each evening, and they would talk, laugh, and share their dreams. She told him of her long life, of how she had meditated for centuries to become human. And Hứa Tiên, in turn, told her of his simple desires: a family, a life filled with peace and love.

Despite the warnings of others—whispers of the dangers of loving a creature not of this world—Hứa Tiên could not resist her charms. He fell deeply in love with her, and soon they married in secret, hidden away from the fearful eyes of the villagers.

But peace, as it often does, could not last. **Fong Thiên**, a Buddhist monk who had heard rumors of the supernatural bride, grew suspicious. He believed that the love between a man and a creature like Bạch Xà could bring nothing but ruin. With his knowledge of ancient rituals, he set out to expose Bạch Xà for what she truly was.

One night, as Hứa Tiên and Bạch Xà lay in the quiet of their home, Fong Thiên arrived. He began chanting ancient mantras, and the air grew heavy with the weight of spiritual energy. The ground trembled, and a great light filled the room.

"Reveal yourself!" Fong Thiên shouted, his voice a command. "Show your true form, serpent!"

The air shifted, and before Hứa Tiên's eyes, the beautiful woman he loved began to shimmer and change. Her graceful human form was replaced by a magnificent white serpent, her eyes still glowing with the same love and sorrow she had shown him.

Hứa Tiên's heart broke as he watched the transformation, but in that moment, he understood the depth of her sacrifice. She had given up her true form for him, for their love.

"No! Don't!" he cried, reaching out to her. But the monk, with his unyielding beliefs, was relentless. He summoned divine forces to separate them, and the serpent-woman was forced to flee.

Bạch Xà, now a snake once again, slithered away, disappearing into the depths of the river. Hứa Tiên, unable to follow her, collapsed in despair. The love they shared was torn apart by the hand of fate.

Years passed, and Hứa Tiên grew old, his heart never forgetting the love he had lost. He would visit the river each night, whispering her name, hoping that one day she would return. And though the villagers spoke of her in fearful tones, Hứa Tiên never stopped believing in the love they had shared.

For in the heart of the river, beneath the water's surface, Bạch Xà lived on, forever waiting for the moment when love would once again reunite them.

Bạch Xà | 259

35.

Gumiho, the Nine Tailed Fox

Korean Mythology

The **Gumiho** (also known as **Kitsune** in Japanese and **Huli Jing** in Chinese) is a powerful and mystical fox spirit deeply embedded in Korean folklore. Traditionally, the Gumiho is depicted as a shape-shifting creature that starts life as a fox but can transform into a beautiful woman. Often associated with both malevolent and benevolent traits, the Gumiho's nature varies depending on the story. In older myths, the Gumiho was portrayed as a fearsome, bloodthirsty predator, while in more recent tales, she is sometimes depicted as a tragic, misunderstood figure. The Gumiho is infamous for her desire to consume human hearts or livers, using her captivating beauty and charm to lure men to their doom.

Gumiho (Korean Mythology)

In her fox form, the Gumiho is usually depicted as a sleek, beautiful creature with nine long, flowing tails. Her fur is often a deep, radiant white or golden hue, symbolizing her mystical power.

When the Gumiho transforms into a human form, she is typically shown as an extraordinarily beautiful woman with enchanting eyes, long black hair, and a figure that can captivate anyone. However, her true fox-like nature is often revealed by her slightly pointed ears, sharp eyes, or sometimes by a single hidden tail, which she must hide at all costs to avoid being discovered.

The Gumiho possesses the ability to shape-shift at will, taking on both human and fox forms. In some versions of the legend, the Gumiho can transform into a fully human woman, while in others, her fox form retains some supernatural traits, such as her glowing eyes or the ability to change her appearance instantly. The Gumiho is also known for her ability to seduce and manipulate her victims, often using charm and allure to trap them. Her most notorious power is her hunger for human hearts or livers, which she needs to consume to maintain her life force or transform into a full human.

Cultural Significance:

The Gumiho is a powerful symbol in Korean folklore, representing both the dangers of temptation and the complexities of duality. In earlier myths, the Gumiho was often feared as a dangerous monster—her very existence was a reminder of the threat posed by hidden desires and dark forces. Over time, however, the Gumiho has been reimagined in popular culture, sometimes as a tragic figure trying to become human, adding layers of complexity to her character. In modern tales, the Gumiho is often depicted as a symbol of the struggle between the natural world and human society, with many stories exploring themes of identity, transformation, and redemption.

Notable Legends and Tales:

The most famous tale involving the Gumiho is the story of a young man who is tricked by a Gumiho in the guise of a beautiful lady. The fox spirit lures the man into a trap, planning to feast on his heart. However, the man, either through wit or divine intervention, manages to expose her true nature, and in some versions, the Gumiho is ultimately redeemed and transformed into a full human after a long process of purification and repentance.

Short Story: "The Heart of the Gumiho"

In a small village nestled between rolling hills, there was a legend of a mysterious woman who lived at the edge of the forest. She was said to be so beautiful that no man could resist her charms. Her name was **Sooyeon**, and her hair shimmered like the night sky, long and black, flowing in waves like the rivers of the world. She lived alone in a small cottage, with the winds always whispering about her presence, though no one had ever seen her in the daylight.

Jiho, a young farmer from the village, had heard stories of the enchanting Sooyeon from his friends and elders. But there was one thing that caught his attention more than her beauty: the whispers that her allure was unnatural, that something about her made men disappear. The rumors spoke of men who had ventured into the forest, lured by her soft voice or the delicate music she played on a hidden flute, only to vanish without a trace.

One evening, as Jiho was walking home from the market, he felt an inexplicable pull toward the woods. The night was deep, the stars hidden behind thick clouds, but his feet moved as though guided by a force beyond his control. He wandered deeper into the forest, the silence broken only by the rustle of leaves in the wind.

Suddenly, he heard it—a soft melody, like the sound of a flute, floating on the air. It was a song that beckoned, its haunting notes dancing through the trees. Jiho felt his heart race, his body moving on its own accord toward the sound. As he neared the clearing, he saw her—a figure standing in the moonlight, draped in white, her back to him. Her long hair shimmered like silver, and her presence radiated an otherworldly beauty.

Sooyeon turned, her eyes locking with Jiho's. She smiled, and in that moment, everything else seemed to fade away. "Come closer, Jiho," she said, her voice soft like the breeze. "I've been waiting for you."

Despite the stories, Jiho felt no fear. There was only a strange warmth, a pull in his chest that told him he was where he was meant to be. As he walked toward her, his mind grew foggy, his thoughts becoming distant. Her beauty, her voice, it all consumed him. She extended her hand, and he took it without hesitation.

But as his fingers touched her skin, he saw it. For a brief moment, her eyes flashed, and something darker flickered within them. Her human appearance wavered, revealing a glimpse of something much older, much more ancient beneath the surface. Jiho's heart skipped a beat. He stepped back, suddenly realizing the danger he was in.

"You... you're not human," Jiho whispered.

Sooyeon's smile faltered. She looked at him with a strange mixture of sadness and longing. Her form began to shift, the beauty of a woman melting away to reveal the sleek, white body of a massive fox, her nine tails swaying behind her like serpents.

"I have lived for centuries, Jiho," the Gumiho said, her voice now low and resonant, full of ancient power. "I am cursed, bound to hunger for the hearts of men. But I do not wish to harm you. I have fallen in love with you."

Jiho stood frozen, his heart pounding in his chest. "Why me? Why do you do this?"

The Gumiho's expression softened. "I once was human, Jiho, but I was transformed into this creature, doomed to feed on the hearts of those I love. I have taken many lives, and I have tried to fight the urge. But the hunger... it is too great."

Tears welled in her eyes as she looked at him, pleading. "Please, Jiho, save me. I cannot control this anymore. If you leave, I will destroy myself in the process of trying to keep the hunger at bay."

Jiho's mind raced. The power to destroy her was in his hands, but the love he felt for this creature was undeniable. The choice was his: to save his own life or risk it to save her.

He looked into her eyes, and in that moment, he knew what he had to do. "I will not leave you, Sooyeon," he said, stepping forward.

He took her in his arms, feeling her powerful form trembling beneath his touch. "We will face this together," he whispered.

But Sooyeon, realizing the gravity of what was happening, closed her eyes. She could feel her old nature surging up, the darkness rising within her like a wave. Her tails lashed violently, and her form flickered between that of a woman and a fox.

The Gumiho's body began to pulse with energy, and the transformation intensified. With one final cry, the Gumiho collapsed, her body shuddering in anguish. The world around them seemed to ripple, and for a brief moment, Jiho felt his life slip away. But then, with a flash of light, the transformation stopped.

Jiho opened his eyes to find himself alone in the clearing. Sooyeon was gone, but the moonlight that had once been heavy with despair now felt peaceful. He gazed around, and in the distance, he saw a single, white tail flickering in the shadows.

Gumiho (Korean Mythology)

PART VII
SHADOWS OF SOUTH ASIA

Stories from South Asia: A Tapestry of Gods, Beasts, and Spirits

South Asia, a region known for its diverse cultures, languages, and traditions, is equally renowned for its vast array of mythological creatures, spirits, and legendary beings. Spanning the countries of India, Pakistan, Bangladesh, Nepal, Sri Lanka, and beyond, the myths of South Asia reflect the complexities of the natural world, the balance between good and evil, and the intricate relationship between humans and the divine.

In this section, we delve into the rich and vibrant folklore of South Asia, exploring the extraordinary creatures that populate the myths and legends of the region. From the terrifying demons of **Hindu** and **Buddhist** traditions, like the **Asura** and **Rakshasa**, to the mystical beings such as **Nagas** (serpent spirits) and the shape-shifting **Matsya** (fish incarnations), the stories from South Asia offer a fascinating glimpse into the region's cultural and spiritual diversity.

South Asian mythology often brings together gods, demons, animals, and spirits that perform important roles in the creation of the world, the maintenance of cosmic order, and the protection of nature and people. Be it the noble and heroic **Vishnu**, the tempestuous **Shiva**, or the trickster **Maya**, each deity or creature embodies the virtues, flaws, and complexities of human existence.

The region's legendary creatures also offer a compelling lens into the values of the various civilizations that have flourished here. Many of the myths contain lessons on morality, respect for nature, the consequences of unchecked power, and the balance between order and chaos. These stories are not just cautionary tales—they are living traditions that continue to shape the cultural fabric of South Asia.

In this section, we will journey through the stories of these mythological creatures, exploring their origins, powers, and cultural significance. We will uncover the myths that define and shape the very heart of South Asia, where deities and beasts walk side by side, and where every myth is both a warning and a guide to understanding the world around us.

Nagas, the Guardians of Treasure

36.

Bangladeshi Ghosts: The Spirits that Haunt the Land

Bangladeshi Phantoms

Bangladesh, a country with a rich history and cultural tapestry, has an equally deep and varied collection of supernatural tales. From the bustling streets of Dhaka to the quiet rural villages, spirits and phantoms walk among the living, each with their own unique backstory, motives, and behaviors. The ghosts of Bangladesh are not just figments of imagination; they are interwoven with the nation's folklore, cultural practices, and religious beliefs, forming an integral part of the collective consciousness.

A Guide To Bangladeshi Ghosts

This guide will take you through some of the most famous and eerie ghosts of Bangladesh—spirits that have lingered in the folklore of the region for generations. Some are vengeful, while others are tragically bound to the mortal realm due to unresolved conflicts. Regardless of their origins, each one serves as a reminder of the unknown forces that continue to shape the living world.

1. The Bhūt (Bhoot)

A Restless Spirit

The most common ghost in Bangladeshi folklore is the *Bhūt*, a restless spirit that is either created by a violent death or by unfinished business. Bhūts are typically seen as malevolent, lingering in areas where they were wronged—such as battlefields, homes, or forests. Their appearance is often described as a shadowy figure, wearing tattered clothes, with an expression of anger or sorrow.

The *Bhūt* is believed to arise from the souls of those who died unjustly, prematurely, or violently. It is said that a *Bhūt* will continue to haunt the living until its unfinished business is resolved, whether that means avenging its death, seeking forgiveness, or gaining peace.

Notable Haunting Locations:

- *Old Dhaka's narrow streets* are notorious for sightings of the *Bhūt*. Locals claim to have heard eerie wails emanating from abandoned buildings.
- *The Sundarbans*, with its thick, fog-laden swamps, is said to be home to many *Bhūts*, especially those who perished in the war or natural disasters.

---

2. The Churels

Vengeful Spirit

The *Churel* is one of the most infamous female spirits in Bangladeshi folklore, often depicted as a beautiful woman from afar, with long, flowing hair and a seductive appearance. Upon closer inspection, however, her true form is revealed—her feet are reversed, and her face is that of a decayed, monstrous corpse. She is known for preying on men, luring them into the wilderness or near bodies of water before draining their life force.

The *Churel* is said to be the spirit of a woman who died during childbirth or in a state of intense emotional trauma, often connected to betrayal by a lover or husband. Consumed by jealousy or rage, her spirit takes on a horrific form, seeking revenge on men, especially those who stray from their wives.

Notable Haunting Locations:

- *Deserted areas near rivers* or *forests*, where men are known to wander alone at night. The *Churel* is said to be particularly active in such secluded locations.

- *Remote villages* where young women died tragically or in childbirth, where it is rumored her spirit may linger.

Ghosts | 269

3. The Kalo Bhoot (Black Ghost)

Poltergeist

The *Kalo Bhoot* is known for its association with darkness and malice. It is said to be a shadowy entity that can cause objects to move or cause disturbances in the household. Unlike other ghosts that appear as human figures, the *Kalo Bhoot* is formless and often manifests as a dark shape that moves swiftly, often leaving an ominous presence in its wake.

The *Kalo Bhoot* is believed to be the spirit of someone who was consumed by evil thoughts or jealousy. It is also thought to be the spirit of someone who lived a life full of deceit, anger, or malice. After death, their soul transforms into this dark, oppressive force that seeks to spread negativity wherever it goes.

Notable Haunting Locations:

- *Village homes*, where the *Kalo Bhoot* is said to manifest during moments of familial strife or unhealed emotional wounds.
- *Old houses* that have been abandoned or left to decay, where the malevolent energy of the spirit may be strongest.

---

4. The Jinn of the Sundarbans

Supernatural Entity

The *Jinn* are spirit beings in Islamic folklore, and in Bangladesh, the *Jinn* are particularly connected to nature and the wild places of the earth. The *Jinn* of the Sundarbans are believed to be powerful beings who have dominion over the forest and its creatures. They can be both helpful and vengeful, depending on their mood or the treatment they receive from humans.

The *Jinn* are thought to be created from smokeless fire, and they are ancient spirits who existed long before humanity. The *Jinn* of the Sundarbans, specifically, are thought to have been there since the creation of the world, guarding the sacred forests. They can be summoned or befriended through proper rituals, but those who fail to show respect or make demands of the *Jinn* may find themselves cursed.

Notable Haunting Locations:

- *The Sundarbans*, particularly deep within its mangroves and swamps, where the dense foliage

makes it easy for the *Jinn* to remain hidden and unapproachable.
- *Isolated riverbanks* where fishermen and travelers may encounter these powerful beings, either in human or animal form.

---

5. The Bhoot Pret (Evil Spirit)

Evil Spirit

The *Bhoot Pret* is an especially wicked form of spirit, often associated with causing harm to the living. It is described as a grotesque figure, with pale skin, hollow eyes, and long, unkempt hair. It is often seen wandering in dark, desolate places, waiting for the opportunity to possess or harm humans.

This spirit is believed to be the soul of someone who lived a life of cruelty or wickedness. It is said that after dying, this evil soul cannot find peace and continues to cause havoc on the living. Some stories suggest that the *Bhoot Pret* may possess the bodies of the living, causing them to behave erratically or dangerously.

Notable Haunting Locations:

- *Cemeteries* or *graveyards*, particularly those associated with sudden or violent deaths.
- *Abandoned temples* or *isolated shrines*, where the spirit may lurk in wait for those who pass by.

---

6. The Pretatma

Wandering Soul

The *Pretatma* is a wandering spirit that roams the earth, often in search of food, water, or peace. Unlike other malevolent ghosts, the *Pretatma* is seen as a pitiful figure, cursed to wander eternally due to unfulfilled desires or unfinished business.

The *Pretatma* is believed to be a soul that was trapped between life and death, often because it was unable to fulfill its desires or because of the way it lived. Some legends tell of *Pretatma* spirits being the souls of those who were greedy in life, unable to pass on due to their unquenchable thirst for material wealth or unkind deeds.

Notable Haunting Locations:

- *Ruins of old homes* or *villages*, where souls are believed to be stuck between worlds.
- *The outskirts of villages* at the edge of forests, where the *Pretatma* can be seen wandering in search of rest.

---

7. The Dooth (Messenger of Death)

Harbinger of Death
The **Dooth** is a shadowy figure that represents death itself. It is often described as a tall, gaunt figure with an expressionless face, dressed in dark robes, and carrying a scythe or staff. The **Dooth** is known for appearing just before someone is about to pass away, silently watching over them as they approach their final moments.

The **Dooth** is said to be the physical manifestation of death itself, a spirit that walks among the living to guide souls to the afterlife. While it is not an evil spirit, it is feared for its connection to mortality and its presence before a person's passing.

Notable Haunting Locations:

- **Hospitals** or **deathbeds**, where the **Dooth** is said to appear to those who are about to die.
- **Graveyards**, especially at night, where it is believed to guide new souls to the afterlife.

Bangladesh's ghostly folklore is rich with a wide variety of spirits, from vengeful beings seeking retribution to wandering souls in search of peace. Each of these ghosts, whether they come from ancient times or more recent stories, reflects the country's deep spiritual beliefs, fears, and cultural heritage. While these stories may frighten, they also remind the people of Bangladesh to live in harmony with the world around them and to respect the forces beyond the living world. The ghosts of Bangladesh are ever-present, not only in folklore but in the collective psyche of the nation.

Ghosts | 273

37.

Vetala: The Reanimated Spirits of the Dead

Hindu Mythology

Name: Vetala
Type: Paranormal Entity, Reanimated Corpse, Spirit of the Dead
Habitat: Charnel Grounds, Cemeteries, Sacred Sites, Remote Villages
First Sightings: Ancient Hindu Folklore, references dating back to at least the 11th century in texts like the *Vetala Panchavimshati*

The Vetala

The **Vetala** is a powerful and malevolent spirit found in Hindu mythology, known for its haunting presence and ability to possess the dead. Unlike traditional ghosts, the Vetala is not a wandering soul or spirit of the deceased; rather, it is a paranormal entity that animates corpses, taking them as vessels to move and interact with the living. These spirits are often depicted as hostile, dangerous beings trapped in a state between life and death, dwelling in places like charnel grounds and cemeteries where corpses are laid to rest.

The Vetala is a terrifying figure that embodies both death and the supernatural. In its traditional form, it is described as a reanimated corpse with a grotesque, decaying appearance. The creature's possession of the dead body allows it to move, speak, and interact with the living, though it is only the vessel for the Vetala's intelligence, power, and malign intent.

Physical Appearance:

The appearance of a Vetala varies based on the corpse it possesses, but it is typically depicted as a walking, animated cadaver with hollow eyes, rotting flesh, and an eerie, unnatural demeanor. The Vetala often has the power to manipulate the body it inhabits, using it to interact with others, causing fear and confusion. In some traditions, it may even appear as an intangible, shadowy figure, depending on how it chooses to present itself.

Abilities and Powers:

The Vetala is known for several supernatural powers:

Possession of Corpses: The Vetala can enter the bodies of the dead, using them as vessels to move, speak, and interact with the world of the living. The creature may possess a body at will and leave it just as easily, making it an elusive and dangerous entity.

Time Manipulation: Vetala are unaffected by the normal laws of space and time. They have deep knowledge of past, present, and future events, making them capable of predicting or influencing the course of human lives.

Mental Influence and Madness: One of the Vetala's most terrifying abilities is its power to induce madness in humans. It is said that the Vetala can drive people to insanity, cause violent outbursts, or manipulate the thoughts and emotions of those around it.

Cursing and Killing: Vetala can bring death, especially through miscarriage or child-killing, as well as spreading pestilence and illness. It is believed that their presence alone can cause harm to entire villages or groups of people.

Shape-shifting: The Vetala can assume various forms, including that of a black cloud or shadow, making it nearly impossible to track. This ability enhances its role as an unpredictable and elusive force of nature.

Habitat and Behavior: The Vetala is traditionally said to dwell in desolate, eerie places such as charnel grounds, cremation sites, and cemeteries—places where the dead are laid to rest and where the boundary between life and death is thin. It is also linked to sacred places, especially in regions where it is revered or feared, such as the Konkan region, where the Vetala is worshipped in certain temples dedicated to *Betal*, a form of Bhairava (a fierce manifestation of Shiva).

Despite its affinity for the dead, the Vetala is not a mere mindless creature; it possesses deep knowledge of human nature, and its motives are often complex. It may be drawn to powerful individuals, especially those engaged in the occult, or to places where its power can be harnessed by sorcerers or witches. While some Vetala act as guardians of sacred spaces, protecting villages or temples from evil forces, others may act purely out of malevolence, tormenting the living with their dark abilities.

Mythological Context:

Origin Story: The Vetala is believed to have originated as a spirit caught in the twilight zone between life and death. Some accounts suggest that they were created from the residual energies of the dead or by the malevolent will of sorcerers seeking to control the dead. According to Hindu lore, the Vetala is a demonic force that haunts the margins of the afterlife, unable to fully transcend to either the realm of the living or the dead.

Symbolic Meaning: The Vetala represents the fear of death, the unknown, and the power of spirits that defy the natural order. It is a manifestation of the corruption of life and death, embodying both the decay of the body and the unrest of the spirit. In a cultural context, the Vetala also serves as a reminder of the frailty of life and the consequences of tampering with the spiritual realm.

Notable Legends and Tales: The Vetala is famously featured in the *Vetala Panchavimshati*, a collection of twenty-five stories that feature the Vetala as one of the central characters. In these tales, King Vikramaditya is tasked with capturing a Vetala, who resides in a tree, hanging by its feet from a rope. The Vetala offers the king stories, followed by difficult moral riddles, each of which must be answered correctly. The tales highlight the Vetala's trickster nature and its ability to outwit the king at every turn. After 24 riddles, Vikramaditya fails to answer the final question, at which point the Vetala reveals the true evil nature of the sorcerer who sent the king on his quest, ultimately aiding the king in defeating him.

Cultural Variations and Worship:

In the Konkan region of India, the Vetala is often referred to as **Betal**, and it has a more complex and sometimes protective role. Betal is worshipped as a guardian spirit, believed to have the ability to protect villages and families from evil. Shrines dedicated to Betal are often located in remote forests or by rivers, where the Vetala's influence is strongest. In these regions, it is common to perform rituals to honor Betal, seeking its favor and protection.

Notable Locations:

- **The Betal Temple in Amona, Goa**: This sacred space is dedicated to Betal, a form of Vetala, and is known for its connection to Bhairava. Devotees visit this temple to ask for blessings, protection, and to appease the Vetala spirit.
- **Charnel Grounds and Cemeteries**: The Vetala is typically associated with places of death and decay. In particular, areas where cremations take place are believed to be more likely to house the Vetala.

Interesting Facts and Beliefs:

- **Mantras and Exorcism:** The Vetala can be repelled or even banished through the chanting of specific mantras or by performing the correct funerary rites. These rituals are often used by those seeking to rid themselves of the Vetala's influence or to free a possessed body.
- **Sorcery and Captivity:** Many sorcerers and shamans believe that the Vetala can be captured and turned into a servant. Some texts describe the Vetala as being used by witches to help in occult practices, serving as a supernatural entity to aid in divination, prophecy, or to create powerful spells.
- **Symbol of Unresolved Death:** The Vetala's existence in the liminal space between life and death suggests that it is a spirit that never found closure, forever trapped in a twilight state. It is both a reminder of the importance of proper death rites and an embodiment of the terror associated with spirits that cannot move on.

King Vikramaditya and The Vetala

The Curse of the Vetala

"The Haunted Tree"

King Vikramaditya had long been known for his wisdom, but his greatest test came in the form of a challenge from a mysterious sorcerer. The sorcerer, jealous of the king's power and knowledge, sent him to capture a Vetala—a spirit known for its wits and cunning.

The Vetala resided in an ancient tree in the middle of a desolate cremation ground, hanging upside down from its roots. It was said that the Vetala could answer any question, but only if the questioner could solve the riddle it posed.

Vikramaditya, ever determined, set out to capture the Vetala. As he approached the tree, the eerie cries of the Vetala filled the air, an unholy wail that seemed to rattle the bones of the living. The spirit's eyes glowed with an otherworldly light, and it spoke to the king, offering him a riddle.

"Answer my riddle, O king, and you shall be free. Fail, and you will remain in my grasp forever," the Vetala's voice echoed.

With every riddle the Vetala posed, King Vikramaditya answered correctly, his wisdom shining through. But as they neared the twenty-fourth question, the king stumbled. The Vetala grinned, its twisted, decaying form filled with malicious delight.

"Do you not know the answer, great king?" the Vetala taunted, its voice like a thousand echoes in the night.

In his desperation, Vikramaditya gave the wrong answer. The Vetala howled in triumph, but then, something unexpected happened. Impressed by the king's resolve, the Vetala spoke once more, its voice softer this time.

"Your heart is true, King Vikramaditya. The sorcerer who sent you here is the true enemy. Beware, for his evil designs will undo you."

The Vetala then bestowed upon the king a gift—an amulet of power that would allow him to defeat the sorcerer. With the Vetala's help, Vikramaditya was able to turn the tables, defeating the sorcerer and returning peace to his kingdom.

But the Vetala's gift came with a price. Though the creature was no longer a threat, its presence lingered in the king's mind forever, a reminder of the fine line between life and death, and the dark power of the spirits trapped in the world beyond.

King Vikramaditya and The Vetala

280 | Vetala

38.

Barmanou: The Wild Man of the Chitral and Karakoram

Pakistani Folklore

Name: Barmanou
Type: Cryptid, Bipedal Humanoid Primate
Habitat: Chitral and Karakoram mountain ranges, Northern Pakistan
First Sightings: Documented reports since the late 20th century, folklore possibly extending much further back

---

Barmanou.

The **Barmanou** is a mysterious, bipedal humanoid primate cryptid that inhabits the rugged, mountainous regions of northern Pakistan, particularly in the Chitral and Karakoram ranges. It is often compared to the more famous cryptids, such as the Yeti of the Himalayas or the Almas of Central Asia. The term "Barmanou" is derived from the Khowar language, but it has spread to other regional languages, including Urdu, Shina, Pashto, and Kashmiri. While local names for the creature may vary, the Barmanou is recognized throughout the region as a wild man or an ape-like figure that roams the mountains.

Sightings of the Barmanou have been reported primarily by shepherds and local residents who dwell in the highlands and remote areas. These reports often describe a creature that is both human-like and apelike, resembling a large, upright primate, similar to the Western concept of Bigfoot. The creature's presence in the folklore of northern Pakistan has made it a subject of fascination and speculation, especially given its resemblance to other cryptids found across the world.

Physical Appearance:

The Barmanou is typically described as a large, bipedal primate, standing between 6 and 7 feet tall. Its body is covered in dark, shaggy hair, with most reports mentioning that the creature's face resembles that of an ape—broad and flat, with deep-set eyes and a wide, strong jaw. The Barmanou's posture is erect, though its movements are often described as being more ape-like, with long, muscular arms and an animalistic gait. Some accounts also claim that it wears animal skins draped over its back and head, adding to its wild and primal appearance.

Eyewitnesses report that the creature's overall physique appears robust and powerful, capable of moving swiftly through the rugged terrain of the mountainous regions. Its feet are said to be wide and bear large, human-like toes, which adds to the humanoid nature of the creature.

Abilities and Powers:

While the Barmanou does not exhibit any known supernatural abilities, its physical prowess and stealth in its environment are key traits that make it a formidable cryptid. The creature is believed to be highly agile and capable of navigating steep mountain slopes and dense forests with ease. Additionally, it is often reported to be nocturnal, with sightings of the Barmanou occurring primarily during the night or in the early morning hours.

One of the most disturbing aspects of the Barmanou's folklore is its alleged tendency to abduct women. Local legends claim that the creature kidnaps young women and attempts to mate with them. While the veracity of these reports is highly speculative, they contribute to the creature's eerie reputation.

Habitat and Behavior:

The Barmanou's habitat is the secluded and largely inaccessible mountainous regions between the Pamirs and the Himalayas, specifically within the Chitral and Karakoram ranges. These regions are known for their remoteness, with few human settlements and vast stretches of uncharted wilderness, making them ideal for a cryptid like the Barmanou to remain hidden from the world.

Behaviorally, the Barmanou is a solitary creature, rarely seen in groups. It is reported to be elusive and secretive, often shying away from human contact. Most sightings occur when shepherds, herders, or hikers accidentally stumble upon its territory. It is known to produce strange, guttural sounds that echo through the mountains, which is described as primitive and bestial, much like an animal's growl or howl.

While some reports suggest that the Barmanou can be aggressive if provoked, other accounts indicate that it is more likely to flee from humans than engage in direct confrontation. However, its massive size and apparent strength make it a formidable creature, and its ability to move silently through the wilderness only adds to the aura of fear surrounding it.

Mythological Context:

Origin Story: The Barmanou's roots can be traced back to the folklore of the northern regions of Pakistan, particularly in the mountainous areas near the Chitral valley. According to local legends, the Barmanou is a wild man, a creature of the mountains that has coexisted with human settlements for centuries, though it is rarely seen. The creature is considered to be both a protector and a harbinger of misfortune. In some traditions, it is seen as a guardian of the mountains, while in others, it is regarded with fear as an omen of death or disaster.

Symbolic Meaning: The Barmanou symbolizes the untamed wilderness and the dark forces that reside within it. Its connection to both the animal kingdom and human-like characteristics reflects the tension between civilization and nature. The creature's ability to exist in the liminal space between human and animal is an embodiment of the fear of the unknown and the mysterious regions where human influence has not yet reached.

Notable Legends and Tales: One of the key stories surrounding the Barmanou is the tale of its encounters with shepherds and villagers. In these stories, the Barmanou is described as a creature of great strength and intelligence, capable of evading human detection and surviving in the harshest environments. The creature's alleged habit of abducting women has also given rise to various cautionary tales, warning against venturing too far into the mountains alone.

Cultural Variations and Names:

While the name "Barmanou" is the most widely used in the region, the creature is known by different names in various parts of Pakistan:

- **Betal** (in the Konkan region)
- **Vetal** (in other parts of Pakistan and northern India)
- **Vetal** (a form that is sometimes linked with the Vetala in Indian folklore)
- **Shah Barmanou** (a local variant name used in some areas)

The Barmanou is often considered the Pakistani equivalent of Bigfoot, though it occupies a different cultural and ecological niche, reflecting the rich folklore and mythology of South Asia.

Notable Locations:

The Chitral Valley: A known hotspot for Barmanou sightings, this region is remote and rugged, making it ideal for such a cryptid to remain elusive.

The Karakoram Range: A vast, mountainous region stretching across northern Pakistan, where the Barmanou is said to roam.

Shishi Kuh Valley: A known site for cryptid activity, where researchers like Jordi Magraner reported hearing strange, guttural sounds that could only be produced by a creature with a primitive vocal apparatus.

Cryptid Research and Exploration:

The initial search for a bipedal humanoid in Pakistan was conducted by Jordi Magraner, a Spanish zoologist residing in France, between 1987 and 1990. He authored a paper titled "Les Hominidés reliques d'Asie Centrale," focusing on the Pakistani cryptid known as the wild man. In the 1990s, he further investigated the Barmanou.

Loren Coleman noted that Magraner "gathered over fifty firsthand accounts of sightings, with all witnesses identifying the reconstruction of Heuvelman's homo pongoides, referred to as the 'apelike man'–specifically, a living Neanderthal. They selected homo pongoides as their identification for the Barmanu from Magraner's collection of illustrations featuring apes, prehistoric humans, indigenous people, monkeys, and the Minnesota Iceman."

In 1994, during an expedition in the Shishi Kuh Valley, Magraner and his team reported hearing unusual guttural sounds that were described as emanating from a primitive, animal-like creature. Despite these sightings and sounds, no concrete evidence was found to conclusively prove the Barmanou's existence. Magraner, tragically, was murdered in Afghanistan in 2002.

Modern Sightings and Cultural Impact:

Despite the lack of physical evidence, the Barmanou remains a subject of fascination and speculation. Sightings continue to be reported by locals, and the creature's image has become a part of regional folklore, often invoked in stories of the supernatural. The Barmanou has also entered popular culture, inspiring cryptid hunters, filmmakers, and enthusiasts, who continue to search for evidence of the creature's existence.

The Barmanou remains one of the most enigmatic and elusive cryptids of South Asia, continuing to captivate those who seek to uncover the truth behind the legends of the wild man of the Chitral and Karakoram ranges. Whether the Barmanou is a forgotten relic of prehistory, a misunderstood wild animal, or a genuine cryptid, its place in the folklore of northern Pakistan ensures that it will remain a subject of intrigue and mystery for generations to come.

Barmanou: The Wild Man of the Chitral and Karakoram

39.

Devil Bird (Ulama): Sri Lanka's Screaming Omen

Sri Lankan Folklore

Name: Devil Bird / Ulama
Type: Mythical Creature, Supernatural Avian Entity
Habitat: Sri Lankan Jungles, Forests, and Remote Areas
First Sightings: Ancient Sri Lankan Folklore, reports dating back centuries

---

The Ulama.

The **Devil Bird** or **Ulama** is a mysterious and terrifying creature from Sri Lankan folklore, best known for its chilling, bloodcurdling shriek that echoes through the jungles at night. Its cry is said to resemble the sound of a soul in torment or a human being in extreme agony, often described as a "soul-screaming" wail that strikes fear into anyone who hears it. The creature's call is so unsettling that it is believed to be an omen of death, with villagers associating its appearance or cry with misfortune, chaos, and inevitable death.

While the identity of the Devil Bird is still a matter of debate, several candidates have been proposed based on its described sound and possible sightings. Some believe it to be the **forest eagle-owl** (*Bubo nipalensis*), others speculate it might be the **crested honey-buzzard** (*Pernis ptilorhynchus*), or perhaps various types of **eagles**. However, some folklorists and wildlife experts suggest that the true identity might be the **Ceylon highland nightjar** (*Caprimulgus indicus kelaarti*), known for emitting strange, eerie calls in the night. Despite these theories, no one has been able to conclusively identify the creature, and its true nature remains a mystery.

The **Ulama**, also referred to as **Yak Kurulla** (devil bird) in Sri Lankan folklore, has connections to other folklore figures from South Asia. In India, it is linked with tales of the **Churail** or **Chudail**, a vengeful ghost of a woman, further intensifying the fear surrounding the creature. Its haunting scream continues to haunt the cultural psyche of the region, with its call often being heard in areas rich with dense foliage and untamed wilderness.

Abilities and Powers:

Unsettling Cry: The Devil Bird's primary power lies in its bone-chilling, human-like scream, which is said to resemble a woman's anguished wail. This sound is often heard at night, deep in the forests, and is so terrifying that it can induce panic, unease, and even physical reactions such as hair-raising fear and frozen heartbeats. The shriek is believed to be a direct link to the supernatural, with many believing it signifies the presence of a cursed or malevolent force.

Omen of Death: The cry of the Ulama is widely considered an omen, particularly associated with impending death or catastrophe. It is thought that when the bird calls, disaster or misfortune will soon follow. This belief has permeated the folklore of both Sri Lanka and parts of India, where the bird is seen as a harbinger of doom. Those who hear the call often feel a deep, instinctual fear that something terrible is about to occur.

Invisibility: Despite the frequency of its calls, the Devil Bird is rarely seen. The elusive nature of the creature only adds to the sense of dread surrounding it. Some suggest that the Ulama has the ability to remain hidden in the dense jungle, calling out its haunting screeches without ever being directly witnessed.

Habitat and Behavior:

The **Ulama** is said to reside in the remote, untamed jungles and forests of Sri Lanka, with the majority of reported sightings occurring in areas like **Yala National Park**, where the creature's unsettling cry has been heard by several wildlife experts, including the renowned British hunter and writer, **Jim Corbett**. The forests of Sri Lanka, dense with towering trees and thick undergrowth, provide the perfect environment for such a mysterious creature to remain elusive.

The creature's cry is most commonly heard at night, adding to its terrifying reputation. The exact behavior of the Devil Bird is unclear, but it is assumed to be nocturnal, using its terrifying call as a form of communication, possibly for mating or territorial purposes. However, no confirmed sightings of the bird during the day or night make it difficult to understand its full range of behaviors.

In folklore, the Ulama is also said to embody the soul of a tragic and vengeful figure, particularly the **soul of a woman wronged by the betrayal of her husband**. This association ties the Devil Bird's cries to themes of loss, sorrow, and vengeance, amplifying its malevolent reputation.

Mythological Context:

Origin Story: The most popular tale in Sri Lankan folklore that explains the origin of the Devil Bird involves a horrific act of betrayal and the tragic consequences that followed. According to the story, a husband, filled with jealousy and suspicion, kills his own child, cooks the body, and serves it to his wife. When she discovers the truth, devastated by the horrific act, she flees into the jungle and curses everyone she encounters, never to return. It is believed that the Devil Bird's scream is a manifestation of the woman's anguished cry upon realizing the death of her son.

Symbolic Meaning: The Devil Bird represents vengeance, loss, and the unseen forces that linger in the wild, both in the literal and metaphorical sense. It symbolizes the power of grief and despair to transcend life and death, taking the form of a creature that haunts the living with its terrible cry. It is an embodiment of sorrowful spirits who have not found peace, forever tormenting those who hear its wail with a reminder of the atrocities and misfortunes that have occurred.

Notable Legends and Tales: The Devil Bird appears in various stories, not just as an omen of death but as a creature tied to the dark, twisted elements of human nature. In these tales, it is often the direct result of human wrongdoing, such as betrayal, murder, or neglect. In more recent lore, the creature is frequently described as a supernatural harbinger, marking the end of an era or the fall of a person or village.

The Ulama Devil Bird of Sri Lanka

Interesting Facts and Cultural Variations:

Cultural Associations with Other Folklore: The Ulama shares similarities with the **Banshee** of Irish folklore, a female spirit who screams as an omen of death. This connection has fueled speculation that the Devil Bird's origins might stem from ancient mythologies that traveled from Ireland to South Asia. Similarly, the Devil Bird is also linked to the **Churail** or **Chudail**, a ghostly female spirit in Indian folklore, whose wailing scream is said to foretell doom or death.

Auditory Mystery: The true identity of the Devil Bird remains a mystery. While there are several theories regarding which bird species might be responsible for the eerie cries, including the forest eagle-owl or the Ceylon highland nightjar, no confirmed visual identification has ever been made. The cry of the Ulama is considered unique, with experts like Jim Corbett stating that it cannot be compared to any other sound in the jungle, cementing the creature's supernatural status.

Rarity of Sightings: Despite numerous reports of hearing the Devil Bird's scream, actual sightings are rare. This adds to its aura of mystery, as no one has been able to photograph or film the bird during its vocalizations. The creature's elusive nature has led to continued fascination with the folklore surrounding it.

The Call of the Ulama

"The Screams of the Jungle"

It was late at night when Ravi, a young traveler from Colombo, found himself wandering deeper into the dense jungle of Yala National Park. He had heard the local legends of the **Devil Bird**, the **Ulama**, and the terrible shrieks that it made. He had scoffed at the stories, believing them to be nothing more than exaggerated tales told around campfires.

But as he moved through the darkened forest, an unease began to settle in his stomach. The jungle, so alive with the sounds of insects and distant animals during the day, was silent now. The air felt thick, oppressive, as if the very forest itself was holding its breath.

Suddenly, the silence was shattered. A bloodcurdling scream, like the cry of a soul in torment, ripped through the air. Ravi froze. The scream echoed through the jungle, causing the hairs on his neck to rise. It was unlike any animal sound he had ever heard—a terrifying, unearthly wail that made his heart race.

He tried to move, but his feet felt rooted to the ground, paralyzed by fear. Another scream followed, closer this time, filled with such agony and despair that it seemed to tear through the very fabric of the night.

The legends were true. The **Ulama** was real.

Ravi turned to run, but as the final scream echoed in his ears, a shadow loomed ahead, flickering between the trees. He felt the weight of something ancient and dark pressing against him, its presence consuming the air around him. It was too late to escape. There was one more scream that night, and it was not the scream of a Devil Bird.

The jungle fell silent again.

The Ulama Devil Bird and Ravi

40.

Asuras and Devas: A Cosmic Battle

Hindu and Buddhist Mythology

Asura (Hindu and Buddhist Mythology)

In **Hindu** and **Buddhist** mythology, **Asuras** are a class of powerful, often malevolent beings who frequently oppose the gods (Devas) in their quest for supremacy. The term **Asura** originally referred to gods or divine beings, but over time, especially in post-Vedic texts, it came to represent a category of demonic entities. Asuras are usually depicted as powerful and destructive beings who possess immense strength, magical abilities, and control over the elements. They are often associated with chaos, darkness, and the forces of evil, but they also embody qualities such as pride, ambition, and desire for power.

Asuras are commonly depicted as large, intimidating figures, often with multiple heads, arms, or eyes. Their appearance can be monstrous, with features that evoke fear, such as sharp fangs, claws, and terrifying expressions. In some depictions, Asuras may possess human-like forms but with exaggerated features—such as a towering, muscular body or an array of appendages—that showcase their immense power and supernatural nature.

Asuras possess significant supernatural abilities, including shape-shifting, the power to control natural forces (like storms and fire), and the ability to cast potent spells or curses. They are often shown to have immense strength, which they use to challenge the Devas and attempt to overthrow the cosmic order. Despite their evil nature, some Asuras are known for their intelligence and cunning, making them formidable opponents. However, their greed and ambition often lead to their downfall, as they seek power at the expense of righteousness.

In Hindu mythology, Asuras represent the forces of chaos and ego that constantly challenge the harmony of the universe. They are often seen as symbols of unrighteousness, materialism, and hubris. The eternal struggle between the Asuras and the Devas is depicted in many texts, including the **Mahabharata** and **Ramayana**, where their battles represent the clash between good and evil. In Buddhism, Asuras are seen as beings who are driven by their desires and attachments, preventing them from attaining enlightenment. They serve as a reminder of the dangers of unchecked ambition and the consequences of living in opposition to cosmic order.

The Asura

The Battle of the Asuras and the Devas

In the beginning, the **Asuras** and the **Devas** were once allies, united by the shared goal of protecting the cosmic order. But as time passed, their unity fractured. The Devas, driven by their

296 | Asura and Devas

devotion to **Brahman** and the pursuit of dharma, believed in harmony and balance, while the Asuras, filled with ambition and desire for power, sought to bend the universe to their will.

The Devas, who resided in the heavens, were beings of light, and they represented purity, truth, and righteousness. They were entrusted with the protection of the universe, ensuring that it thrived in harmony. The Asuras, on the other hand, inhabited the netherworld, ruled by pride, anger, and envy. They coveted the dominion of the heavens, believing that they too were worthy of the power and glory the Devas enjoyed.

For centuries, tensions simmered between the two factions, each growing stronger and more determined to seize the universe's ultimate power. The turning point came when **Indra**, king of the Devas, sought the **Amrita**, the nectar of immortality, hidden deep within the **Ocean of Milk**. The Devas knew that consuming the nectar would ensure their reign forever, solidifying their place in the universe. But the Asuras, hungry for power, had the same idea.

A battle was inevitable.

The moonlight shimmered on the calm waters of the ocean as the Devas and the Asuras gathered, each preparing for what would become the fiercest battle the world had ever seen. In the sky, **Brahma**, the creator, watched silently, his hand resting on his great lotus, as he knew that the time for action had come.

Indra stood at the head of the Devas, his mighty **Vajra** (thunderbolt) crackling with divine energy, ready to strike at his enemies. Beside him was **Vishnu**, his blue form calm and serene, as his eyes glimmered with wisdom. Together, they prepared for the battle that would decide the fate of the universe.

On the other side, the Asuras assembled under the leadership of **Ravana**, a towering figure of monstrous power. With a body as fierce as a lion's and eyes burning with rage, Ravana stood proud. His followers, including **Bali** and **Vritra**, stood beside him, their minds sharp and their hearts driven by envy. The Asuras had long waited for this day, and their ambition burned like an unquenchable fire.

The battle began with a deafening roar, as the Devas and Asuras clashed with all their might. Indra's thunderbolt struck the earth, causing the ground to tremble, while Ravana's sword sliced through the air with deadly precision. The heavens rang with the sound of clashing weapons, and the very elements seemed to falter as the forces of light and darkness collided.

For hours, the battle raged, neither side yielding. But the Devas, though mighty, were beginning to falter against the Asuras' sheer strength and cunning. The tide of the battle seemed to favor the forces of darkness as Ravana's monstrous strength and the Asuras' manipulation of powerful magic began to overwhelm the Devas.

In the midst of the chaos, Vishnu, knowing that victory was slipping from the Devas' grasp, turned to Brahma for guidance. With a calm, steady voice, Brahma spoke:

"Vishnu, the balance of the universe is at stake. It is not strength alone that will win this battle, but unity and wisdom. You must guide the Devas with your wisdom, for they cannot win through force alone."

Vishnu nodded solemnly. In a flash, he transformed into his mighty **Narasimha** avatar—half-man, half-lion—a form of terrifying power that embodied both divine strength and justice. With a roar that echoed through the heavens, Vishnu leaped into the fray.

The sight of Narasimha struck fear into the hearts of the Asuras. His claws, sharp as divine weapons, tore through their ranks with ferocious speed. Ravana, though a mighty warrior, could not match the relentless force of Vishnu's divine avatar. The Asuras, who once believed they would triumph, were now on the backfoot, overwhelmed by Vishnu's fury.

As the Devas rallied behind their newfound strength, led by Vishnu's incarnation, the Asuras were forced to retreat. Ravana, though powerful, was no match for the mighty Narasimha. The once-proud leader of the Asuras fell to his knees, his massive form crumbling under the weight of Vishnu's divine justice. With one final, mighty roar, Vishnu struck Ravana down.

In the aftermath of the battle, the Devas stood victorious, their power restored. Yet, their triumph came at a great cost. The heavens, once filled with peace, now lay scarred by the conflict. The Asuras, though defeated, had not been completely vanquished, and the seeds of future conflict were sown.

Indra, looking down at the battlefield, turned to Vishnu. "How long will we have peace?" he asked, his voice filled with both gratitude and uncertainty.

Vishnu smiled gently, his form returning to its peaceful state. "Peace comes with balance, Indra. The Asuras will always rise again, for the forces of darkness are eternal. But so too is the light. As long as there is unity, wisdom, and righteousness, the Devas will stand firm. And so shall we—until the next battle is fought."

Narasimha—half-man, half-lion—a form of terrifying power that embodied both divine strength and justice

41.

Rakshasa, Naga and Matsya

South Asian mythology

Rakshasa (Hindu and Buddhist Mythology)

In Hindu and Buddhist mythology, **Rakshasas** are malevolent, supernatural beings or demons that are known for their evil nature, fearsome appearance, and insatiable hunger for human flesh. They are often depicted as shape-shifters, capable of disguising themselves in various forms, which they use to deceive and terrorize their victims. Rakshasas are believed to inhabit remote forests, cremation grounds, and other dark, desolate places. They are typically associated with chaos, destruction, and the corruption of the natural order, and they often act as obstacles to divine heroes.

Rakshasas are often described as grotesque and terrifying in appearance. They can be shown as large, powerful beings with sharp teeth, claws, and horns. Some depictions present them with multiple arms or heads, further emphasizing their monstrous and intimidating nature. Their eyes are usually described as glowing or red, and their features are often distorted, making them appear otherworldly and terrifying. Despite their fearsome forms, Rakshasas are also known for their ability to change shape and appearance, allowing them to blend into human society or assume the guise of beautiful women or wise sages to deceive others.

Rakshasas are powerful shape-shifters, able to take any form they desire. They are also known for their ability to possess and control others, casting dark spells and curses to harm their enemies. In many legends, they are shown as capable of consuming vast amounts of food, particularly human flesh, and they often torment humans by kidnapping or eating them. Some Rakshasas are also gifted in dark magic, including necromancy and the ability to summon other demons. Their supernatural strength and cunning make them formidable foes, capable of wreaking havoc on those who oppose them.

In Hindu mythology, Rakshasas are often viewed as the embodiments of disorder, chaos, and moral corruption. They are seen as beings who reject the divine order and indulge in excessive desires and passions, which ultimately lead to their downfall. In the **Ramayana**, the most famous Rakshasa is **Ravana**, the king of Lanka, who kidnaps **Sita** and becomes a primary antagonist to the hero **Rama**. Rakshasas serve as powerful reminders of the dangers of unrighteousness and the importance of adhering to dharma (cosmic law) in the battle between good and evil.

Naga (Hindu, Buddhist, and Jain Mythology)

The **Naga** is a divine or semi-divine serpent-like being that appears across several South Asian mythologies, including Hinduism, Buddhism, and Jainism. In Hinduism, Nagas are considered guardians of treasures, water sources, and wealth, often associated with rivers, lakes, and the ocean. They are typically depicted as human-serpent hybrids, with the upper body of a human and the lower body of a serpent. In Buddhist and Jain traditions, Nagas hold a similar role, often as protectors of sacred sites or deities.

Nagas are often shown with the upper torso of a human, usually a royal or majestic figure, and the lower body of a serpent, complete with multiple coils. They are often adorned with jewelry, crowns, and other symbols of their divine status. Some versions of Naga mythology depict them with a multitude of heads, representing their vast power and spiritual significance. In certain depictions, the Naga is shown with an elegant and graceful appearance, while others emphasize their more fearsome, dragon-like traits.

As powerful serpentine beings, Nagas possess various supernatural abilities. They can control water, summon rain, and guard precious treasures, particularly those related to wealth and spiritual knowledge. In many myths, they are also capable of shape-shifting into human forms or other animals. They are protectors of sacred knowledge and sometimes act as guardians of certain deities or spiritual truths. Nagas are also known for their ability to heal and bring prosperity, symbolizing fertility and the natural cycles of life.

In Hindu and Buddhist mythology, Nagas represent the duality of creation and destruction. While they are protectors of the natural world and symbols of wealth and abundance, they can also be vengeful and destructive if angered. The **Mahabharata** and **Ramayana** feature Nagas as both allies and adversaries, highlighting their complex nature. Nagas are also important figures in Jainism, where they are often associated with the protection of sacred spaces and the embodiment of spiritual purity.

Matsya (Hindu Mythology)

Matsya is one of the **Dashavatara**, the ten principal incarnations of the Hindu god **Vishnu**, and it takes the form of a giant fish. Matsya is often depicted as a massive fish, sometimes shown with a human head or in combination with human features. This incarnation of Vishnu is primarily associated with saving the ancient scriptures (the **Vedas**) and rescuing the sage **Manu** from a great flood.

Matsya's appearance is that of a giant fish, often shown with a human face or torso. The fish itself is depicted as enormous, capable of carrying sacred texts and a boat that contains the sage Manu and the seven sages (Saptarishi) to safety during the deluge. The fish is often shown with vibrant, divine colors, symbolizing its heavenly nature and its role in the preservation of the universe.

Matsya's primary ability is its immense size and strength, which allows it to rescue the Vedas and protect life during the flood. Matsya is also credited with being a guide, leading Manu's boat through the waters of the great deluge. In this sense, Matsya is both a protector and a savior, ensuring the survival of humanity and divine knowledge during times of catastrophe.

Matsya represents the divine intervention of Vishnu in times of great peril. As the protector of life and knowledge, Matsya's story reflects themes of survival, divine protection, and the preservation of sacred knowledge. This myth is often interpreted as a metaphor for renewal and the cyclical nature of creation, where destruction makes way for new beginnings.

These mythical beings—Rakshasa, Naga, and Matsya—each play vital roles in South Asian mythology, embodying themes of creation, destruction, protection, and transformation. Through their stories, they serve as powerful symbols that reflect the moral and spiritual values of the cultures they represent, teaching lessons about the balance between light and dark, good and evil, and the eternal struggle for cosmic order.

42.

Vishnu, Shiva, and Maya

South Asian Mythology

Vishnu (Hindu Mythology)

Description:

Vishnu is one of the principal deities of Hinduism, known as the **preserver** of the universe. He is part of the holy trinity (Trimurti) in Hindu belief, alongside **Brahma** (the creator) and **Shiva** (the destroyer). Vishnu's primary role is to maintain the cosmic order (dharma) and ensure the preservation of life and the universe. His worship spans across numerous sects of Hinduism, with his devotees seeing him as the supreme god, a compassionate and benevolent deity who guides humanity through cycles of creation and destruction.

Vishnu is typically depicted as a majestic figure with four arms, each holding significant items: a **conch** (symbolizing the cosmic sound of creation), a **discus** (Chakra, symbolizing the wheel of time and law), a **mace** (Gada, representing power and protection), and a **lotus flower** (representing purity and spiritual liberation). He is usually shown with a blue complexion, which signifies his association with the infinite sky or the cosmic ocean. Vishnu is often portrayed with a serene and regal appearance, sitting or standing on a lotus, exuding divine tranquility.

Vishnu possesses immense power, including the ability to maintain balance in the universe by both preserving and renewing it. His divine ability to incarnate in various forms, known as **avatars**, is central to his role. Through these incarnations, Vishnu descends to the earthly plane whenever dharma (righteousness) is under threat. His avatars include the **Matsya** (fish), **Kurma** (tortoise), **Varaha** (boar), **Narasimha** (man-lion), and the most famous **Rama** and **Krishna**, who are central to the epics **Ramayana** and **Mahabharata**.

Vishnu is seen as the protector of the cosmos, who intervenes to restore order when it is threatened by chaos or evil. His compassion and commitment to righteousness make him a beloved figure in Hinduism. He is revered not only for his acts of preservation but also for his role in the spiritual development of humanity, teaching devotees how to live according to dharma.

Shiva (Hindu Mythology)

Shiva, known as the **destroyer** or **transformer** within the Hindu trinity, plays a vital role in the cosmic cycle of creation, preservation, and destruction. Unlike Vishnu, whose role is to preserve the universe, Shiva's function is to destroy or dissolve the universe at the end of each cycle to allow for regeneration. Though his role may seem grim, destruction in the Hindu worldview is seen as necessary for the clearing of old energies, creating the space for new life and spiritual progress.

Shiva is often depicted with a third eye, a crescent moon on his head, and matted hair. He holds a **trident** (Trishula), which symbolizes the three aspects of existence—creation, preservation, and destruction. His skin is usually depicted as ash-colored, reflecting his connection with both life and death. Shiva's body is often adorned with serpents, which signify his control over death and transformation. His posture is often meditative, showing him as the embodiment of **yoga** and inner peace.

Shiva's abilities extend far beyond his destructive nature. As the god of transformation, he can dissolve the universe and remold it again, making him a symbol of both death and rebirth. He is also the patron god of **yoga**, **meditation**, and **asceticism**, and is believed to be the supreme master of spiritual discipline. Shiva's powers also extend into the realm of the supernatural, where he commands the elements, can summon storms, and is associated with the wild, untamed forces of nature.

Shiva's paradoxical nature, as both the destroyer and creator, is central to his worship. He is revered for his power to purify the world through destruction, his control over chaos, and his role as a teacher and protector of spiritual seekers. Devotees see Shiva as a god who transcends worldly concerns and provides liberation from the cycle of birth and death.

Maya (Hindu Mythology)

Maya in Hindu mythology refers to the illusion or power that creates the physical world. Maya is not a god in the traditional sense but a concept that personifies the illusion of the material world and the veil that prevents individuals from seeing the ultimate truth. Maya is often associated with the goddess **Durga**, as she represents the illusory power that binds beings to the material world, preventing them from recognizing their divine essence.

In a broader context, Maya is seen as the force that causes the world to appear as real, even though it is ultimately an illusion. It is through Maya that individuals experience suffering and attachment, but it is also through recognizing the illusory nature of the world that one can attain enlightenment.

Maya is often depicted as a beautiful and powerful goddess, adorned in fine garments and jewelry, symbolizing the allure and entrapment of the material world. Her form is often radiant, captivating, and mesmerizing, reflecting her ability to enchant and deceive.

Maya's primary ability is to create the illusion of the physical world. This illusion binds individuals to the cycle of life, death, and rebirth (samsara), causing them to identify with their ego and material possessions. However, Maya also holds the power to lift this illusion, helping individuals realize the ultimate truth of **Brahman**, the unchanging reality beneath the surface of the world.

Maya represents the transient, ever-changing nature of the physical world. She is both a force of illusion and an essential concept in Hindu philosophy, teaching that everything we perceive with our senses is ultimately an illusion, and that true knowledge comes from transcending the material world to realize the oneness of the divine.

"The Dance of Shiva"

In the distant mountain cave, the air was thick with the scent of incense and the hum of distant drums. **Shiva**, the lord of destruction, sat in his usual meditative pose, his body still and tranquil,

312 | Vishnu, Shiva, and Maya

yet his mind raced with thoughts of the world. The cosmos, teetering on the edge of another cycle, awaited his divine intervention. It was the time for **Pralaya**, the cosmic dissolution.

As the drums grew louder, Shiva's third eye opened, casting a fierce, fiery gaze across the world. His dance, the **Tandava**, would soon begin—the dance of creation and destruction. His massive form, adorned with snakes and ash, rose from his seat and began to move. With every step, the mountains trembled. With every turn, the sky cracked open, and lightning danced across the heavens.

The **Devas** and **Asuras** watched, knowing that this destruction was not one of cruelty but of rebirth. It was necessary for the old to be destroyed so that new life could emerge. The world, in its current form, was exhausted—its energy spent—and it was time for renewal.

Shiva's movements grew more wild, and his celestial trident sliced through the air, bringing the destruction of the old age. The **Nagas**, the serpents of the deep, slithered from the earth, feeling the ground shake beneath them. **Vishnu**, the preserver, and **Brahma**, the creator, stood in silence, understanding that their roles in the divine cycle were coming to an end, only to begin again in the next great age.

As Shiva spun, his body covered in the ashes of the previous age, the world was consumed in flames. Mountains crumbled, rivers dried, and the oceans swirled. Yet, beneath this wild destruction, there was peace. Shiva's dance was not one of chaos for chaos's sake—it was a dance of transformation. The old was fading, but the new was being born.

Finally, after what seemed like an eternity, Shiva halted. His eyes, burning with the fire of the cosmos, looked upon the remnants of the world. The destruction was complete, but the seeds of a new world were already sprouting in the ashes. With a final, graceful step, Shiva returned to his meditative pose, his dance done.

In the stillness that followed, **Maya** descended, veiling the world in her illusions once again. The Earth, now reborn, would once more fall under her spell, and beings would once again be caught in the cycle of life and death. But in the hearts of those who understood Shiva's dance, the truth remained clear—the dance of life and death was endless, but each cycle brought them closer to the realization of the ultimate truth: the eternal, unchanging **Brahman**.

Vishnu, **Shiva**, and **Maya**—three fundamental aspects of Hindu philosophy—represent the ongoing dance of the cosmos: creation, preservation, and destruction. Each story and myth surrounding these figures is a reflection of the eternal cycles of life, and a reminder that in the destruction of one world, another is born.

PART VIII
SHADOWS OF AFRICA

Africa, a land rich in cultural diversity, is home to some of the most fascinating and terrifying creatures in the world of mythology. From the jungles of West Africa to the vast rivers of Southern Africa, the myths and legends of this vast continent are filled with creatures that embody the raw power of nature, the depths of the human imagination, and the forces of the spiritual world. The stories surrounding these creatures often reflect the complex relationship between humans and the natural world, with these beings serving as protectors, avengers, or even embodiments of chaos and fear.

African Creatures: Mythical Beasts and Folkloric Guardians

The **Dingonek**, an elusive and feared creature from East Africa, strikes terror into the hearts of those who hear its tale. First encountered near Lake Victoria, it is described as a hybrid between a **sea serpent**, a **leopard**, and a **whale**, a creature that haunts the waters and is capable of monstrous feats. **Sasabonsam**, from the folklore of West Africa, is a vampiric being that stalks the forests, with iron teeth, bat-like wings, and the ability to dangle its legs from trees to ensnare its victims. The **Tibicena**, known in the Canary Islands as the offspring of the dark gods, takes the form of a wild dog with glowing red eyes and long black fur, terrorizing villages and hunting the unwary in the night.

In the deep forests of the West, the **Sasabonsam** and **Obia**, both monstrous beings, serve as symbols of both the power and danger of witchcraft. The **Obia**, an enormous beast that kidnaps young girls to wear their skin, serves as an allegory for the fear of witchcraft and dark magic among African communities, with a long history in the African Diaspora. And from the southern regions, the **Nyami Nyami**, the river god of the Zambezi River, evokes reverence and fear, his power over the river both a blessing and a curse for the people living near it.

These creatures, steeped in the rich traditions of African mythologies, are not merely beings of fear; they are metaphors for the struggles and complexities of life. They embody the unpredictability of nature, the weight of ancestral beliefs, and the delicate balance between human existence and the supernatural world. Whether guardians of the underworld, enforcers of justice, or mere harbingers of doom, the creatures of African folklore continue to capture the imagination, shaping the culture, rituals, and beliefs of millions across the continent.

This section dives into the legendary creatures of Africa, exploring their origins, physical descriptions, abilities, and the roles they play in the cultural landscapes of their respective regions. From the **serpent spirits** of Southern Africa to the **vampiric demons** of West Africa, these creatures reveal the depths of Africa's mythological richness and the powerful symbolism embedded within these stories.

Shadows of Africa

43.

Dingonek, East African Cryptid

East African Cryptid

The **Dingonek** is a mysterious and elusive creature reported to inhabit the waters around **Lake Victoria** in East Africa, particularly near the **Maggori River**. First brought to widespread attention by big-game hunter **John Alfred Jordan** in 1907, the creature has since been the subject of various eyewitness accounts and articles that attempt to explain its nature. The Dingonek is described as a terrifying hybrid, combining aspects of a serpent, a leopard, and a whale, and it is noted for its formidable size and strength.

The Dingonek

Eyewitnesses describe the Dingonek as being around 14 to 16 feet (4.3 to 5 meters) long, with a **lioness-like head** marked by the appearance of a **leopard**. Its back is broad and shaped like a **hippopotamus**, and it is covered with **scales** resembling those of an **armadillo**. The most striking features of the Dingonek are its two **long white fangs**, which protrude like tusks from the upper jaw, and its **broad fin-tail**, which it uses to navigate the swift currents of the Maggori River.

The creature is often described as a "reptilian bounder," a term that suggests its movements on land or water are slow and deliberate, but still powerful enough to overwhelm those who come into contact with it. It is believed to move primarily in the water, where it can remain submerged for long periods, but is also known to venture ashore to leave distinctive clawed tracks resembling those of a reptile.

Despite several sightings and testimonies from trusted sources, the Dingonek remains an enigma. The descriptions of the beast are consistent, but no concrete evidence has ever been found. Many scholars have speculated that the creature may be a relic of a prehistoric species, possibly a descendant of ancient **saurians** that survived undisturbed in the region's remote waters.

Physical Appearance:

- Length: 14 to 16 feet (4.3 to 5 meters)
- Head: Resembling a lioness, but with markings akin to a leopard
- Body: Broad like a hippopotamus, scaled like an armadillo
- Tail: Large, finned, used for navigating through the water
- Fangs: Long, protruding white fangs capable of piercing through a man's body
- Claws: Large, reptilian claws that can leave imprints similar to those of a hippopotamus, but with a sharper, more dangerous edge.

The Dingonek is also believed to be capable of withstanding human weapons, as accounts from hunters like Jordan reveal that a .303 rifle shot fired at the creature did little to stop it. This has only added to the mythos surrounding the creature, with some theorizing that it may be a rare and unclassified reptile or amphibian, possibly immune to common forms of attack.

Cultural Significance:

The Dingonek has held an aura of mystery and fear in East African folklore, particularly around Lake Victoria. In the local communities, the creature is often linked with both awe and terror. The natives of the region, particularly those around the **Maggori River**, have long spoken of the **"Luquata,"** a similar giant water reptile, which was said to bring blessings of fertility and good harvests, but also to carry an ominous presence, signaling disaster or misfortune. The creature's appearance is considered a harbinger of bad luck or natural disaster by the local people, further embedding it within the cultural fabric of the region.

Over the years, the Dingonek has become a part of the region's cryptozoological lore, fueling theories about the survival of prehistoric creatures and the possibility that unknown species continue to exist in the unexplored corners of the Earth.

Notable Legends and Tales:

The most prominent tale of the Dingonek comes from **Edgar Beecher Bronson's memoir**, *In Closed Territory* (1910), where he recounts the experiences of big-game hunter **John Alfred Jordan** and his encounter with the beast in 1907. The creature was described as a monstrous hybrid, combining characteristics of land and aquatic animals, and Jordan's account was accompanied by vivid descriptions of the beast's size and appearance.

In 1913, **Charles William Hobley** published an article in the *East Africa Natural History Society* in which he discussed further sightings of similar creatures, reinforcing Jordan's original description. Hobley speculated that the creature might be an undiscovered species of large reptile or a surviving member of a prehistoric group of creatures, perhaps something akin to a giant, aquatic dinosaur.

The Dingonek's sightings have led to further research and intrigue among cryptozoologists, with many dismissing it as an exaggerated myth while others believe there may be a kernel of truth in the numerous, consistent eyewitness accounts.

"The Dingonek's Wake"

The Maggori River was swollen with the rains of the season, its waters rushing relentlessly through the jungle, carrying with it the remnants of the storms that had plagued the region. John Alfred Jordan sat at his campsite, surrounded by his trusted hunting party. The night was thick with the sounds of the wilderness, but there was an uneasy silence in the air, a tension that was palpable even in the midst of nature's symphony.

Mataia, his native guide, approached him with an urgent look in his eyes. "Master Jordan," he whispered, "the Lumbwa have seen it. The beast—the Dingonek."

Jordan stiffened. The name was one that had been spoken in hushed tones around campfires, in the villages by the riverbanks, but he had always dismissed it as superstition. The Lumbwa were known for their tall tales, their fear of the unknown, but Jordan's instincts told him that something was different this time. He had heard the rumors for years, but now, faced with the possibility of the creature being real, his curiosity burned hotter than ever.

"Show me," Jordan commanded.

Mataia led him and his small party toward the river. The sun had dipped below the horizon, leaving only the muted glow of twilight, and the jungle around them seemed to hold its breath. The only sound was the steady rushing of the river, and then, in the distance, something shifted in the water.

The creature appeared like a ghost in the mist, its massive body floating lazily in the current. Jordan's heart skipped a beat as he beheld it: a creature of impossible proportions, its back broad like a hippo, yet its scales glinted in the fading light like armor. The long, white fangs protruded from its mouth, and its head resembled that of a great leopard, but larger, more terrifying.

For a moment, everything stood still. The creature seemed to be unaware of their presence, its slow movements barely disturbing the water. But Jordan's eyes never left it, mesmerized by its sheer size and power.

Suddenly, the beast stirred. With a violent movement, it turned toward the riverbank, its eyes locking onto Jordan's party. The world seemed to slow as Jordan's breath caught in his throat. His instincts screamed at him to run, but his legs were frozen in place.

Without warning, the beast surged forward, its broad fin-tail swishing through the water as it propelled itself toward the shore. Jordan's rifle was in his hands before he even realized it, his finger pressing against the trigger. The bullet rang out, but the creature didn't flinch.

Panic set in. The creature was not slowed. It was unstoppable, a force of nature that defied the very laws of the world.

"Mataia, Mosoni, run!" Jordan shouted, grabbing the closest member of his party and pulling him toward the jungle. The rest of the men followed, but Jordan couldn't stop himself from looking back. The Dingonek was moving toward them, its eyes wild, its massive claws digging into the riverbank as it began to climb out of the water.

They ran deeper into the jungle, the sounds of the creature's pursuit fading as the dense foliage swallowed them whole. The darkness of the night seemed to grow deeper, as if the very jungle was alive and closing in around them.

Eventually, they stopped, panting and terrified, and Jordan leaned against a tree, his hands trembling. "We've seen it. There's no mistake. The Dingonek is real."

His heart still pounded in his chest, and he knew that the creature—whatever it was—was still out there, somewhere in the jungle, waiting. And in the silence of that night, with the jungle pressing in around them, Jordan felt an eerie certainty that they had only scratched the surface of the mystery of the Dingonek.

The beast had shown itself, but Jordan couldn't shake the feeling that the true nature of the creature—its origin, its purpose—was far greater and more dangerous than anyone could comprehend. The Dingonek, it seemed, had just begun to reveal its secrets.

the Dingonek of East Africa

44.

Tibicena, North African Demon

North African Cryptid

The **Tibicena**, also known as **Guacanchas** in the Canary Islands' pre-Hispanic mythology, is a legendary creature that inhabits the caves and mountains of these volcanic islands. These monstrous beings are believed to be demons or genies, born from the dark god **Guayota**, who is often equated with evil or malignant forces. Tibicenas are described as enormous wild dogs, their bodies covered with long, thick, black fur and their eyes glowing a vivid red. Their menacing appearance and ferocious nature make them one of the most fearsome creatures in Guanche lore.

Tibicena (Guacanchas) – Mythology of the Canary Islands

The Tibicena's most feared trait is its ability to attack at night, preying on livestock and even humans. Their actions were said to be guided by the malignant will of **Guayota**, who sought to bring terror and death to the world. These creatures were often associated with evil omens, and their presence was considered a bad sign, portending misfortune or disaster for those who encountered them. The Tibicena was a symbol of the raw, untamed forces of nature, feared by the ancient inhabitants of the Canary Islands for their nocturnal raids and their connection to the darker aspects of the world.

The Tibicena is described as a **large wild dog** with a formidable presence. Its body is covered in long, dark fur that appears almost black in the shadows of the night. Its most striking feature is its **glowing red eyes**, which are said to pierce the darkness and instill terror in anyone who looks into them. The creature's fangs are sharp and large, capable of tearing through flesh with ease, while its massive size makes it an imposing figure. Tibicenas were often said to have an almost supernatural agility, moving silently through the dark caves and mountains they called home.

In some versions of the myth, they are depicted as having the ability to shape-shift, sometimes appearing as smaller, more inconspicuous animals before transforming into their full, monstrous form to strike fear into their victims. Their powerful bodies and predatory nature make them one of the most dangerous creatures in Guanche mythology.

Habitat and Behavior:

Tibicenas are believed to live in **deep caves**, often hidden in the mountains of the Canary Islands. These caves, sometimes referred to as "**Cueva del Tibicena**" (Cave of the Tibicena), are considered sacred or cursed places by the locals, where these creatures are said to reside. The Tibicenas were particularly active at night, when they would come out of their lairs to hunt and terrorize the islanders. It is said that they were capable of tracking down and attacking livestock or people, often with little warning, making them a constant source of fear for the ancient inhabitants.

Though they were primarily nocturnal hunters, there are accounts of Tibicenas being able to move swiftly during the day as well, although they were much less common in daylight hours. They were often seen as **messengers of death or misfortune**, and many believed that if you ventured too close to their caves or mountains, you would be marked for a horrible fate.

Mythological Context:

The Tibicena is deeply tied to the **Guayota** mythos, as it is said to be one of his offspring. **Guayota**, a dark and malevolent god in the Guanche pantheon, was believed to dwell inside the heart of the volcano **Teide** on Tenerife, where he was said to have trapped the sun. The Tibicena, in this myth, were the demon's agents—creatures created to carry out his will and spread fear, suffering, and death. The Tibicena, therefore, embodied the destructive and chaotic power that Guayota wished to unleash upon the world.

The legends of these creatures served as a cautionary tale for the inhabitants of the Canary Islands, reinforcing the importance of respecting the natural world and the unseen, supernatural forces that governed it. The Tibicena's connection to **death and darkness** made them symbolic of the evil that could lurk in the unknown, while their terrifying presence acted as a reminder of the consequences of angering the forces of nature.

Cultural Significance:

In the islands' traditional beliefs, the Tibicena was both feared and respected. Their ability to prey on livestock or humans and their connection to Guayota imbued them with an air of mystery and terror. They were often considered omens of death, with their appearance marking a forthcoming disaster or tragedy. Some believed that the Tibicena's attacks on livestock were a way to appease Guayota, a practice linked to the darker rituals that were said to occur in the caves and mountains where the creatures were believed to reside.

Over time, as the Guanches' culture and beliefs gave way to Spanish influence, the Tibicena faded from common belief but remained a staple of island folklore, continuing to be passed down through stories and legends. In modern times, these myths have influenced literature, films, and other forms of popular culture, cementing the Tibicena's place as a fearsome and enigmatic figure in the mythology of the Canary Islands.

The Tibicena of the Canary Islands

"The Curse of the Tibicena"

On the northern shores of Tenerife, nestled beneath the shadow of the towering **Teide**, a young shepherd named **Carlos** made his living tending to his flock. The rugged land was wild and untamed, and Carlos was familiar with the dangers of the mountains, where the air was thick with mystery and ancient whispers.

But the greatest fear of the locals wasn't the mountain itself–it was the **Tibicena**, the terrifying creature said to haunt the caves in the distant hills. Carlos had grown up with stories of the wild dogs with glowing red eyes, of the monstrous fangs that could tear through the strongest of creatures. His mother had often warned him, "Never go near the caves after dark. The Tibicenas are always waiting."

One evening, as Carlos returned home from the hills, he noticed something unusual–a disturbance in the air. The once calm evening had turned cold and eerie, and the sounds of the mountain's night creatures seemed to have vanished. He glanced around, unease rising in his chest. It was then that he saw it: a shadow darting across the edge of the forest, too swift to be any common animal.

His heart raced as he followed the figure with his eyes. There, in the distance, at the mouth of the cave–the Tibicena stood. It was larger than anything he had ever imagined, its body a mass of dark fur, with eyes glowing like the red embers of a dying fire. It was a beast of nightmares, its fangs gleaming in the dim light of the setting sun.

Carlos froze, his instincts screaming at him to run. But he had no time–he could already hear the creature's slow, steady steps, each one growing louder. The Tibicena was coming closer.

He glanced back at his flock, grazing peacefully nearby. He couldn't leave them to the beast. He had to protect them, and himself.

Suddenly, a plan formed in Carlos's mind. He dashed to a nearby rock formation, quickly gathering stones and piling them together. His breath came in quick gasps as he worked, the urgency of the moment pressing against him. When he was ready, he hurled a stone into the air, hoping to distract the Tibicena long enough to escape.

The beast's head whipped around, its eyes locking on him. The growl that rumbled from its throat sent a chill through his bones, but Carlos didn't hesitate. He grabbed his staff and ran toward the herd, hoping he could lead them to safety before the Tibicena could catch up.

The chase was brutal. The Tibicena pursued him relentlessly, its growls echoing through the mountains as it closed the gap. Carlos could feel its breath on his neck, the sound of its claws scraping the rocky ground growing nearer.

But just as the creature lunged, Carlos spotted an opening–a narrow path between two cliffs that he knew would lead to a hidden cave where the Tibicena couldn't follow. With one final burst of speed, he sprinted toward the path, the creature just a heartbeat behind him.

Carlos dove into the cave, his body slamming against the cold rock. The Tibicena stopped at the entrance, its fiery red eyes peering in, but it could not fit through the narrow opening. It howled in frustration before turning away, its massive body retreating back into the darkness.

As Carlos sat in the quiet cave, the adrenaline slowly fading from his body, he realized that he had narrowly escaped the wrath of the Tibicena. But the terror of the encounter stayed with him, a lingering reminder that the creature was never truly gone.

And as the sun rose the next morning, Carlos made a vow never to forget the stories his mother had told him—about the Tibicena, the demons of the mountain, who would always be watching, waiting for the right moment to strike.

For now, though, Carlos was safe. But the mountain held many secrets, and the Tibicena was never far behind.

The Tibicena chases Carlos

45.

Sasabonsam, Vampire of the Akan

West African folklore

The **Sasabonsam**, or **Asanbosam**, is a vampire-like creature deeply rooted in the folklore of the Akan people of **West Africa**, particularly from the regions of **southern Ghana, Côte d'Ivoire, Togo**, and among the Akan-descended enslaved peoples of **18th-century Jamaica**. The Sasabonsam is typically described as a terrifying and predatory creature, part **ogre** and part **vampire**, that lives in the high trees of dense forests. It is said to have a humanoid form with bat-like features and is known for its deadly territorial nature, feeding on humans who stray too close to its domain.

Sasabonsam (Asanbosam) – West African Mythology

The Sasabonsam's most distinctive physical traits are **iron teeth, pink skin, long red hair**, and **iron hooks for feet**. These hooks enable the creature to securely perch in trees, where it often hides, ready to pounce on any unsuspecting prey below. It is often depicted as having **bat-like wings**, which can span up to **20 feet**, giving it the ability to swoop down quickly on its victims. It is said to be extremely territorial, and its home is usually in the upper branches of large trees, where it can ambush intruders and protect its domain with unrelenting aggression.

Physical Appearance:

- **Size:** Often described as humanoid in shape but with **bat-like wings** spanning up to **20 feet**.
- **Coloration: Pink skin**, contrasting with its vibrant, **red hair**, which is wild and untamed.
- **Teeth and Feet:** The creature's most notorious feature is its **iron teeth**, which it uses to tear into its victims. Its **feet are iron hooks**, perfect for anchoring itself to tree branches.
- **Legs:** Long and **unusually twisted**, with feet that point both forward and backward, which enhances its ability to entangle prey.
- **Eyes: Large, bloodshot eyes** that gleam with malice, signaling its predatory nature.
- **Wings:** Bat-like wings that can span up to **20 feet**, giving it the ability to fly and swoop down quickly from the trees.

Habitat and Behavior:

The Sasabonsam resides primarily in **dense forests** of **West Africa**, where it claims a vast territory in the high treetops. These forests are its domain, and it fiercely defends it from human intrusion. According to legend, it **feeds on the blood** of those who wander too close to its lair. It is especially dangerous for hunters and travelers who are unaware of the dangers lurking in the trees.

While the Sasabonsam is most active at night, it is believed to remain hidden in the daytime, resting in its lair. Its nocturnal nature aligns it with other mythological vampire creatures, but its ability to fly and the use of its hooks make it unique among similar beasts.

Cultural Significance:

In the folklore of the Akan people, the Sasabonsam represents both the dangers and the balance of nature. Its predation on humans reflects the precariousness of life in the forest, where survival depends on knowing the natural laws and respecting them. The Sasabonsam, in this regard, enforces these laws, punishing those who break the unwritten rules of the land.

The creature's association with **iron**, **hooks**, and **teeth** places it within a larger cultural context of magical protection, where iron is often seen as a material that can ward off evil. In some stories, people who are wise enough to recognize the signs of the Sasabonsam's presence can avoid falling victim to its traps. However, those who are caught are often never seen again, leaving behind only strange, twisted **footprints** or **claw marks** on the earth.

The Sasabonsam is often depicted in **art**, particularly in carvings and figurines that represent the creature's fearsome qualities. These representations, like the famous **Sasabonsam figure** at The British Museum, highlight the creature's status as both a terrifying monster and a symbolic enforcer of the natural order.

"The Lair of the Sasabonsam"

Beneath the thick canopy of trees, the air was heavy with the scent of earth and decay. The jungle was alive, a chorus of insects, the rustling of leaves, and the occasional distant growl of a predator. Yet, in the midst of all the sounds, there was a silence that felt unnatural.

Kofi, a seasoned hunter from the village, was no stranger to the forest. He had navigated its dangers for years, but this journey felt different. There was a weight to the air, as though the very trees themselves were holding their breath.

As he ventured deeper into the forest, Kofi's mind lingered on the tales his grandmother had told him—tales of the **Sasabonsam**, the terrifying creature that lived in the highest branches of the trees, a monster of iron teeth and bloodshot eyes. The elders warned him never to enter the forest without respect for the unseen forces that governed it. But Kofi had always dismissed the stories as superstition, the product of a generation too afraid to face the wilds.

Until today.

He moved cautiously, aware of every sound, every movement in the jungle. His spear was in hand, but it felt heavy, as though the weight of centuries of myth pressed upon it. He had heard stories from fellow hunters—of friends who had vanished into the forest, never to return. They had spoken of a creature, a dark figure that hung from the trees, watching, waiting.

As he neared the riverbank, Kofi saw it—the unmistakable marks in the earth. Claw-like impressions, wider than a man's hand, deep and unnatural, stretching toward the water. His breath caught in his throat. **The Sasabonsam.**

Before he could react, a low growl rumbled from above. He looked up, his heart hammering in his chest.

There, high above him, perched upon the branches of an ancient baobab tree, was the creature. Its eyes gleamed like twin embers in the darkening twilight, glowing a bloodshot red. Its long, twisted legs dangled down, the iron hooks scraping the bark of the tree with a horrible sound.

Kofi froze. The Sasabonsam had seen him.

Suddenly, with the speed of a lightning strike, the creature's massive wings unfurled, spanning a terrifying twenty feet. It swooped down, its claws extended, aiming for Kofi. He barely had time to react as the creature's hooks scraped past his face, missing him by inches.

The sound of the Sasabonsam's wings was deafening, and Kofi's instincts kicked in. He grabbed his spear and hurled it into the air, aiming for the creature's heart. The spear hit its mark, but the Sasabonsam barely flinched. Instead, it screeched, a sound so loud it seemed to shake the very trees.

Kofi scrambled backward, his heart racing. The Sasabonsam circled above him, its wings cutting through the air like a storm. The creature was playing with him, toying with its prey. He knew it would take him if he didn't act fast.

With a surge of adrenaline, Kofi bolted into the dense underbrush, the Sasabonsam hot on his heels. He could feel the creature's eyes burning into his back as it pursued him through the jungle.

He leapt over a fallen tree, barely avoiding the claws of the Sasabonsam that slashed the air behind him. Kofi's legs were growing heavy, but he knew he had to keep running. The forest was alive, the shadows closing in, and the Sasabonsam was relentless.

Just when he thought his strength would fail him, he burst through the trees into a small clearing. He turned to face his pursuer, his breath ragged and sharp. The Sasabonsam hovered above him, its red eyes burning with fury.

With one last desperate cry, Kofi lifted his spear high. The creature paused, watching him, as if considering whether to finish him off. But Kofi wasn't ready to die. With all his remaining strength, he hurled the spear once more.

This time, the spear struck the creature in its side, and with a shriek that could shatter glass, the Sasabonsam recoiled, its wings flapping wildly. For a moment, everything was still.

And then, as quickly as it had come, the Sasabonsam disappeared into the trees, vanishing into the shadows of the forest.

Kofi stood alone in the clearing, the eerie silence pressing down

The Sasabonsam of West Africa

46.

Obia, The Witches Creature

West African folklore

The **Obia**, also known as **Obeah**, is a dark and sinister creature originating from **West African folklore**, with strong ties to the Caribbean, particularly Jamaica, where the term has evolved to describe witches, magic, and spells. In the traditional West African context, the Obia is described as a **massive, malevolent animal**, often thought to be sent by witches to terrorize villages. Its primary function is to kidnap young girls, stealing their skins to wear as a coat. This act of wearing the skin is symbolic of the witch's power to disguise themselves, reinforcing their supernatural and malevolent abilities.

Obia (Obeah) – West African Folklore and Caribbean Mythology

The Obia is commonly believed to be **a tool or familiar of witches**, used to carry out dark magic and summon evil spirits. Its animalistic form is often described as a large, predatory beast–often a beast of burden or one resembling a **hyena**, **lion**, or **panther**–which can strike terror into any village it targets. The creature itself is capable of striking fear into the hearts of its victims, and the witches who command the Obia are known to have **intimate knowledge of dark magic**. In some versions of the myth, the Obia is seen as the embodiment of the witch's power and their connection to the **supernatural world**.

In the Caribbean, the concept of the **Obia** evolved beyond a mere beast and became synonymous with **witchcraft and sorcery**. In this context, the term is used to describe the magic itself, as well as the practitioner of that magic, known as an **Obiaman** or **Obiama**. The belief in the Obia, and the practices associated with it, spread across the Caribbean through African slaves brought to the islands, where the art of Obia was practiced secretly in the shadows, feared and respected by locals.

In Jamaica, the term **Obia** also became associated with witchcraft that was believed to be powered by connections with **the devil**. Practitioners of Obia, called **Obeahmen** or **Obeahwomen**, were believed to have the power to **curse or bless**, control spirits, and bring misfortune or prosperity. They were thought to use their dark magic to punish wrongdoers, avenge betrayal, and even predict the future.

Physical Appearance:

The Obia itself is described as a **massive, predatory animal**, often with **hyena-like features** or resembling a **giant panther or lion**. In some versions, it is said to have **glowing red eyes**, adding to its supernatural and terrifying aura. Its fur is dark, often black or mottled, and it is sometimes described as having **claws or sharp talons**. The most striking and eerie aspect of the Obia is its ability to **wear the skin of the young girls it kidnaps**, using it as a **coat** to blend in among humans and further terrorize the villagers.

The Obia is not always described in purely animalistic terms, as it is often seen as a manifestation of **dark sorcery**—an entity that is controlled and manipulated by witches, embodying their power. When summoned or controlled by an **Obiama** (witch), the Obia can take on a more **ethereal form**, often appearing as a shadowy creature, a **specter of death**, or a **horrifying figure** meant to instill fear and obedience.

Abilities and Powers:

- **Shape-shifting:** As a shape shifter the Obia is capable of **wearing the skin of its victims**, often young girls, which gives it the ability to hide among humans and attack when least expected. This ability allows it to blend into society, creating terror among those who may

have unknowingly encountered it.
- **Supernatural Strength:** The Obia is described as having immense physical strength, capable of overpowering adults and dragging them into the forest to meet their demise.
- **Dark Magic Connection:** The creature's true power lies in its connection to the witches, or **Obeah practitioners**, who summon and control it. The **Obiamen** and **Obiawomen** who command the creature possess knowledge of **occult rituals**, allowing them to use the Obia for **punishments**, **curses**, and **fortune-telling**.
- **Night-Time Attacks:** The Obia is typically associated with night raids, where it strikes without warning. Its attacks are swift and terrifying, usually leaving no trace of its presence except for the eerie signs of **animal tracks** or **human remains**.

Cultural Significance:

The Obia has deep cultural roots in West African societies, particularly within the **Akan people**, where the practice of **Obia** referred to the magic and spiritual rituals used for both good and bad purposes. It is a practice that can be traced back to **African traditional religions**, where powerful figures could invoke spirits or communicate with the **ancestral world**.

As African slaves were brought to the Caribbean, they carried with them the knowledge of **Obia**—a spiritual practice that survived in secret due to its association with **the devil** and its perceived danger to colonial powers. It was said to be a **subversive practice** that allowed enslaved peoples to gain some form of control over their oppressors, using the power of Obia to curse, harm, or fight back against the system.

The **Obiaman** or **Obiama**—the practitioner of Obia—was often a figure of great fear and respect in Caribbean communities. While feared for their potential to curse, cause illness, or bring bad fortune, Obiamen and Obiama were also seen as spiritual healers who could cure ailments or provide **spiritual protection**. The Obia was seen both as a tool of **destruction** and **empowerment**.

"The Curse of the Obia"

It was just after dusk when **Kwame**, the village elder, heard the telltale signs—the rustling in the trees and the low growl that seemed to reverberate in the air. The **Sasabonsam**, or so he had believed, was nothing more than a myth—until now. There was something else in the air, something darker, more menacing.

He had heard the whispers in the village—whispers of the **Obia**. Children were going missing, one by one, disappearing into the dense forests that bordered their village. What had once been dismissive stories of wild animals had begun to take on a darker edge. Women spoke in hushed tones, afraid to mention the creature by name, but their fear was palpable.

Kwame had lived long enough to know that there were things beyond understanding in the world, things that couldn't be explained by rational thought. He had seen the magic of the **Obiamen**, the witches who wielded power that seemed to stretch beyond the realm of the living. And now, it seemed, that dark magic had manifested in a creature—a **monster** that lurked in the shadows of the trees.

"Kwame, there is something in the forest," said **Kofi**, the village hunter, his voice trembling. "I saw it. It was not an animal. Not any beast I've ever seen. It had red eyes. It wore the skin of a girl... I know it."

Kwame's heart sank. The creature—the Obia—had come.

"Do not speak of it," Kwame replied sternly. "The Obia is no mere beast. It is a curse, a punishment sent by the **Obiama**. The witches have sent it here."

The two men hurried to the clearing, their hearts heavy with dread. The **Obia** had made its move—this time, it was not simply a tale to tell around the fire. The creature was real, and it had taken yet another victim.

They reached the clearing and froze. There, in the darkness, hung the twisted body of a young girl, her face unrecognizable, the skin stripped from her bones. The **Obia** had claimed her, just as the legends foretold.

But in the distance, there was a sound—a noise that stopped their hearts cold. **The growl.**

Before them, standing between the trees, was the **Obia**, its eyes glowing a fierce red, its massive form outlined in the moonlight. It was the size of a great lion, but with the dark, twisted fur of a hyena. Its fangs were iron, glinting in the moonlight, and the long, twisted legs hung from the branches above, ready to strike.

Kwame stepped forward, trembling but resolute. "You will not take another life," he whispered, his voice low but firm.

The Obia's head tilted, and with a slow, deliberate motion, it stretched its wings wide, the eerie, bat-like appendages spreading like a shadow over the clearing.

Kwame gripped his charm, the **iron amulet** passed down through generations, and whispered an incantation. The wind picked up, the trees creaked, and the Obia hissed, its red eyes narrowing in fury.

Then, with a scream, the Obia leapt from the trees. But it was not Kwame it sought—it was Kofi, whose legs faltered in fear.

In that moment, Kwame knew: the only way to stop the Obia was not through magic, but through courage.

With a cry, Kwame lunged forward, driving the amulet into the creature's heart. The Obia screeched, a sound that shattered the night, and collapsed, its body crumbling into the earth.

The forest was still. And in the silence, Kwame realized that the curse had been lifted—for now.

But the shadows lingered, and the stories of the Obia would live on.

The Obia of West Africa

47.

Nyami Nyami – The Zambezi River God

Southern African Mythology

The **Nyami Nyami**, also known as the **Zambezi River God** or **Zambezi Snake Spirit**, is a powerful deity of the Zambezi River, particularly revered by the **Tonga people** who inhabit the Zambezi Valley. As one of the most important gods in their folklore, the Nyami Nyami is believed to be both a protector and a provider, controlling the river's flow and ensuring the sustenance of the people living along its banks. The Nyami Nyami is typically depicted as a **serpent-like** being, often with the **body of a snake** and the **head of a fish**, but variations of its appearance may also include it being portrayed as a **river dragon** or even a **whirlpool**.

Nyami Nyami – The Zambezi Snake Spirit

This deity's immense size and power are said to be both awe-inspiring and terrifying, with some depictions showing it as having **massive snake-like coils** with **fish-like features**, symbolizing its dominion over both the **land and water**. Its **eyes** are said to glow, reflecting the river's depths, and it is commonly associated with the **spiritual realm**, particularly in the **Kariba Gorge**, where it is believed to reside with its wife.

Physical Appearance:

- **Body**: The Nyami Nyami is traditionally described as having the **body of a giant serpent** or dragon, symbolizing its deep connection to water and its immense strength.
- **Head**: Its head is typically portrayed as that of a **fish** or sometimes a **whirlpool**, a symbolic representation of the river's power and its ability to control the flow of water.
- **Size**: The creature is believed to be enormous, its body sprawling across vast sections of the river.
- **Wings**: Some versions describe it as possessing wings or fins, further connecting it to both terrestrial and aquatic realms.

Abilities:

- **Water Control**: The Nyami Nyami is believed to have the power to **control the river**, both its flow and its depths. It is said to have the ability to flood the land or calm the waters based on its will.
- **Protection and Provision**: The Nyami Nyami is revered as a protector, safeguarding the people who live along the river and providing them with sustenance, especially in difficult times.
- **Anger and Wrath**: The Nyami Nyami's wrath is feared, particularly if it is disturbed or angered. The construction of the **Kariba Dam**, which separated the Nyami Nyami from its wife, is said to have triggered a series of floods and calamities.

Habitat and Behavior:

The Nyami Nyami is believed to reside in the **Zambezi River**, particularly around the **Kariba Gorge** and was said to live alongside its wife. During the construction of the Kariba Dam it is said Nyami Nyami was separated from his wife. The separation of the two spirits is central to the **Kariba legend**. The river god is

> also connected to the **underworld**, and many of its powers and behaviors are tied to the natural and spiritual forces that govern both the physical world and the afterlife.
>
> The Nyami Nyami is both a **benevolent** and **terrifying** presence, providing food and protection to the people when respected, but capable of immense destruction when its wrath is provoked. Its relationship with the Tonga people reflects a **balance of reverence and fear**, as they believe the god controls the river's resources and must be appeased in times of hardship or threat.

Cultural Significance:

The Nyami Nyami is deeply embedded in the cultural fabric of the Tonga people, who see him as both a **spiritual protector** and an active force in the river's life cycle. The deity's power extends beyond mere superstition— it is a central part of the people's connection to the river. The **Kariba Dam** project, which was built across the Zambezi River, is said to have deeply offended the Nyami Nyami, causing a rift between the river god and its wife, and triggering a series of devastating floods.

The Tonga people believe the Nyami Nyami will one day destroy the dam, reuniting with its wife and restoring the river to its former state. This belief is sustained through **earth tremors** that occur around the Kariba area, which the people interpret as the Nyami Nyami's continued struggle to reunite with its wife, separated by the dam.

Legends:

The most famous and documented myth about the Nyami Nyami is the **Kariba legend**, which tells of the river god's fury at the construction of the Kariba Dam. This legend involves the destruction of the dam and the devastating floods that followed, which were attributed to the anger of the Nyami Nyami. The floodwaters, which claimed the lives of many workers and wiped out much of the dam's progress, were believed to be a direct result of the Nyami Nyami's power.

The Kariba Legend tells how the **Tonga people** lived peacefully in the Zambezi Valley, relying on the river for their sustenance. But when the dam project was initiated, they were forced to leave their homes, and the peaceful valley was overtaken by heavy machinery and floodwaters. The construction of the dam was seen as a grave offense to the Nyami Nyami, and when the floods struck, they were believed to be the wrath of the river god, furious at being disturbed. The Tonga people performed sacrifices to appease the Nyami Nyami, which included offering animals like a **black calf** to the river in hopes of retrieving missing workers' bodies after they mysteriously vanished.

Despite the dam's eventual completion, the Tonga people believe that the Nyami Nyami will eventually destroy it, causing the river to return to its natural flow.

"The Wrath of Nyami Nyami"

It was in the late afternoon when the sky over the Zambezi River grew unnaturally still. **Khamisi**, a seasoned fisherman from the village near **Kariba Gorge**, stood by the riverbank, his eyes scanning the horizon. He had heard the warnings from the elders, tales passed down through generations, of a time when the **Zambezi River** would rise in fury. But nothing had prepared him for the silence that now hung in the air.

The river was calm, almost too calm. The usual ripples that danced across the surface were gone, replaced by an eerie stillness that seemed to stretch for miles. The heavy machinery on the far side of the gorge, working relentlessly on the construction of the **Kariba Dam**, seemed distant and insignificant.

"**Nyami Nyami**," Khamisi whispered under his breath.

The elder had told him that the river god was angry—angry at the great dam being built across the Zambezi, which cut off the river from its very heart. They had disturbed the sacred waters, the home of the river god. And now, it seemed, the god had come.

Suddenly, the air thickened with a heavy, suffocating pressure. Khamisi stumbled back as the ground beneath him rumbled. The trees along the river's edge began to sway, despite there being no wind.

Then, from the depths of the river, a sound like a great **roar** echoed through the gorge. The water began to churn violently, creating massive waves that crashed against the shores. Khamisi's heart raced as the ground trembled beneath his feet.

Through the swirling water, a massive shape emerged—a **serpent-like creature**, its scales glistening like water-drenched stone. Its eyes were **glowing red**, filled with the fire of ancient anger. The **Nyami Nyami** had risen.

The river god rose higher, twisting through the water like a snake, its body long and immense, stretching across the river in a way that seemed to defy nature. The **whirlpool** at its head spun violently, and Khamisi realized that this was not just a flood. It was **wrath**.

The creature's roar split the air as the ground trembled with the force of the river god's power. Khamisi turned and ran, but the force of the current swept him from his feet. He could hear the voices of the elders in his mind, telling him that only appeasing the **Nyami Nyami** would bring peace.

As the **Nyami Nyami** rose higher from the waters, the ancient spirit of the Zambezi, Khamisi understood one thing. The river god would not be satisfied until the **Kariba Dam** was destroyed. Until the Zambezi returned to its natural flow.

But it was too late. The god had already spoken. The ground shook again, and the roar of the Nyami Nyami was the last sound Khamisi heard before the world fell into darkness.

Nyami Nyami of the Zambezi River

Epilogue

Shadows and Whispers

As we return to the light...

As the final whispers of ancient creatures and forgotten legends fade into the winds of time, one truth remains undeniable: myth and folklore are the heartbeat of the land. They have shaped cultures, transcended generations, and woven themselves into the very fabric of human existence. The creatures in these pages—some fierce, some mischievous, some sorrowful—embody the mysteries of the world, the balance between light and shadow, the natural and the supernatural. They are the guardians of realms unseen and the keepers of secrets buried beneath the earth, in the oceans, and deep within the forests.

But these stories, while captivating, also serve a deeper purpose: they are reminders of our connection to the past, the forgotten tales of those who walked this earth before us. Each legend, whether from the outback of Australia, the misty swamps of the American South, or the shadowed forests of Europe, carries within it lessons of respect, humility, and caution. The creatures we fear or revere are reflections of the forces we cannot control—nature, time, death, and the unknown. They remind us that even in the face of the most extraordinary beings, we remain small, fragile, and bound to the earth we call home.

As you close this book, remember that the stories do not end here. For every legend shared, there are countless others waiting to be unearthed, whispered on the wind, or buried deep within the hearts of those who still believe in the magic of the world. The Bunyip's call still echoes in the waters, the White Lady wanders in the moonlight, and the Wild Hunt rides beneath the darkened skies. They wait, not just in the pages of books, but in the spaces between the living and the dead, in the quiet moments when you pause to listen.

Perhaps, in your travels or quiet moments of reflection, you will hear their calls. Perhaps, if you venture into the forests or gaze into the deep waters, you will catch a fleeting glimpse of one of these creatures. And maybe, just maybe, you will find that the world of myth is not so far removed from our own.

After all, as long as we tell their stories, the creatures live on.

JG Baigent

Shadows of Glossary

Shadows and Whispers

Abere

Abere is a demoness from Melanesian mythology. She is portrayed as a "wild" woman with young female servants. She is said to reside in marshes.

Adlet

The Adlet (or Erqigdlet) are a race of creatures in the Inuit mythology of Greenland, as well as the Labrador and Hudson Bay coasts.

African mythologies

African mythology is a collection of stories and beliefs about supernatural beings, heroes, and other figures that influence human life

Afterlife

The afterlife, or life after death, is the idea that some aspect of a person continues to exist after their physical body dies. It's a belief that's common to many religions, and is often based on teachings in their scriptures or traditions.

Ahp

A nocturnal female spirit of Southeast Asian folklore. It manifests as the floating, disembodied head of a woman, usually young and beautiful.

Airlangga

Airlangga Anantawikramottunggadewa (born 1002 in Bali, Indonesia – died 1049 in Java), was the only king of the Kingdom of Kahuripan.

Akan people

The Akan people are an ethnolinguistic group of people who primarily live in Ghana, with some also living in Ivory Coast and Togo

Alchemists

Alchemists were people who practiced alchemy, a medieval chemical science and speculative philosophy that involved the pursuit of transforming less valuable metals into gold, finding a cure for disease, and discovering a way to extend life.

Alicanto

The Alicanto is a nocturnal mythological bird of the desert of Atacama, pertaining to Chilean mythology.

Almas

The Almas is an ape-like cryptid reported from Central Asia. They are said to inhabit the Asian mountain regions of the Pamir and the Caucasus

Amaru

Amaru is a serpent deity in Andean mythology that symbolizes wisdom, power, and the connection between the spiritual and earthly realms. Amaru is associated with the water economy, and is often depicted as a guardian spirit of sacred sites like rivers, lakes, and mountains. Amaru is also featured in shamanic traditions, where the serpent is seen as a conduit between the two realms

Amrita

a Sanskrit word that means "immortality". It is a central concept within Indian religions and is often referred to in ancient Indian texts as an elixir.

An bhean bhán

"An bhean bhán" in Irish translates to "the white woman," with "bean" meaning "woman" and "bán" meaning "white"; it is often used in Irish folklore to refer to a supernatural being similar to a banshee, associated with death or misfortune, due to the white color symbolizing death shrouds.

Androktasiai

The Androktasiai were the personifications of manslaughter in Greek mythology, daughters of the goddess of strife Eris.

Animalistic form

characteristic of animals, physicality and body shape of an animal, particularly in being physical and instinctive.

Ao

Ao is a giant sea turtle in Chinese mythology. The creator goddess Nüwa cut off Ao's legs and used them to support the sky after Gong Gong damaged Mount Buzhou.

Ao Guang

Ao Guang, revered as the Dragon King of the Eastern Seas, holds a significant position in Chinese mythology. As one of the four Dragon Kings, he governs the East Sea with authority and wisdom,

Ares

Ares is the Greek god of war and courage. He is one of the Twelve Olympians, and the son of Zeus and Hera.

Asanbosam

The Asanbosam, also known as the Sasabonsam, is a vampire-like creature from Akan folklore. It is said to live in the forests of West Africa, enforcing the rules of the forest by preying on those who wander into its territory

Asin

Asin, a man-eating female giant from the folklore of the Alsea tribe

Asura

Asuras (Sanskrit: असुर) are a class of beings in Indian religions. They are described as power-seeking beings related to the more benevolent Devas

Asuras

Asura, in Hindu mythology, class of beings defined by their opposition to the devas or suras (gods).

Aswang

Aswang is a term in Filipino folklore for a variety of evil, shape-shifting creatures, including vampires, ghouls, witches, and werewolves. Aswangs are also known to consume the innards of corpses. The term is used as an umbrella term for these creatures, which can also be human-beast hybrids, usually dogs, cats, or pigs.

Athena

Athena or Athene, often given the epithet Pallas, is an ancient Greek goddess associated with wisdom, warfare, and handicraft

Azure Dragon

The Azure Dragon is a dragon god and one of the Four Symbols in Chinese constellations

Bạch Xà

Lady White is a thousand-year-old snake who, through centuries of meditation and self-discipline, has managed to attain human form.

Bai Suzhen

Bai Suzhen (Chinese: 白素貞), also known as Lady Bai is a one-thousand-year-old white snake spirit

Bai Ze

Mythical creature with the head of a man and the body of an ox, often with three eyes on each flank and horns on its back.

Baihu

Baihu (白虎) is a white tiger from Chinese mythology and one of the Four Symbols of the Chinese constellations

Bailongma

The White Dragon Horse, known as Bai Long Ma, and Yu Long

Baku

The Baku, otherwise known as the dream eater, is a mythological being or spirit in Chinese and Japanese folklore which is said to devour nightmares.

Barmanou

The Barmanou is allegedly a bipedal humanoid primate cryptid that inhabits the mountainous region of northern Pakistan.

Barong

Barong (Balinese: ◇◇◇◇) is a panther-like creature and character in the Balinese mythology of Bali, Indonesia. He is the king of the spirits.

Bashe

Bashe are evil spirits from Chinese mythology that take the form of gigantic snakes infamous for their ability to devour elephants.

Basket Woman

The Basket Women is an Ogress, a marauding giant common to the folklore of many Northwest Coast tribes. She catches humans, especially naughty or careless children.

Batibat

Filipino folklore describes the batibat as ancient, obese, female demons who live in trees.

Betal

Betal, also known as Vetala, is a ghost figure in Hindu folklore, often depicted as a spirit who inhabits cremation grounds and trees, and is most famous for the "Vikram and Betal" stories where a king named Vikram must answer riddles posed by Betal to escape his grasp; essentially, Betal is a trickster ghost who tests the intelligence of those who encounter him.

Bhoot Pret

Bhoot pret is a term that refers to ghosts and evil spirits in Hindu mythology and ancient Vedic texts.

Bifang

one legged green crane with red stripes or spots and a white beak. is a bad omen of a fire disaster.

Bigfoot

Bigfoot also commonly referred to as Sasquatch is a large, hairy mythical creature said to inhabit forests in North America

Bipedal Humanoid Primate

A bipedal humanoid primate is a primate that walks on two feet, or a hominid. The term "bipedal" comes from the Latin words bi (two) and ped (foot).

Bixi

Bixi, or Bi Xi (Wade–Giles: Pi-hsi), is a figure from Chinese mythology. One of the nine sons of the Dragon King, he is depicted as a dragon with the shell of a turtle.

Bloody Bones

Bloody Bones is a bogeyman figure in English and North American folklore whose first written appearance is approximately 1548. As with all bogeymen the figure has been used to frighten children into proper deportment. The character is sometimes called Rawhead, Tommy Rawhead, or Rawhead-and-Bloody-Bones.

Bo Beast

The Bo is a carnivorous Unicorn-like beast from Chinese folklore. An inhabitant of mountainous terrains, this rare creature is shaped like a white horse.

bogeyman

an imaginary evil spirit or being, used to frighten children.

Boogeyman

The bogeyman is a mythical creature typically used to frighten children into good behavior.

Boyi

n Chinese mythology, Boyi is a legendary beast that resembles a sheep but has nine tails, four ears, and eyes on its back. It is said that a person who wears Boyi's fur will never be afraid.

Brahma

Brahma is a Hindu god and member of the trimurti, a trinity of gods that create, maintain, and destroy the world

Brazilian folklore

Brazilian folklore, with cultural elements of diverse origin found in Brazil, comprising folk tales, traditions, characters and beliefs regarding places, people, and entities.

Bunyip

The bunyip is a legendary, man-eating monster from Australian Aboriginal folklore that lives in the country's waterways

Calan Gaeaf

Calan Gaeaf is the name of the first day of winter in Wales, observed on 1 November. The night before is Nos Galan Gaeaf or Noson Galan Gaeaf, an Ysbrydnos ("spirit night") when spirits are abroad. Traditionally, people avoid churchyards, stiles, and crossroads, since spirits are thought to gather there.

Call of the sirens

In Greek mythology, sirens are female humanlike beings with alluring voices; they appear in a scene in the Odyssey in which Odysseus saves his crew's lives.

Calon Arang

Calon Arang is a character in Javanese and Balinese folklore dating from the 12th century. Tradition calls her a witch, a master of black magic.

Cánmǔ

Cánmǔ (蚕母, the "Silkworm Mother"), is a goddess whose cult is related to that of Houtu (the "Queen of the Earth") and to that of the Sanxiao

Cánshén

Cánshén or Cánwáng (蚕王 "Silkworm Ruler") is the deity of silkworm and sericulture in Chinese religion.

Capelobo

The Capelobo is a bipedal monster with a strong body covered in fur, perfectly round hooves, alongated razor sharp claws and the head of an anteater.

Celtic mythology

Celtic mythology is the body of myths belonging to the Celtic peoples

changeling

A changeling was a substitute left by a supernatural being when kidnapping a human being.

Chullachaki

The Chullachaki or Chullachaqui, also known as the Shapishico, is a mythical forest creature of the Peruvian and Brazilian Amazonian jungle

Churel

The Chural is also the name of a mythical creature that resembles a woman. It is also known as Charail, Churreyl, Chudail, Chudel, Chuṛail, Cuḍail, or Cuḍel. In India, the Chural is the ghost of a woman who died while pregnant and haunts lonely places. Some believe that a woman becomes a Chural if she dies in childbirth or due to neglect.

Coi Coi-Vilu

The Mapuche god of water (or goddess, in some versions found in Chiloé) and, according to Mapuche myths (later also found in Chiloé), supreme ruler of the sea.

Colombian folklore

Colombian traditional folk tales and stories about legendary creatures, which are transmitted orally and passed on to new generations.

Cosmological hierarchy

Cosmological hierarchy refers to the idea that the universe has a structure that is present on all scales, from individual galaxies to superclusters.

Cronus

Cronus was the youngest of the Titans, the children of Gaia (Earth) and Uranus (Heaven). He was the king of the Titans and ruled during the Golden Age. Cronus was associated with agriculture, and his festival, the Kronia, celebrated the harvest.

cryptid

A cryptid is an animal that some people believe exists but has never been proven to do so. Cryptids are often associated with difficult-to-reach habitats, and many are said to be supernatural or mythical. However, not all cryptids are supernatural, and some popular cryptid legends grow to include these characteristics.

cryptobotanic

Cryptobotany is the study of various exotic plants which are not believed to exist by the scientific community, but which exist in myth, literature or legend.

Cryptozoological

Cryptozoology is the study of animals that are legendary, unknown, or extinct, and whose existence is disputed or unsubstantiated. It is considered a pseudoscience and subculture.

Cu bird

The Cu bird is a bird from a Mexican folklore that is unhappy with its looks.

Curupira

The Curupira is a mythological creature present in the Tupi-Guarani myths in the Amazon rainforest of Brazil.

Dao

A White Lady (or woman in white) is a type of female ghost. She is typically dressed in a white dress or similar garment, reportedly seen in rural areas

Dashavatara

The Dashavatara (Sanskrit: दशावतार, IAST: daśāvatāra) are the ten primary avatars of Vishnu, a principal Hindu god.

Deity

A deity or god is a supernatural being considered to be sacred and worthy of worship due to having authority over the universe, nature or human life.

Demogorgon

Demogorgon is a deity or demon associated with the underworld.

Demon

an evil spirit or devil, especially one thought to possess a person or act as a tormentor in hell.

Denglong

Denglong is one of the sons of the Dragon King, and has the habit of guarding. He is said to have horns like a deer, head like a camel, ears like a cat, eyes like a shrimp, mouth like a donkey, hair like a lion, neck like a snake, belly like a Shen, scales like a koi, front paws like an eagle, and rear paws like a tiger.

Deuan

A White Lady (or woman in white) is a type of female ghost. She is typically dressed in a white dress or similar garment, reportedly seen in rural areas

Devas

In Hinduism, devas are god-like beings or angels that are often divided into groups based on their association with the forces of nature, such as the sky, air, or earth. Devas are said to be in an eternal battle against darkness, and each one represents an aspect of the Infinite God. For example, Agni is the deva of fire

Devil Bird

The Ulama, or Devil Bird, is a creature from Sri Lankan folklore that is said to make blood-curdling shrieks in the jungle at night. The Ulama's cry is believed to be a portent of death.

Dilong

Dilong is a Chinese dragon name that is also used to mean "earthworm" in traditional Chinese medicine and Geosaurus in zoological nomenclature.

Dingonek

The Dingonek is a mythical, chimera-like creature from Western Africa that is said to be a cross between a scorpion and a walrus

Dooth

a shadowy figure that represents death itself.

Dreamtime

The Dreaming is used to represent Aboriginal concepts of "Everywhen", during which the land was inhabited by ancestral figures, often of heroic proportions or with supernatural abilities.

Durga

Durga is a Hindu goddess and a major aspect of the supreme goddess, Devi, or Shakti. She is a symbol of strength, motherhood, protection, and destruction, and is often depicted with many arms, riding a lion or tiger, and fighting a demon.

El Cucuy

El Cucuy is a mythical monster from Spanish and Portuguese folklore that is similar to the bogeyman. El Cucuy is said to come at night to take away children who are disobedient. The more naughty the child, the hungrier El Cucuy becomes. Once captured, the child is either devoured or disappears

Elizabeth Báthory.

Countess Elizabeth Báthory of Ecsed was a Hungarian noblewoman and alleged serial killer from the powerful House of Báthory, who owned land in the Kingdom of Hungary. Báthory and four of her servants were accused of torturing and killing hundreds of girls and women from 1590 to 1610.

English folklore

English folklore consists of the myths and legends of England, including the region's mythical creatures, traditional recipes, urban legends, proverbs, superstitions, dance, balladry, and folktales that have been passed down through generations, reflecting the cultural heritage of the country.

Erinyes

The Erinyes were the three ancient Greek goddesses of vengeance and retribution who punished men for crimes against the natural order.

Esoteric

understood by or meant for only the select few who have special knowledge or interest.

European folklore

European folklore is the folklore of the Western world, and includes many traditions shared across European cultures

Fairies

Fairies are mythical creatures that are often described as having supernatural qualities and appearing human-like

Fates

In Greek mythology, the Fates, also known as the Moirai, are three sister goddesses who determine the destiny of mortals

Feilian

a Chinese wind spirit from a southern tradition, later identified with and subsumed under the primary wind deity Fengbo.

Feilong

Feilong, winged dragon that rides on clouds and mist

Folklore

the traditional beliefs, customs, and stories of a community, passed through the generations by word of mouth.

Foo Dogs

Typically made of stone, they are also known as stone lions or shishi (石獅; shíshī). They are known in colloquial English as lion dogs or foo dogs / fu dogs.

Freyja

Freyja is a Norse goddess associated with love, fertility, war

Furies

The Furies are goddesses of vengeance in ancient Greek and Roman mythology

Fuzhu

The Fuzhu is described as being a white deer with four horns. It is gentle and likes to keep itself clean.

Gaia

In Greek mythology, Gaia also spelled Gaea is the personification of Earth. Gaia is the ancestral mother—sometimes parthenogenic—of all life.

Germanic mythology

Germanic mythology consists of the body of myths native to the Germanic peoples, including Norse mythology, Anglo-Saxon mythology, and Continental Germanic mythology.

ghost of Matilda

Margaret Pomeroy is suspected to be one of the ghosts that stalks Berry Pomeroy castle and is known as the White Lady.

Ghoul

an evil spirit or phantom, especially one supposed to rob graves and feed on dead bodies.

Goblin

A small, grotesque, and often mischievous humanoid creature that appears in European folklore.

Greek mythology,

Greek mythology is a collection of myths and folklore from ancient Greece that is now considered part of classical mythology.

Guacanchas

a mythological creature of the Guanches, pre-Hispanic inhabitants of the Canary Islands.

Guayota

Guayota, in Guanche mythology of Tenerife (the Canary Islands), was the principal malignant deity and Achamán's adversary.

Gumiho

The gumiho is a nine-tailed fox from Korean folklore that can shapeshift and is often depicted as a vicious monster

Gwyn ap Nudd

Gwyn ap Nudd is a Welsh mythological figure, the king of the Tylwyth Teg or "fair folk" and ruler of the Welsh Otherworld

Hades

Hades in the ancient Greek religion and mythology, is the god of the dead and the king of the underworld

Hanako-san

Hanako-san is the ghost of a World War II-era girl who was killed while playing hide-and-seek during an air raid, that she was murdered by a parent or stranger.

Harbingers of doom

A harbinger of doom is a sign, a warning of bad things to come.

Heian period

The Heian period was a time in Japan from 794 to 1185 that was marked by cultural, political, and social change

Hellequin

Leader of the Wild Hunt and Fairy King

Hipag

The Hipag are ferocious spirit of war who are invoked by warring expeditions to provide courage. They are also invoked in kinship controversies and in sorcery

homo pongoides

Homo pongoides is a term used to describe a creature that was believed to be a new species of ape-like man. The term was coined by Belgian cryptozoologist Bernard Heuvelmans, who named the creature after the pongids, a type of anthropoid ape. Heuvelmans published his notes about the creature in a 1969 paper in a Belgian scientific journal

Hong

Hong or jiang is a Chinese dragon with two heads on each end in Chinese mythology, comparable with Rainbow Serpent legends in various cultures and mythologies.

Hứa Tiên

Lover of the white snake

Huan Beast

A beast that resembles a normal wild cat, except that it has three tails and one single eye. The sound it makes is loud enough to be heard over 100 beasts.

Huli Jing

Huli jing (Chinese: 狐狸精) are Chinese mythological creatures usually capable of shapeshifting, who may either be benevolent or malevolent spirits.

Hulijing

Huli jing (Chinese: 狐狸精) are Chinese mythological creatures usually capable of shapeshifting, who may either be benevolent or malevolent spirits.

Humanoid form

Having human characteristics or form; resembling human beings

Hybrid

a hybrid is the result from combining the qualities of two organisms of different varieties, subspecies, species.

Imugi

Imugi is a Korean mythological creature that is a lesser dragon or proto-dragon that resembles a giant serpent

Indra

Indra is the king of the devas and Svarga in Hinduism. He is associated with the sky, lightning, weather, thunder, storms, rains, river flows, and war.

Jacob Grimm

Jacob Ludwig Karl Grimm, also known as Ludwig Karl, was a German author, linguist, philologist, jurist, and folklorist. He formulated Grimm's law of linguistics, and was the co-author of the Deutsches Wörterbuch, the author of Deutsche Mythologie, and the editor of Grimms' Fairy Tales

Jiangshi

A jiāngshī, also known as a Chinese hopping vampire, is a type of undead creature or reanimated corpse in Chinese legends and folklore.

Jiaolong

Jiaolong is a dragon in Chinese mythology, often defined as a "scaled dragon"; it is hornless according to certain scholars and said to be aquatic or river-dwelling.

Jin Chan

Jin Chan (also known as Chan Chu) is a greedy three-legged toad with a gold coin in her mouth that will help draw wealth into your life.

Jinn

a spirit inhabiting the earth but unseen by humans, capable of assuming various forms and exercising extraordinary powers.

Kaitiaki

Kaitiaki is a Māori term that refers to a guardian or protector of the land, sea, and sky.

Kalaviṅka

In Sanskrit, "kalaviṅka bird"; a mythical bird from the Himālaya mountains with a call said to be far more beautiful than that of all other birds.

Kalo Bhoot

A supernatural creature, usually the ghost of a deceased person, in the popular culture, literature and some ancient texts of the Indian subcontinent.

Kaperosa

Kaperosa a female who commited suicide because of hatred or being betrayed by her husband or fiance, murdered, other's said. They are souls who don't rest.

Kappa

Kappa, in Japanese folklore, a type of vampirelike lecherous creature that is more intelligent than the devilish oni and less malevolent toward men.

Kasu

a nocturnal female spirit of Southeast Asian folklore. It manifests as the floating, disembodied head of a woman, usually young and beautiful.

Kayeri

The Kayeri is a giant, plant-like humanoid cryptid from the folklore of the Cuiba people of Colombia and Venezuela.

Kitsune

Kitsune are supernatural fox spirits from Japanese folklore with a variety of paranormal abilities

Krasue

a nocturnal female spirit of Southeast Asian folklore. It manifests as the floating, disembodied head of a woman, usually young and beautiful

Kurma

Kurma (Sanskrit: कूर्म, lit. 'Turtle' or 'Tortoise'), is the second avatar of the Hindu preserver deity, Vishnu.

Lady in the Lake

A ghostly figure that is searching for her murdered daughter

Lady of White Rock Lake

One of the best-known Dallas legends is the so-called "Lady of White Rock Lake," a ghostly figure who is said to haunt the park's environs

Lake Tianchi Monster

Lake Tianchi Monster is the name given to what is said to be a lake monster that lives in Heaven Lake (known as Cheonji in Korean)

Legend

A legend is a genre of folklore that consists of a narrative featuring human actions, believed or perceived to have taken place in human history.

Leyaks

According to Balinese belief, Leyak is a normal human who practice dark magic and need embryonic blood to survive.

Luan

The luan (traditional Chinese: 鸞; simplified Chinese: 鸾; pinyin: luán; Wade-Giles: luan²) is a mythological bird in East Asian mythology. The name is sometimes reserved for males, while female luan are called Jīnjī

Magical protection

protective magic is a type of magic intended to turn away harm or evil influences, as in deflecting misfortune or averting the evil eye.

Malay folklore

Malay folklore refers to a series of knowledges, traditions and taboos that have been passed down through many generations in oral, written and symbolic.

Malevolent

having or showing a wish to do evil to others

Manawa-Tāne

Mānawa-tāne. The dwelling of the Ponaturi. The country they inhabited was underneath the waters, but they had a large house on the dry land.

Māori mythology

Māori mythology is a collection of oral tales about the origins of the world and the Māori people, often involving gods and supernatural events

Matsya

Matsya (Sanskrit: मत्स्य, lit. 'fish') is the fish avatar of the Hindu god Vishnu. Often described as the first of Vishnu's ten primary avatars,

Maya

Vaishnavism, Māyā is an epithet, or a manifestation of the Hindu goddess Lakshmi, who with Vishnu are together revered as the personification of the Absolute.

Melanesian cultures

Melanesians are the predominant and indigenous inhabitants of Melanesia, in an area stretching from New Guinea to the Fiji Islands.

Mengkuang

Mengkuang is a Malay word for the screw pine, a shrub or tree that is native to tropical regions in Southeast Asia and the Pacific Islands. The leaves of the mengkuang plant are a versatile material for weaving and thatching, and are used to make a variety of traditional crafts.

Mexican folklore

Mexican folklore is a rich tradition of supernatural stories that have been passed down through generations. These tales often feature ghosts, witches, mythical creatures, and haunted locations.

Monster of Lake Tota

The Monster of Lake Tota is a legendary aquatic animal known in many works as Diablo ballena, or the 'devil whale'. The monster is an inhabitant of Lake Tota in present-day Colombia

Moon Rabbit

The Moon rabbit or Moon hare is a mythical figure in both East Asian and indigenous American folklore, based on interpretations that identify the dark markings on the near side of the Moon as a rabbit or hare.

Muki

The muki is a goblin-like creature in the mythology of the Central Andes in Bolivia, Peru, Ecuador and Colombia. He is known to be a miner.

Mulyawonk

To the Ngarrindjeri people of the River Murray, the bunyip was known as the Mulyawonk who, in a dreamtime moral story, protected the river and the fish.

My Ladye

A White Lady (or woman in white) is a type of female ghost. She is typically dressed in a white dress or similar garment

Myth

a traditional story, especially one concerning the early history of a people or explaining some natural or social phenomenon, and typically involving supernatural beings or events.

Mythical creatures

A mythical creature is an imaginary animal or being that exists in folklore, myths, or legends, but not in real life. Mythical creatures are often supernatural, with unique characteristics and abilities, and may have metaphorical significance.

Mythological

relating to, based on, or appearing in myths or mythology.

mythological creatures

A legendary creature (also called a mythical creature or mythological creature) is a type of fantasy entity, typically a hybrid, that has not been proven to exist.

mythology

Mythology is the study of myths, which are stories that are often about gods and goddesses and are meant to explain natural phenomena or beliefs

Myths and legends

A myth is a traditional story or legend, generally about the ancient history of a population of people. A myth includes supernatural events and characters. Legends often teach lessons about factual historical characters.

Naga

Naga, in Hinduism, Buddhism, and Jainism, a member of a class of mythical semidivine beings, half human and half cobra.

Nagas

Nagas are half-human and half-serpent, and are often depicted as strong and handsome. They can take human or part-human form, and are also known as dragons and water spirits.

Narasimha

Narasimha is known primarily as the 'Great Protector' who specifically defends and protects his devotees from evil and destroys evil.

Nian

In Chinese mythology, Nian is a ferocious, lion-like beast that lives in the sea or mountains. On New Year's Eve, Nian would come ashore to eat people and livestock.

Nue

A Japanese chimera having the head of a monkey, the limbs of a tiger, the body of a Japanese raccoon dog, and the front half of a snake for a tail.

Nyami Nyami

Nyami Nyami is a dragon-like river god and a central figure in the cultural beliefs of the Tonga people who live along the Zambezi River in Zambia and Zimbabwe

Obeah

In West African folklore, an obeah is a giant animal that witches use to kidnap young girls and wear their skin.

Obeah practitioners

Obeah practitioners, also known as Obeahmen or Obeahwomen, are people who practice the form of witchcraft known as Obeah. Obeah originated in West African religions and has been practiced in many places

Obia

In West African folklore, Obia is a giant animal that witches send to kidnap girls from villages. In the Bay Islands of Honduras, Obia is also a term for a witch or the spells they cast.

Occult

a term that describes a range of supernatural and esoteric beliefs and practices that are often outside of organized religion and science. The word "occult" comes from the Latin word occultus, which means "hidden, clandestine, or secret".

Occult rituals

Occult rituals are practices that involve the use of supernatural powers, secret knowledge, or an interest in the paranormal. The term "occult" refers to a category of supernatural beliefs and practices that includes magic, spirituality, alchemy, astrology, divination, extra-sensory perception, and parapsychology

Odin

Odin is a Norse god associated with many aspects of life, including war, death, wisdom, and magic

ogre

An ogre is a large, hideous humanoid monster of mythology, folklore and fiction.

Onryō

In Japanese traditional beliefs and literature, onryō are a type of ghost (yūrei) believed to be capable of causing harm in the world of the living.

Orestes

In Greek mythology, Orestes or Orestis was the son of Agamemnon and Clytemnestra, and the brother of Electra.

Panlong

Panlong is an aquatic dragon resembling a jiaolong 蛟龍 "river dragon; crocodile" in Chinese mythology, an ancient motif in Chinese art, and a proper name.

Paranormal Entity

A paranormal entity is a supernatural being or disembodied spirit that some people believe exists, but is not scientifically explainable

Penanggalan

The Malay penanggalan, a vampiric creature that, by night, detaches its head and organs from its body to go hunting for humans.

Peng

Peng or Dapeng (大鵬) is a giant bird that transforms from a Kun giant fish in Chinese mythology.

Perchta of Rožmberk

Perchta was a daughter of Ulrich II. von Rosenberg, and she was married off to Jan from Lichtenstein against her will in 1449. She quite suffered from that marriage because her husband mentally and physically mistreated and tormented her, as far as we can gain from her private letters.

philosopher's stone

an unknown substance, also called "the tincture" or "the powder," sought by alchemists for its supposed ability to transform base metals into precious ones, especially gold and silver

Philosophers

A philosopher is a person who seeks wisdom or enlightenment, or a student of philosophy

Pishtaco

The pishtaco is a monster from South American folklore that steals the fat from its victims

Pluto

Pluto was the Roman god of the underworld. In Roman myth, when someone died, they traveled to the Underworld. Pluto was originally named Hades, but the name became more commonly associated with the underworld itself.

Ponaturi

The Ponaturi are a group of hostile creatures (goblins) who live in a land beneath the sea by day, returning to shore each evening to sleep.

Pretatma

Pretatma is a Hindi word that translates to "spirit" in English. A spirit is a supernatural being or ghost.

Prom Dress Girl

A White Lady (or woman in white), a female ghost. She is typically dressed in a white prom dress.

Qinglong

Qinglong, or the Azure Dragon, is a dragon god that represents the forces of the Five Regions' Highest Deities. It is one of the Four Symbols of the Chinese constellations and symbolizes the east and spring.

Rainbow Serpent

The Rainbow Serpent or Rainbow Snake is a common deity often seen as the creator God, known by numerous names in different Australian Aboriginal languages.

Rakshasa

Rakshasa, in Hindu mythology, a type of demon or goblin. Rakshasas have the power to change their shape at will and appear as animals, as monsters, or in the case of the female demons, as beautiful women.

Rakshasas

Rākshasa are a race of usually malevolent beings prominently featured in Hinduism, Buddhism, Jainism and Folk Islam.

Rangda

In Balinese mythology, Rangda is a demon queen and half-witch who leads an army of evil witches against the forces of good, represented by Barong.

Rātā

In Māori mythology, accounts vary somewhat as to the ancestry of Rātā. Usually he is a grandson of Tāwhaki and son of Wahieroa.

Ravana

Ravana is a demon-king of the island of Lanka and the chief antagonist in the Hindu epic

Ramayana. In the Ramayana, Ravana is described as the eldest son of sage Vishrava and Kaikasi. He abducted Rama's wife, Sita, and took her to his kingdom of Lanka, where he held her in the Ashoka Vatika.

Rawhead and Bloody Bones

Bloody Bones is a bogeyman figure in English and North American folklore whose first written appearance is approximately 1548. As with all bogeymen the figure has been used to frighten children into proper deportment. The character is sometimes called Rawhead, Tommy Rawhead, or Rawhead-and-Bloody-Bones.

Renaissance mythography

Renaissance mythography was the retelling of classical Greek and Roman mythology in the context of the Renaissance, a period of rediscovery of classical antiquity.

Running Lady

The White Lady (also known as the "Running Lady") of Beeford, East Yorkshire resides on the "Beeford Straight", a stretch of road between Beeford and Brandesburton. Motorists have reported her apparition running across the Beeford Straight toward the junction of North Frodingham.

Sasabonsam

The Asanbosam, also known as the Sasabonsam, is a vampire-like creature from Akan folklore. It is said to live in the forests of West Africa, enforcing the rules of the forest by preying on those who wander into its territory.

serpent-like

Serpent-like means something resembles a serpent or snake. For example, you might describe a riverbed as serpentine if it's twisted and curves throughout a canyon floor

Sexagenary Cycle of astrology

The Chinese sexagenary cycle is used to record the Chinese calendar. The inner ring has 10 elements (heaven stems) and the outer ring has 12 elements (earth branches), which represents the Chinese zodiac. Every year the inner ring and outer ring rotate one step clockwise, for a total of 60 combinations.

Shah Barmanou

The Barmanou (or Barmanu or Baddmanus) is allegedly a bipedal humanoid primate cryptid that inhabits the mountainous region of northern Pakistan.

shape shifter

A shapeshifter is a mythical or fictional figure that can change their form or identity at will.

Shenlong

The spirit dragon from Chinese mythology who is the dragon god of the tempest and also a master of rain.

Shiva

Shiva is a Hindu god who is part of a triumvirate of three gods responsible for the creation, upkeep, and destruction of the world. Shiva is the destroyer who re-creates the world, and Hindus believe his powers are used to destroy illusions and imperfections. Shiva is seen as both the source of good and evil, and is known for his untamed passion. Shiva is often depicted as dancing, and is known as Shiva Nataraja.

Skin-walkers

Skinwalkers are supernatural beings from Navajo folklore that can transform into animals, possess them, or disguise themselves as them

South American folklore

South American folklore is the study of the customs, beliefs, and cultural traditions of Latin American countries. It includes a variety of myths, legends, and stories that provide insight into the values and beliefs of the indigenous people of South America.

South American mythology

South American mythology is a rich and diverse collection of stories and legends that reflect the beliefs and values of the indigenous people of South America. These myths often include creation stories, and can also explain the supernatural connection between humans and animals.

Specter

a visible disembodied spirit

Spectral woman

A spectral woman is a woman who is associated with the Gothic genre and the idea of the phantasmatic aspects of language and the fragile thresholds of the mind and body. The word "spectral" can mean relating to or suggesting a specter, or relating to or made by a spectrum.

Spiritual world

The spiritual world is a realm that some believe is controlled by a divine spirit and is inhabited by spirits, both good and evil

Squawkowtemus

Female spirit that resides in swamps. Its cries lure people close. If it touches them, they die.

Supernatural

The meaning of THE SUPERNATURAL is things that cannot be explained by science and seem to involve ghosts, spirits, magic, etc

Superstition

Superstition is a belief or practice that is considered irrational or supernatural by non-practitioners. It can also refer to a negative attitude towards the supernatural, nature, or God.

Suscon Screamer

"The Suscon Screamer" is the ghost of a teenage girl killed on her prom night on Suscon Road as she was hitchhiking to get back home.

Taniwha

In Māori mythology, a taniwha is a large, supernatural creature that lives in water or caves, and can be either harmful or protective to humans

tapu

Tapu is a Polynesian concept that means something is sacred, holy, or forbidden, and involves rules and prohibitions. It can also be defined as a "spiritual restriction". In Māori culture, tapu is a strong force that can be applied to people, objects, or places. For example, a graveyard or church might be considered tapu.

Tāwhaki

In Māori mythology, Tāwhaki is a semi-supernatural being associated with lightning and thunder.

Teju Jagua

Teju Jagua is the first son of Tau and Kerana and one of the seven legendary monsters of Guaraní mythology.

Ten Ten-Vilu

The Mapuche god of earth and fertility (or goddess in some versions found in Chiloé); he has a generous spirit and is the protector of all life on Earth.

Tengu

In Japanese folklore, the tengu are supernatural, mischievous beings that are often depicted with human and bird-like characteristics

the Bhūt

The meaning of BHUT is an especially malevolent spirit : ghost, demon, goblin.

The Boiuna

Boiuna (translated as "Black Snake") is a mythological creature in Brazilian mythology. It is also known as the Cobra-Grande

The Chi

Chi means either "a hornless dragon" or "a mountain demon" (namely, chīmèi 螭魅) in Chinese mythology.

The Kayeri

The Kayeri is a giant, plant-like humanoid cryptid from the folklore of the Cuiba people of Colombia and Venezuela.

the Obia

An obia is a giant animal that witches send into villages to kidnap girls and wear their skin.

the Sasabonsam

The Sasabonsam is a mythical vampiric creature from the folklore of the Akan people of Ghana, Côte d'Ivoire, Togo, and 18th century Jamaica

Tibicena

A Tibicena, also known as Guacanchas, was a mythological creature of the Guanches, pre-Hispanic inhabitants of the Canary Islands. Tibicenas were imagined to be demons or genies who had the bodies of great wild dogs with red eyes, covered by long, black fur. They lived in deep caves inside the mountains.

Tjukurrpa

Tjukurrpa refers to origins and powers embodied in country, places, objects, songs and stories. It is a way of seeing and understanding the world and connects people to country and to each other through shared social and knowledge networks.

Tonga people

The Tonga people of Zambia and Zimbabwe, also called "Batonga", are a Bantu ethnic group. They are related to the Batoka people, but are different culturally and linguistically from the Tsonga people of South Africa and southern Mozambique.

Transmutation

the action of changing or the state of being changed into another form.

Trolls

an ugly creature depicted as either a giant or a dwarf.

Ulama

The Ulama, or Devil Bird, is a creature from Sri Lankan folklore that is said to make blood-curdling shrieks in the jungle at night. The Ulama's cry is believed to be a portent of death.

Uranus

In Greek mythology, Uranus is the god of the sky and heavens, and a symbol of masculinity. He is one of the primordial gods and is also known as Ouranos.

Urban legend

a story that appears mysteriously and spreads spontaneously in various forms and is usually false; contains elements of humor or horror

Vajra

A vajra is a ritual object that symbolizes the properties of a diamond and a thunderbolt

Vampire

A vampire is a mythical creature that subsists by feeding on the vital essence of the living. In European folklore, vampires are undead humanoid creatures

vampire-like

A vampire-like being is a creature that is similar to a vampire in some way. A vampire is a mythical creature that subsists by feeding on the vital essence of the living usually blood.

Varaha

Varaha (Sanskrit: वराह, Varāha, "boar") is the avatara of the Hindu god Vishnu, in the form of a boar. Varaha is generally listed as third in the Dashavatara, the ten principal avataras of Vishnu.

Vetal

Vetal is king of ghosts. The konkan desh is ruled by Vetal and his ghosts.

Vetala

A vetala is a paranormal entity in Hindu mythology that is often described as a vampire. Vetala are evil spirits from Hindu folklore with varying shapes and forms who haunts cemeteries and takes demonic possession or control of corpses

Vishnu

Vishnu is a Hindu god who is the preserver and protector of the universe. He is one of the three gods in the Hindu triumvirate, along with Brahma and Shiva, who are responsible for the creation, upkeep, and destruction of the world

Vritra

Vritra is a danava in Hinduism. He serves as the personification of drought, and is an adversary of the king of the devas, Indra.

Weiße Frauen

The Weisse Frau ("White Lady") in German lore is a beautiful matron said to protect children. Wearing all white, she is thought to be benevolent and sad.

Weredog

A weredog is a creature similar to a werewolf – it is a shapeshifter. Instead of a man turning into a wolf, it's a man turning into a dog

West African folklore

West African folklore is rich with tales of animals, tricksters, and supernatural beings that teach morals and offer insight into West African culture

White Lady

A White Lady (or woman in white) is a type of female ghost. She is typically dressed in a white dress or similar garment, reportedly seen in rural areas and associated with local legends of tragedy.

White Lady of Avenel

The White Lady of Avenel is the most common reported apparition in Avenel, Virginia. The apparition is thought to be Mary Frances "Fran" Burwell, a member of the Burwell family of Virginia.

White Lady of Balete Drive

The White Lady was a young woman who tragically lost her life in a car accident on Balete Drive and haunted the road in pursuit of her killer.

White Lady of Radford

The White Lady in question was one of several girls living at the erstwhile mansion house at Radford in the eighteenth century.

White Lady of Whopsy

The White Lady of Wopsy is a ghost story from Pennsylvania about a ghostly hitchhiker who haunts the misty, wooded lookout area of Wopsononock Mountain. The story is said to have originated from a real tragedy that happened on the mountain roads of Pennsylvania

White Snake

Bai Suzhen (Chinese: 白素貞), also known as Lady Bai is a one-thousand-year-old white snake spirit

White Witch

A ghostly figure in white that haunts the historic district of Fremont, California. She is said to roam the old train tracks and Niles Canyon at night, drifting silently through the mist. Some say she beckons drivers with a mysterious allure, only to vanish without a trace.

Wild Hunt

The Wild Hunt is an ancient myth of a spectral or otherworldly hunting party that sometimes appears at night.

will-o'-the-wisp

A will-o'-the-wisp is a mysterious, glowing light that appears in the night sky, particularly over marshes, swamps, or bogs. It is also known as ignis fatuus, which is Latin for "foolish fire".

Witchcraft

Witchcraft is the practice of magic or sorcery, and the belief in the ability to use supernatural powers to harm others

Witches

a person, especially a woman, who professes or is supposed to practice magic or sorcery; a sorceress

Witte Wiwer

Witte Wieven (translation: White Women) are nocturnal apparitions commonly found in the East and Northern parts of the Netherlands and Germany

wrathful demon

A wrathful demon is a fearsome, demonic being that is a characteristic feature of Mahayana and Vajrayana Buddhism. These deities are often alternative manifestations of peaceful deities, such as Buddhas, Bodhisattvas, or Devas.

Xuanwu

Black Tortoise or Turtle, one of the Four Symbols of Chinese astronomy · Xuanwu (god) ("Dark Warrior")

Y Ladi Wen

Spectral apparition of a woman dressed in white, known in Welsh oral tradition. A common bogy reputed to warn children about bad behaviour.

Yak Kurulla

The Devil Bird is a creature that is said to make blood-curdling shrieks that sound like humans in the jungles at night.

Yee naaldlooshii

Yee naaldlooshii is a Navajo word that translates to "by means of it, it goes on all fours" and refers to a type of skinwalker, a malevolent witch in Navajo folklore that can transform into an animal.

Yeti

The Yeti is an ape-like creature purported to inhabit the Himalayan mountain range in Asia.

Yokai

Yokai is a catchall Japanese word for ghosts, demons, monsters, shapeshifters, tricksters, and other kinds of supernatural beings and mysterious phenomena.

Yūrei

Yūrei are ghosts in Japanese folklore that are similar to the Western concept of ghosts. The word "yūrei" is made up of two kanji characters: 幽, which means "faint" or "dim", and 霊, which means "soul" or "spirit"

Zhenniao

The Zhenniao are depicted as poisonous birds with purple abdomens and green-tipped feathers, along with long necks and scarlet beaks.

Zhulong

Zhulong /ˈdʒuːlɒŋ/ or Zhuyin /ˈdʒuːjɪn/, also known in English as the Torch Dragon, was a giant red solar dragon and god in Chinese mythology.

Zhuque

The vermillion bird. It is described as a red bird that resembles a pheasant with a fire-colored plumage and is perpetually covered in flames.